THE

THUNDER

BEFORE

THE

STORM

THE THUNDER BEFORE THE STORM

THE **Autobiography** OF
Clyde Bellecourt
AS TOLD TO **Jon Lurie**

MINNESOTA
HISTORICAL
SOCIETY PRESS

www.mnhspress.org

The Minnesota Historical Society Press is a member of the Association of American University Presses.

Manufactured in the United States of America

10 9 8 7 6 5 4 3 2 1

∞ The paper used in this publication meets the minimum requirements of the American National Standard for Information Sciences—Permanence for Printed Library Materials, ANSI Z39.48-1984.

International Standard Book Number
ISBN: 978-1-68134-019-7 (hardcover)
ISBN: 978-1-68134-124-8 (paper)
ISBN: 978-1-68134-020-3 (e-book)

Library of Congress Cataloging-in-Publication Data
Names: Bellecourt, Clyde H. (Clyde Howard), 1936– author. | Lurie, Jon, 1967– author.
Title: The thunder before the storm : the autobiography of Clyde Bellecourt / as told to Jon Lurie.
Other titles: Autobiography of Clyde Bellecourt
Description: Saint Paul, MN : Minnesota Historical Society Press, [2016] | Includes index.
Identifiers: LCCN 2016026452 | ISBN 9781681340197 (hardcover : alk. paper) | ISBN 9781681340203 (ebook)
Subjects: LCSH: Bellecourt, Clyde H. (Clyde Howard), 1936– | Ojibwa Indians—Biography. | American Indian Movement. | Wounded Knee (S.D.)—History—Indian occupation, 1973—Personal narratives. | Oglala Indians—Biography. | Human rights workers—United States—Biography. | Indians of North America—Government relations—1934– | Indians of North America—Politics and government.
Classification: LCC E99.C6 B425 2016 | DDC 323.1197/073092 [B]—dc23
LC record available at https://lccn.loc.gov/2016026452

This and other Minnesota Historical Society Press books are available from popular e-book vendors.

For Peggy

CONTENTS

THE

THUNDER

BEFORE

THE

STORM

PROLOGUE: THE DAMN TRUTH

YOU CAN PRAY ALL DAY AND NIGHT, but if you don't work damn hard you ain't gonna get what you want. That's the way I believe, you know?

You see a tornado coming, know what you do?

Put your tobacco out and pray.

You know what you do next?

Head for the basement.

The Creator will help you, but you've got to help yourself.

We in the American Indian Movement made a decision when we formed in 1968: if need be, we'd give our lives for what we believed. No longer would we allow our people to be victimized without fighting back.

Despite that commitment, I personally never carried a gun. Despite the physical threats against our people, it was my policy, even at Wounded Knee, never to carry a weapon. I believe in the Sacred Pipe, and I believe that those who carry the pipe have different responsibilities than those who take up arms.

The story of the American Indian Movement has been told many times, but so far it's been told incorrectly, as I see it, by people who never did the damn hard work of revitalizing Indian communities.

This book is the whole truth, and nothing but the truth, so help me God. This is my story, the way I remember it. Other people remember it differently, and they can write their own books. I'm not pulling any punches; I'm just telling it like it is, and like it was before the American Indian Movement came along to help our people help themselves.

Indian people had no legal rights centers, job training centers, community clinics, Native American studies programs, or Indian child welfare statutes. There were no Indian casinos or Indian schools, no Indian preference housing. We were prohibited by federal law from practicing our spirituality. It was illegal for us to be us in our own country. The Movement changed everything for Indian people.

I knew from the minute the American Indian Movement first assembled that we were on a collision course with organized religion, the Bureau of Indian Affairs (BIA), and white European education.

I didn't know it was going to happen so fast—but just five years after we started, we were surrounded by US military forces at Wounded Knee, on the Pine Ridge Reservation in South Dakota.

As soon as we saw those troops coming in over the hills surrounding Wounded Knee, we issued a Red Alert. We told our people to spread the word throughout Indian Country: bring your camping gear here with you. Bring your weapons with you. Bring anyone you know who is a demolition expert. Bring your snipers, your communications people. We had Vietnam vets come in who had just returned from the war with these skills. This was how we swelled our ranks and armed ourselves.

We did this in response to the fact that we were surrounded by the FBI, GOONs (so-called Guardians of the Oglala Nation), rancher-vigilantes, US Marshals, and several branches of the military. When you added up all the firepower we were able to muster, it really didn't amount to shit. But they treated us like we had weapons of mass destruction, a threat to start World War III.

They had tanks, automatic weapons, armored personnel carriers—fighter jets and helicopter gunships flying over.

We didn't know it at the time, but this response to us—the overwhelming force they brought—was part of an FBI plan conceived by J. Edgar Hoover called COINTELPRO (short for Counter-Intelligence Program). It was the government's intention to eliminate all forms of social and political dissent in America.

Indians weren't the only people under attack by the federal government. At that time in America—1960s and 1970s—people were being gunned down, burned out, bombed—people like the Black Panthers, the Weather Underground, and the civil rights activists. They targeted AIM, Black Panthers, Martin Luther King, the Kennedy brothers, Malcolm X. Hoover was so paranoid he even targeted his own personnel.

The reason they targeted AIM wasn't because we had all kinds of weapons—like I said, we didn't have shit. But we knew that 80 percent of all the natural resources left in America were on Indian land: I'm talking about timber, iron, uranium, water, grazing lands, farmlands, silver, gold. . . . When you think about it, the number should actually be 100 percent, because everything the United States has it stole from Native people.

AIM said repeatedly that we intended for Native people to "never give up another inch of land, another ounce of Mother Earth."

We started a movement to take back everything that belonged to us: our spirituality, our languages, our hunting and fishing rights, our water rights, our gold and minerals, our sacred sites—and our children.

We found out that just three years after AIM formed, the federal government had listed us as the number one threat to the "stability and the security of the United States." We learned about this in 1975— during FBI testimony at the Wounded Knee trials—that the government had basically declared war on us; a lot of people were shook up, man. I was happy.

Wow, I thought, *it took just three years. We didn't have no guns, no military force, yet we became the number one threat to the stability and security of the United States.* What an honor, when you think about it.

We knew they would do everything they could to infiltrate the Movement, cause dissension, turn people against one another. That's what COINTELPRO was all about. The FBI was killing people all over the country and, with the help of the CIA, all over the world.

Because of the FBI's campaign to disrupt and discredit the Movement, there has been a lot of misinformation put out about me. Many people think they know me. They say I have a history of violence; they call me a militant and a communist—all of those things the FBI wanted them to believe.

Call me what you want, but I have my own story to tell, and I believe every man deserves the right to tell his story, at least once.

I have fought for Indian people, and with good reason. When the American Indian Movement formed, there was no such thing as Indian religious freedom in America. To achieve that, and our other goals, we had to take on the FBI and many other institutions of power—state and church.

After years of enduring confrontations, beatings, jails, and killings, we in the so-called Red Power Movement saw our efforts rewarded when Congress passed the American Indian Religious Freedom Act. On August 11, 1978, President Jimmy Carter signed the legislation into law. The American Indian Movement, you might say, had been the main lobbyists for that. We went out and took action in the streets, taunting and daring the judicial system to arrest us, to put us in jail, so we could embarrass them in their own courts where we'd turn the tables, put the Americans on trial for crimes against Indian people, crimes against humanity.

Finally, we were free to practice our ceremonies in the open.

At that time the elders started talking about the American Indian Movement as being the fulfillment of prophecy. I felt really good whenever I heard that. It had long been foretold, they said, that our generation would rise up and awaken the people. It made me understand why we had to get our asses kicked and dragged around the country. We did it for our people. And I would do it all over again because I've always believed, you know, that you can pray all you want, but if you don't get out and do the damn hard work, it ain't going to happen.

Well, it happened, and this is how.

1. MY MOTHER'S LIMP

MY SPIRIT NAME IS NEEGAWNWAYWIDUNG, which simply means "The Thunder Before the Storm." I prefer that, of course, over Clyde. I'm a member of the Mississippi Band of the Great Anishinaabe Nation. I was born and raised on the White Earth Reservation in northwestern Minnesota. I was born May 8, 1936.

When I was growing up, we called ourselves the "Chippewa," as we were known by the Europeans, who couldn't be bothered to call us by our proper name. We didn't call ourselves Anishinaabe, like we do today, because we didn't know anything about ourselves.

I was born way out in a place called Elbow Lake. Our home was right next to the lake, with a little sandy beach and nice clear water. It was a two-story house, with five small bedrooms. I'm a middle child in a family of twelve children, and we all got along fine, which was important because our house was crowded. It was not unusual for boys and girls to share beds, especially when it was cold; the fire would go out about 3:00 a.m. If you needed a drink, you would have to go downstairs and use a knife to bust the ice off the top of the water bucket.

I remember having to cut wood when we came home from school to make sure we had enough to last the night and cook breakfast the next morning. We didn't have natural gas and all this stuff they have up there today. We used kerosene lamps to light our home. We had no electricity.

Like most other homes on the reservation, ours also had no running water. We had to go outside and pump our water by hand. In the wintertime, when the well froze, we had to hire somebody to go up to Government Hill, where they kept the big tanks. There was a guy by the name of Frank Warren who would come with his team of horses. Frank had these big, fifty-gallon barrels he put up on his wagon. He would go up to the hill and fill them up—charge maybe fifty cents a barrel. In the summertime, though, we all had running water—rain coming off our roofs and collected in troughs. That's what we used to bathe. How we lived is how families lived on reservations across America.

My great-grandfather on my mother's side, Wainchemadub, also known as Joseph Charette and Joe Critt, left, was a Civil War veteran. He stands next to another well-known Anishinaabe leader named Ojibway in 1910. *MNHS collections*

Gwen, Evanelle, Judy, and me on the steps of our home with dogs in about 1939. *Courtesy author*

I'm at left, holding a rock, next to Vernon, Yvonne, and Carol. Lenny is at center, and Evanelle is at far right. *Courtesy author*

We had to stretch the disability check my father got from the military each month. But we never went hungry. We snared rabbits, trapped muskrats, hunted deer, and fished. We harvested wild rice and blueberries and maple syrup, and somehow we always managed to have a car.

I remember how my father, Charles Bellecourt, used to tell stories as our family sat around the fire at night in a tar paper shack at the rice camp on the White Earth Reservation. He often spoke of his horrible boarding school days.

My father would have done anything to get away from the Carlisle Indian Industrial School in Carlisle, Pennsylvania. Like countless other Indian kids, my father had been stolen from his home on White Earth. He was forced to march and wear uniforms and train to be a good American, to forget his culture. He hated it, and so, he told us, in 1917, at the age of sixteen (along with some forty thousand other Indian kids across the country who had the same idea), my father enlisted in the hell of World War I to escape the hell of boarding school. He wasn't legally old enough to join, but he was a warrior. He lied about his age. The military didn't care how old he was, they just needed warm bodies for the fight. The marines gave him a little training and sent him to Europe to fight the Germans. Like a lot of Indians of his generation, he believed in democracy and freedom—all those things America supposedly stands for.

My father told stories about all the big battles he'd been in. I remember him talking about Belleau Wood, near Paris. He recalled the whole forest being burned down, and all the battling that took place over three weeks in 1918. He survived with seventeen bullet wounds— he had been gassed, and would be bloated the rest of his life. He told us he made it out from behind German lines by covering himself with the dead bodies of fellow marines. When the Allied forces found him three or four days later, they were amazed to find a survivor among a pile of casualties. Until his death in the early 1960s, at the age of sixty-four, he believed that America was a true democracy, a righteous nation.

When I was a child, whenever there was a thunderstorm, I would come downstairs, and my father would be sitting at the window with that thousand-mile stare. The thunder would roar, and my father, reliving his combat experiences, would duck and cover under the table.

My father had a way of making the best of things. He was a big man—six feet two inches and weighing about three hundred pounds—and he told us that he still had gas in his system from the war. We'd go swimming, and he'd float in the water. You could push him down, he'd bubble right back up. We kids used to crawl up on him and dive off. He'd go to these carnivals around Minnesota, and they would pay him to come out there and float in the water. People would go out and push him down, he'd come right back up. He could even lay on his back and fish.

My father really had a great sense of humor; he was also a strong leader. They called him Big Ogimaa, the Big Boss. He was the main organizer of the Indian people in our community. When politicians were running for office, they would always come to my dad and ask for his support. Big Ogimaa was also the literal boss of many of our people, who worked as migrant laborers in the Red River Valley beet and potato fields, on the Minnesota–North Dakota border.

I must have been four or five years old when I started working the fields alongside my family. We loaded trucks and tended beets. In order to tend beets, you have to make sure they grow about eighteen inches from one another, because sugar beets get big. And if you don't thin them, they get crowded out and don't grow to their full potential. Later in the season, we harvested the beets by first plowing them up, a process called topping. We'd pick up those beets with our knives and cut off their roots with a quick swipe, and then the truck would come by and we'd load them. Away they went to one of the Crystal Sugar plants that line Interstate 29 all the way up to the Canadian border.

Our entire family, along with the rest of the crew, lived in big barns during the weeks of the harvest. We'd throw some fresh hay and a couple mattresses down in stalls designed for cows and horses. It was a very hard life, but at least we were all together. My father was disabled, so he didn't work the fields. He earned his money as the supervisor of all the folks from the reservation. The money our family made from doing seasonal farm labor helped us survive the relentless winters.

This was in the era before the reforms brought about by Cesar Chavez, who is one of my heroes and role models. We had no schooling available on those job sites, no real housing, and we earned a meager wage—about six cents for a bushel, when we were harvesting potatoes. We would fill gunnysacks full of them and heave them onto trucks as they came by.

My brother, Charles Bellecourt Jr., with our dad, Charles Bellecourt Sr. They're standing in front of our home in the mid-1940s. *Courtesy author*

We spent our off-hours picking blueberries and searching the prairie for medicinal herbs. Harvest was also a time for us to engage in traditional gathering activities. When we weren't picking beets and potatoes, we'd go to Mitchell Dam up on my reservation and work the lake until the wild rice was gone. Then we'd move about thirty-five miles to Big Rice Lake, and we'd tap out there.

We lived in rice camps as fall came to a close. I looked forward to the rice camps; they would spring up like little villages. People made tar paper shacks maybe a week before they started harvesting the wild rice. Tents, tipis, little cookshacks, and shelters for playing poker—little card rooms—sprung up all over. On the reservation, everyone lived so far apart. Ricing season was a time when I could look forward to seeing all of my friends come together in one place. There would be moccasin games at night, storytelling around the fire, and lots of card games and gambling. The men would gamble bags of wild rice. Winners sometimes went home with a few hundred pounds of rice. Perhaps more than any other time, the rice camps gave us a true understanding of who we were as Ojibwe people.

The elders had complete control over all aspects of the wild rice harvest. In the morning they would send somebody onto the water to get some rice grains. If they were still milky the elders would say, "Well, you can't go on this lake today," or "The sun's shining on that side of the lake, and the rice is ripe over there, so you can only harvest on that side."

Our elders' words were respected by our people as the law. We successfully managed our natural resources for thousands of years by listening to our elders' wisdom. Very seldom would somebody defy the elders and go ricing where they weren't supposed to. If they did, the tribe would kick them off our lakes.

Only when the white men came and made rigid laws that were not in keeping with the best interests of the land and its living creatures did the natural systems start to break down. Today, our wild rice is endangered in many areas where it was once abundant.

The only way successfully to hunt, fish, or gather in those days was to do it in force. If you went out by yourself ricing, hunting, or gathering, the game wardens would find you and take everything you had. If you went out in a party of fifty or sixty people, set up a camp to go rice, they didn't come in and bother you at all. They would listen to the elders; even game wardens would listen to Indian people when we were out in force.

My mother, Angeline, was placed in a boarding school when she was ten years old. She spoke the Ojibwe language fluently, and a little French—there was French-Canadian on my father's side. She could speak English, as well.

I often wondered why my mother always limped. As a child I had a sense her limp was part of some great truth being hidden from me by my parents. My siblings and I often asked her, "Mom, what's wrong with your legs?"

She'd always kind of shush us up. She would tell us to just go to school and learn the English language and study hard, and someday, "You might be president of the United States."

Late at night, when we were all tucked away upstairs in bed, the old people would come to our house. My mother thought we were sleeping, but I wasn't. I'd hear a knock on the door. Old Lady Mitchell, Mrs. Big Bear, and Mrs. Smith would come over. They would greet one another in a strange language. They were really cheerful and chatty.

I would lie awake listening to them tell stories in what I later learned was our Ojibwe language. Sometimes they laughed so hard, they fell right off their chairs. Then the alarm clock would go off early in the morning, and everything was sad, and flat, and English once again.

"Mom," I used to ask, "how come you don't teach us to speak in that beautiful language? I heard you last night talking to Old Lady Mitchell and Mrs. Big Bear; you had such a good time."

"Oh, forget about that," she would say. "That's all in the past now."

It wasn't until I was in my mid-thirties, after the American Indian Movement's 1973 occupation of Wounded Knee, that I found out the truth about my mother's limp. I'll tell you that story, but you'll have to be a little patient, because you need to know other things first.

In my youngest years I lived at home with my family and attended public school. I remember my first confrontation with the church—of course, there would be many more. I was coming home late at night out by St. Benedict's Mission School, and these two fearsome creatures came floating out of the woods and scared the hell out of me. I never saw anything like that in my life—completely black bodies that merged with the darkness, and completely white faces. I ran home. I slogged all the way across the slough, waist deep in mud. My parents thought maybe I got chased by a bear. I told them I saw ghosts in the woods and explained what they looked like. Everybody started laughing at me. They told me these were Catholic nuns out of St. Benedict's Mission.

So from that point on, knowing I was afraid of them, there was always kind of a threat hanging over my head. My parents would say, "If you don't make it in the public school, if you don't go to school every day and toe the line, we're going to send you out there, and let those nuns take care of you."

We all had heard the stories of how strict they were at the mission school. There was a missionary that took in Indian orphans and worked them to the bone in the gardens. They had silent hours and silent days, when kids would be punished for making a sound. If you missed church on Sunday, they'd line you up along the blackboard on Monday morning and whack you with rulers on the hands. It was very strict, sadistic you might say.

Although I was afraid of the nuns, I could not be controlled, and it wasn't long before the threats of sending me to the mission school were made real. As a little boy, I hated school, ran away every chance I got. I loved the woods, and I would rather be out there, fishing and hunting. I was also the kind of kid that never liked church—especially during Lent. You had to go at night and do the Stations of the Cross. So just about every Monday they ordered me and my cousin, Billy Bellecourt, to step forward to receive a beating. Billy and I always hung out. We went out camping, went out to the lakes fishing, and stayed up all night around a fire by some lake. That's what we wanted. That's the way we thought life was supposed to be.

I missed a lot of church, and my hands were beat bloody. They would whack me with the metal side of the ruler and split my knuckles wide open. Of course, I started running away from that, too. If you look at my knuckles today, you'll see they all have scars on them.

At eleven years old, I was finally picked up and placed in jail at Detroit Lakes, Minnesota, on the southern border of the White Earth Reservation. They charged me with truancy and delinquency. They had a court hearing. The judge there was named Judge Peoples. He was always sending children away, putting them in boarding schools, putting them in foster care, splitting up families. Church administrators came to the hearing. My mother and dad, of course, were there. The court decided to give me another chance. They told me they would put me on probation, but I had to go back to the mission school, and I had to apologize. They said I had to go to school every day. I had to go to church on Sunday and all other church services that were held. Otherwise they were going to send me to a place called Red Wing State Training School.

They painted a pretty nice picture of Red Wing back in those days. They said it was a nice farm setting, with horses, and animals, and campouts, and all that stuff. In my mind, I thought, *geez, this has got to be better than going back to those nuns*. I remember still today, my mother crying in the court, begging me to go on probation and go to school, and I wouldn't agree to it. I turned around and told the judge, "I will not return to the mission school." Judge Peoples deemed me "incorrigible" and sent me to the Red Wing State Training School.

They transported me to Red Wing in a van with adult offenders. I was handcuffed between a man who had sexually assaulted four of his grandchildren—they delivered him to Stillwater State Prison—and another guy who was being sent to St. Cloud Reformatory for forty-five years for armed bank robbery.

I found out Red Wing was nothing like the picture that had been painted. I found out it was a very strict, institutional environment—

Me, age eleven or twelve.
Courtesy author

a kind of military academy. We wore uniforms. We marched to church. We shined our boots.

This was the first time I had been off the reservation; I was three hundred miles away from home in an environment where they housed some inmates with long criminal records. It was a transformative experience.

I was placed in a group of boys called Scout Company. I was one of the youngest and one of the smallest boys, the only Indian in the institution at that time. So, of course, I faced a lot of racism. I suffered a lot of beatings from the housefathers and other boys. They had what they called blanket parties. The other inmates would put a blanket over you and beat the hell out of you. That was a rite of initiation. If you told on them, then they would give you another beating. It was a tremendous culture shock to go into that kind of setting.

I wasn't raised Anishinaabe in a traditional sense, where the Indian language was openly spoken, or ceremonies were taking place all the time. Those kinds of things were underground in those days. But I was raised in a traditional fashion as far as hunting and fishing and surviving, harvesting wild rice, spearing and netting fish at night, hiding from game wardens who were constantly harassing us for exercising our treaty rights.

People in the Indian community have a total distaste for any kind of law enforcement. For many of us who grew up on reservations, this started very early in life with the game wardens. As a kid I got in a confrontation with the game warden every day of the week. I remember when we'd go out spear fishing in the spring. My uncle would come to the house in a horse-drawn cart. He'd pick up my dad and me and my brother Vernon and we'd head out to the White Earth River, White Earth Lake, Nett Lake—all those places where the walleye were spawning. We'd go out there, and it was so quiet that if there was a car coming you could hear it thirty miles away. My uncle had that horse so well trained, it would automatically go off the road and into the woods when it heard a car. The horse would keep his back to the road until the car went past, so the game warden wouldn't be able to see the shine of his eyes. Two or three minutes later, after the car passed, that horse would go back on the road, and we'd go out and set our nets and spear some fish.

After pulling in our haul of walleye, the men would filet them, and then we'd take them around to the people—the elderly and the handicapped, who couldn't go fishing no more. Then we'd go home and there'd be a big celebration, a big feast. This is a tradition I honor to this day, to always share with those in need.

Everything we did to support ourselves, we had to hide. When we were caught, they'd confiscate our cars, confiscate our wagons, take our rifles, take our nets, and take our canoes. They would take everything from you. If you didn't have money to pay the fine, you lost it forever. Over the years, our people at White Earth lost millions of dollars of fishing and hunting equipment. So there was always a total distrust for the law enforcement on our reservation.

Those kinds of feelings were reinforced in me after I left the reservation. The first time I was at Red Wing, I was there three years. I
was only supposed to be there three months. But my three months
passed by, and I was given more time, and they just kept tacking time
onto the end of my sentence. What happened to me was a form of
forced relocation. The government was eager to push Indian people
off the reservations. They'd put you in an institution like that, and in
order for you to get out, you had to have the permission of your home
reservation's law enforcement officials and town councils, who were
white. This permission was most often denied. A lot of Minnesota's
Indian families were forced to move into Minneapolis and St. Paul so
their children could come home to them.

During those three years I received one visit from my parents, this
after I had been there for a year and a half. They let us have visits from
home over the Christmas holidays if you were well behaved. Red Wing
was a very long way for my parents to travel—over three hundred
miles from White Earth. The distance was all part of the plan. They
isolated children far from their homes so family members couldn't visit. They tried to break that family bond, robbing kids of the comfort of
loved ones and disrupting the transmission of traditional knowledge
that comes from spending time with elders.

I came in contact with a lot of new things in Red Wing. But there's
one experience I can never forget. I have not talked about it openly
or publicly.

There was a Catholic priest there by the name of Father Hendricks.
He used to do the intake interviews when new inmates arrived. You
had to get your shots and go through psychological evaluations, and
then you had to meet the priest. I first heard about Father Hendricks
from other inmates. They kind of joked about him with me. "Oh, you're
going to see Father Hendricks today," they'd laugh.

I went in there, and he asked me a lot of questions: Did I go to
church on Sunday? Was I a Catholic? I told him my history, and the
next thing I knew, the guy told me to unzip my pants.

I was really embarrassed. I never did that. Even living and growing up with seven sisters and four brothers, I never took my pants

off around them. But he just went ahead and started unzipping my pants; he wanted to look at me. He started feeling me. He asked me to pull my skin back. I didn't know what he was talking about. So he did it himself.

"Oh, you're not circumcised," he said. "You ought to get circumcised."

He later made arrangements for me to get circumcised.

He fondled me for a long time.

Father Hendricks never assaulted me again after that. But I remember going to Cub Scout camp down by Lake Pepin. He was always taking boys into the tent with him at night. I heard a lot of stories about him. I can still hear those little boys crying, "Please, Father, don't hurt me."

I never told my parents. Other kids had tried, and their parents didn't believe them. They thought these Catholic priests were incapable of doing things like that. The kids were accused of lying and were punished. I was too embarrassed to tell my parents, so I silently endured that experience.

Every new inmate did two or three months in Scout Company, then was transferred to another part of the institution. I was put in a company called Washington with all the smallest and youngest inmates. All of the kids played on the same playgrounds and used the same dining facilities. We did jobs together. But we were separated at night from the older inmates.

We had a housefather there by the name of Olson. He was a no-nonsense-type person. You didn't dare step out of line around him. We heard about the beatings he'd administer. Those terrible stories were true. One night, after I'd been in his house five or six months, I was showering with fifteen or so other boys. This young boy that was supposedly gay came up and started messing with me. Without thinking I punched him in the face, and his nose started bleeding, and there was blood all over the water.

The housefather looked in and asked who did that. Of course, the others all said it was me. I was the only Indian in there. He pulled me out of the shower. I didn't have no clothes on. He took one of these radiator brushes, about the size of a yardstick, real hard oak wood. He beat me. I never received a beating like that in my life. I had welts all over my body and knots on my head. He beat me so bad that the night watchman heard the commotion and came and pulled the guy off me. He would probably have killed me. They dressed me, carried me to the infirmary, and then transported me to the hospital.

About three o'clock in the morning, the superintendent of the institution came to see me. He told me it was terrible what this guy did to me, and he was going to reprimand him. He asked me to forgive him, but didn't want me to tell anybody, and absolutely didn't want me to contact my parents.

My parents came to see me a few months after that. I told them exactly what happened to me.

They said, "You must have deserved it. You must have deserved it, or he wouldn't have done that."

I did three years and returned home to the same reservation I had left behind. Of course, once you're in an institution you're labeled, so now anything that happened on the reservation was blamed on me. "That damn Clyde Bellecourt," they said, "he must have done it. He's leading a gang. He runs around doing all these crimes. He's not going to school."

I was sent back to Red Wing at age fourteen for a second round. They called my offense a parole violation, but I really didn't do anything. I just still refused to go to school. I was truant and incorrigible. This time I did two years. It helped that I came into the situation already knowing what to expect. I had a very good friend there. Like me, he would also end up doing time in St. Cloud, and Stillwater. He was a young Black kid named Leroy Cotton. We used to call him Cotton Ball. He was tough. He was short and stocky. He suffered a lot of beatings. Cotton and I teamed up for survival. If somebody jumped Leroy, they had to jump me, too. If they jumped me, they had to deal with Leroy.

The third time I was sent away to Red Wing I ran away. There was another young kid from my home reservation; we were both working in the power plant. On a Sunday, when everybody went to church, we filled up the coal hopper for the boilers, packed a lunch and some water, and ran off. We crawled over the nearby bluff and dashed probably six or seven miles until we thought we were free.

They had a deal there where they'd pay the area's farmers $25 a head if they caught an inmate running away. The next thing we knew, there were cars coming from all over. It was right after church, and many of our pursuers were dressed in their Sunday best. They surrounded us in a wheat field. That was the second-biggest beating I ever got. These grown men threw us to the ground and kicked the living shit out of us.

They brought us back to the facility and put us on the chain gang. We spent nine months there. We toiled shoveling coal, cutting hay, and hauling rocks. We were forced to be completely silent, except during recreation time. When I violated the rules and spoke during silent times, they would punish me by making me stand on line. We had a line drawn across the floor, and you had to stand with your feet together, ramrod straight, with your arms folded. If you stumbled off the line, they made you hold your arms straight out from your sides. You were not allowed to drop them or rest. If you dropped them, they'd come and whack you one. I stood on line one time for thirty-three evenings in a row. I had the record there. I guess I just wanted to be tougher than anybody else.

When all the kids were watching television or playing games, I'd be standing on line until eleven o'clock at night. They had some very sadistic night watchmen and housefathers there. They would sometimes take soaking-wet sheets and hang them over my arms and make me hold them out like that for hours.

These were very difficult times, but the effect on me was positive in the long run. I got very strong. I would later need to rely on my toughness to get me through the many battles ahead, in a war I could not foresee.

Later, when I began fighting for Indian people in the Movement, my mother would hear about me getting beat up, arrested, and shot. She begged me to "forget about the past and think about the future."

Our family in the early 1970s. Mom sits at center right, with folded hands. Ten of her twelve children are in the back row. *Courtesy author*

I would respond, "Mom, if we ever forget about our past, we'll never have a future—our past is our future. Our grandparents thought about us, guaranteed us life, guaranteed that we'd have our culture, have our ceremonies, have hunting and fishing and wild rice. But what do we have to pass on to our children? We have nothing. We try to hunt or fish, they arrest us, beat us up, and even kill us."

I knew my activities caused her stress, but I never knew how much until my brother Vernon confronted me. This must have been about 1970—after I got out of Stillwater State Prison, but before the BIA takeover, before Wounded Knee.

My mom used to go stay with Vernon in Denver for two or three months at a time. Vernon was a very prosperous businessman. He was one of the top hairdressers in America. He built a persona as "Monsieur Vern from Paris." He had never been to France in his life, but no one questioned him because he was so talented. He created popular styles, like those elaborate updos that were in vogue in the 1960s and '70s. He promised to make his clients look like empresses. He ran salons and a school of cosmetology. He was married with children, active in investing and real estate; just a very smart, successful guy.

One day, in early 1969, after one of my mother's visits with Vernon in Denver, he brought her back to Minneapolis, dropped her at home, and came directly to my house. He asked if he could have a few words. I met him out on the sidewalk at Thirteenth and Franklin.

He lit into me, demanding to know how much money I was making in the Movement.

"I'm not making no money," I said.

"Then why are you doing this?" he shouted. "You're driving your mother to her grave. She's having heart problems, she's so worried about you."

"I'm sorry," I said. "She never told me anything like that. I'll talk to her tonight."

"I'm asking you right now to knock this shit off," he said.

"Vernon," I said, "I can't. We got all these good things going. We're helping people. I will never give this up."

I told him about all the problems that Indian people were having. I told him someone had to stand up. The discussion got heated. I really felt bad about what was happening, and I told him, "Vernon, I can't turn around now. I'll talk to Mom and I'll try to get her to not fear these things. But I'm totally committed to what I believe in. There's nothing you or anyone can do to change what is happening. Nothing."

He thought I was crazy. Vernon had been in jail himself when he was young, yet he rose to become a successful businessman. He had a houseboat on the St. Croix River and belonged to a big party crowd that vacationed all over the world.

I told him what I thought of his decadent lifestyle.

He took a swing at me. He told me he didn't want to see me no more. I said fine, and he took off.

A couple nights later, I went to my mother's house and asked if I could talk with her. I tried to convince her that the work I was doing with AIM was not just important but a matter of our people's survival. Of course I was concerned about her heart condition, but I also had to know about the secrets she had been keeping from me since I was little.

"Mom," I asked, "what's wrong with your legs?"

When the weather would change, her knees would swell up. Sometimes she could hardly walk. She would blame her condition on "rheumatism," but somehow I sensed there was much more going on. I was right.

Finally, she told me about the boarding schools. She said, "All your life you've asked me why I don't teach you the Ojibwe language. All your life, you've asked me about my legs, why I still walk with a limp today. The answer to these two questions is the same. When I was a little girl, I went to the boarding schools—not just me, thousands of poor Indian kids like me. They would catch me speaking Indian, and I would have to get down on my hands and knees and scrub the floor and clean out the toilets with a toothbrush. Most of the other ds would be outside playing and having a good time."

Toward the end of her internment in boarding scho

when they hadn't been able to rob her of the Ojibwe language, the nuns tied sacks of marbles to her knees and forced her to scrub floors on them. That crippled her. The rest of her life she had problems with her legs. "Not just me," she said. "Many other stubborn kids like me were forced to scrub floors. All these kids would be playing outside. They'd pound on the school's windows and shout, 'Come outside, Angeline! Come out and play, you don't have to speak that language anymore.'"

When she told me this, I was so angry and so hurt, I locked myself in a room. I didn't go nowhere for a long time. That knowledge seemed to justify everything I was doing in the Movement.

My mother never stopped being stubborn. She had to have a stroke before she would allow me to take her to the hospital. Late one night, not too many months after she told me that story, I took her to Hennepin County Medical Center, in a taxi because she wouldn't go in an ambulance. She fought me all the way to the hospital.

After they admitted her, she told me she wanted to see this old lady named Madge Smith. They were real good friends, grew up together. I promised to get Mrs. Smith the following day. Later that night my mother slipped into a coma.

In the morning I left to get Mrs. Smith, and when I returned, they had my mother hooked up to all these machines. She had told me many times to never, ever let them keep her alive artificially. I wasn't sure what to do. I was the only family member in town at the time.

I called my brother Vern in Denver, and my sister in Seattle—these different places where my family had been relocated off the reservation. I told them about our mother's condition and told them we had to make a decision.

"How will we know what's right?" I asked them.

They both voiced their faith in me, which was very important for me to hear at that time. "You'll know the right thing to do," they said.

I talked to the doctors, and I told them my mom never wanted to b̲ ept on life support. I asked them to please unhook her from all the mä ̲ery. With this Madge Smith standing by me, the doctors and I sign̲ ̲ the paperwork, and they unhooked the medical equipment and removed the breathing apparatus from her mouth. It was a very solemn moment.

Just then my mother started singing. I couldn't believe it. She was singing with a smile on her face. Mrs. Smith bent down and started listening to her, and she looked up at me and winked. Then my mother went silent.

I pleaded with Mrs. Smith, "What was she talking about? What was she singing?"

"Oh," she said, "she was singing about the beautiful lakes, and the wild rice beds, and the birch trees at White Earth. Your mom went home."

She had died right in front of my eyes, but I felt good. I felt so proud, because to the very end of her life my mom never gave up her language. Even though she wouldn't teach it to us, she finally told us the reason why; she didn't want us to be punished like she was. She was protecting us as Indian mothers all over the country were doing— protecting their children by not teaching them the language, and the culture, and the ceremonies. So we were deprived of all that growing up. But it wasn't her fault.

It wasn't her fault.

2. THE DRUM WITHIN THE WALLS

I WAS SIXTEEN YEARS OLD, nearly seventeen, when I was released from Red Wing for the last time. I returned to my family, who now resided in Minneapolis. It didn't take long for me to get into trouble again. It seemed no one in the urban Indian community could get a job. All doors seemed closed to me. I didn't see much of a future. I was used to jail now and thought—because I would see the same Indians on the inside over and over—that this was just the way life worked for Indian people. I got involved with a group of kids one night, and we decided to burglarize a movie theater in north Minneapolis. We were lousy criminals, apparently. We came out of there with no money, got busted, and were placed in juvenile detention in the Minneapolis City Jail, which was supposed to be escape-proof. Nobody had ever escaped from it.

I was in the juvenile detention section, which was on the same floor with the adult offenders. There was a small rectangular screen door on the wall, and a door on the other side that had a knob on it. We were able to fit a comic book through the mesh. We got it wet so it gripped the knob, and we turned it, and the damn door opened. Beyond the door was an elevator shaft, currently unused and undergoing renovations.

So two days after they put me there, the three of us kids planning to escape waited until after dinner and told the matron in charge we were going to bed. She turned out the lights, and we went to work on that door. We were able to pull it open again, and we crawled through. We scaled up to the fifth floor of the building, walked across to the Fourth Street side, and went down the steps.

There was a janitor there doing some cleaning, mopping the hallways. "Hey, where are you guys going?" he said. "What are you guys doing up here?"

"Oh," we said. "We got lost. How do we get out of here?"

"There's the stairs right over there."

So we walked down and right out of the building.

It was in the wintertime, very cold, blustery. We just had little jackets and shirts on. We tried everything we could think of to get some money. We tried snatching some purses but failed. Tried to grab some-one's car keys. We were way too cold to get anything done. Finally, I called my mother. It was about midnight. She started crying when I told her we ran away. She said, "You go back and you turn yourself in right now."

I always tried to listen to my mom, although I didn't always take her advice. So about two o'clock in the morning, we walked back into the Minneapolis jail, stood before the desk sergeant, and told him we ran away.

He said, "Nah, nobody runs away from here. You get the hell out of here right now or we'll put you in jail."

"No, we ran away. If you call up, you'll find out." So he called up to the jailhouse, and they went and checked and found out we had indeed escaped.

We embarrassed them, so before I knew it, I was on a bus bound for St. Cloud State Reformatory, which would be my home for the next few years.

I was put away in St. Cloud three separate times. The first time I was sentenced to thirty-six months. Eight or nine months later I was out on parole. I was convicted again on a whole string of burglaries. I went back and did two more years. I was released again and got in-volved right away with a second-degree robbery with Indian friends I met over the years in Red Wing and St. Cloud. We were convicted and sent back to St. Cloud Reformatory.

Between prison stays I got involved in boxing. I aspired to be the light heavyweight champion of the world. I sought out a man named Harry Davis. Harry was the most prominent Black leader in town, also the boxing coach for the Phyllis Wheatley Community Center in north Minneapolis. I was in great shape; I worked out all the time. I walked into Phyllis Wheatley one day and found Harry. I was the only non-Black person in the building.

I told Harry I wanted to fight for him.

He asked, "Why?"

I told him it was because he had trained all the local champions, and I wanted him to train me to be an elite fighter. He tested me.

Harry put me in the ring with a guy named Jerry Bailey, who weighed 265 pounds. I was six feet one, 170 pounds. This guy Bailey was fighting professionally, had already won the Upper Midwest Heavyweight Championship. I had spent most of my life fighting for my life, and I wasn't afraid to take on this bruiser. I stayed in there for three rounds with Bailey.

I never became a boxing champ, but I did become very close with Harry Davis. My time under his wing was cut short when I was sent back to prison. I had accumulated suspended sentences of up to thirty years. I was told if I ever committed another crime, I would be convicted as a habitual offender, and I'd spend the rest of my life behind bars.

I was approaching twenty-five years old. I decided it was time to turn my life around. And I got an opportunity to do so when I was offered a job in the steam generating plant. Not only was it one of the better jobs in the reformatory; I was also offered the chance to apprentice and earn a license as a second-degree engineer. I liked the work and caught on quickly. I learned how to fire up the boilers and work the water pumps. After earning my second-degree license, I sought to achieve a first-degree license. With that I would be qualified to get an entire power plant online.

I gained a lot of education in the power plant, but I was also getting a different kind of education. We Natives always had the best sports teams in the Minnesota prison system. I was an athlete on all of these teams: football, softball, basketball, and boxing. We excelled in every sport. The inmates would bet on the outcome of games and matches using cigarettes as currency. The odds were always against us because we were like a minor-league team taking on major-league talent, and yet we almost always won.

The prison administration would put together these all-star teams whose players were the very best athletes behind bars in the state of Minnesota. They even brought in professionals, like the Flannigan brothers—Del and Glen—big-time professional boxers, and our Native fighters would whip their asses.

I was in charge of organizing the teams, so I controlled the winnings. When you control the cigarettes inside prison, you have a great deal of power. You can buy goods and services: drugs, booze, protection, food—pretty much anything you can imagine.

Before I could get that first-class engineer's license, the reformatory hired a new power plant supervisor, a German guy who was very racist against Blacks and Indians. I was the only Indian working at the plant, and he hated me. He was dead set on keeping me from completing my education.

This German participated in a plot to have me transferred out of St. Cloud. He wasn't the only one who wanted me out. The warden was concerned about me because I had achieved what he saw as too much power among the inmates. It was true that I pretty much ran the place.

There was a sympathetic priest there by the name of Father Peter Hilaire, who had served inmates in Sing Sing Correctional Facility in New York. He was a really nice guy who genuinely cared about the men. He knew pretty much everything that was happening inside those walls. I'd go to confession not to absolve my sins but to get information from Father Hilaire.

One day I went to confession, and he said, "Hey, if I was you, I would ask for a transfer to Stillwater."

I said, "Why?"

He said, "Because they're going to get you. They're after you. You've raised so much hell. They're going to set you up on something and put you away."

There was a lot of bootlegging going on in prison at the time. Guys were finding ways to make wine using potatoes, yeast, and sugar. This German guy placed one hundred pounds of sugar and a load of potatoes in the power plant locker next to mine. One day the warden called me in and accused me of bootlegging. Soon after, I was summoned to disciplinary court, and of course I didn't admit to anything. But I said, "If your decision is to send me to Stillwater, please give me the opportunity to work in the power plant there so I can finish my education and get my first-class engineer's license."

They agreed.

One morning, shortly after the hearing, the guards grabbed me as I was headed to my cell after breakfast. They threw me in a locked transfer area, then went and packed my things. Two hours later I was on a bus to Stillwater.

When I got to Stillwater, they did not assign me to work in the power plant. They sent me where they sent most of the young Natives, to the damn twine shop. I absolutely refused to work the twine shop, where prisoners made twine for the Minnesota farm industry. I looked at the Indian guys who had worked there; they always had a finger torn off after getting their hands caught in the machinery.

I told the prison officials: "They made a commitment to me; I was going back to the power plant to get my first-class engineer's license." But they didn't listen.

I went on a hunger strike. I fasted for over thirty days. I refused to work. They locked me up in solitary confinement. They sent doctors, social workers, everybody down to see me, to try to convince me to eat. They didn't like my attitude, so they put me in what they called deadlock—twenty-three hours a day locked in my cell. They kept me there for about two and a half months. They took everything from me. But they couldn't break me. First they took my books, then my mattress, then my clothes, then they shut off the lights. For ten days they kept me naked in total darkness. I was ready to die. I wanted to die.

One day, during this desperate period, I heard somebody out in the corridor whistling "You Are My Sunshine." I peeked out of the damn peephole, and it was Eddie Benton-Banai, although I didn't know the man's name at the time. He was a welder, an Anishinaabe prisoner who went around fixing leaky pipes.

Eddie hollered, "Is there a Clyde Bellecourt here?"

I was so angry and depressed that I wouldn't respond.

The cheerful welder returned every day for four days. "Is there a Clyde Bellecourt here?"

During those four days I started having dreams. I dreamed I was an eagle flying over a strange land, which I would later realize was Wounded Knee, the site of the 1890 massacre of Big Foot's band of Lakota. I saw a big circular gathering down below with beautiful painted tipis all the way around the edges. I flew down and looked closer. It was a Sun Dance. There were Indian people dancing, and there were horses dancing. As I watched, the horses started dancing backward, blowing eagle bone whistles. It was just beautiful. I was free and with my people in a sacred land. Then I woke up in goddamn solitary confinement and felt those walls crushing me.

On the fourth day, when I heard my name called, I finally gave in. I said, "Right over here."

He came over to my cell door and stuck his eye in the peephole and said, "I heard a lot about you."

"What are you talking about?" I asked.

"I would like to ask you for your help. I want you to be the co-chief of this new group."

I said, "Why do you want me?"

"You're an organizer; you know how to organize the Indian guys. You controlled the cigarettes in St. Cloud." He had done his homework.

Today Eddie is my brother; he's the grand chief of the great Three Fires Midewiwin Lodge, one of the biggest spiritual movements in America. Back then I knew nothing about him. He was about my age, and he seemed like any other Indian guy in prison. I learned that he was a spiritual person who came from a very traditional background on the Lac Courte Oreilles Reservation in Wisconsin; he spoke only Ojibwe until he was twelve years old. Eddie ended up behind bars for a crime that a white man wouldn't even have been tried for. He was in St. Paul while on leave from the army. He came out of a bar and saw an older white man trying to force an Indian girl into a car. Eddie pushed him, and the man fell and hit his head against the curb. He later died of a brain hemorrhage, and Eddie was convicted of manslaughter.

"You know every single Indian inmate in here," he continued. "You've been from Red Wing to the workhouses to the city jails. You know all the Indian inmates, and they have a lot of respect for you. I've tried talking to them, but they don't want anything to do with what I'm saying. I figured if I can get you to come out and help, we'll be able to put this thing together."

"What exactly are you trying to get them to do?" I asked.

He said, "I met a guy here named James Donahue, he's a social worker, and he has all the Indians' cases, because he *gets* us. He understands where we're coming from. He's always trying to help. He's very interested in knowing why there were so many Indian inmates in here. We make up less than one-half of one percent of the population in the state of Minnesota, but over 20 percent of the inmates in this institution."

Eddie told me that when Donahue was a little boy he had a serious illness, and he spent a lot of time in the hospital. His parents used to bring him books on Indian lore and Native history, and he fell in love with Indians.

Eddie said, "Me and Donahue got together and did a study and found out that every Indian in this institution is in here for alcohol-related crimes. Everybody's here for lesser crimes, like burglary and simple assault. But Indians do the most time. Goddamn rapists and murderers get out before Indians."

They also learned that most of the Native inmates know nothing about their culture. The Indian guys would fight anybody that said anything bad about Indians, but they didn't know what they were defending. Eddie and Donahue saw this great need to educate the Indian prisoners about themselves.

I listened through my cell door. He said, "We're going to put together an Indian culture program. We figure if we can build some pride in these Indian men they'll want to earn high school diplomas, study skilled and technical trades, and start taking the correspondence courses offered by the University of Minnesota."

Eddie explained that while programs existed to help Native men get their lives together—Alcoholics Anonymous, Narcotics Anonymous, anger management classes—none of the Indians were involved in them. There was an associate warden, Dr. Moran, who Eddie said would support anything that might attract Native inmates to these programs.

"Why are you asking me to do all this stuff?" I asked. "I don't know nothing about Indians."

Eddie said, "I'll help you."

The next day he appeared again outside my cell. He brought me a thick book by William Whipple Warren called *History of the Ojibway Nation*. The author was from White Earth, like me. Eddie brought me books like *Black Elk Speaks* and *The Seven Rites* by Black Elk, the Oglala Lakota medicine man. As I began to read them my thoughts, my perspective, my understanding of who I am and where I come from began to shift. This was 1964, the year, I always recall, when everything started to change.

Everything that was not taught me when I was a child was taught to me in those pages—what it really was like to be Indian. I started envisioning what a beautiful way of life we once had.

I wanted to help Eddie, but moreover, I needed to get myself into a situation where I could stop thinking about suicide. I told Eddie if they got me out of solitary confinement, placed me in an honor dormitory—where they had TV and other freedoms and amenities—and got me a job in the power plant, I would help them organize the Native prisoners to participate in his "Indian Folklore Group."

Four days after our initial conversation, Eddie returned with Dr. Moran, who had agreed to my offer. "I'm going to give this thing a chance," he said.

So they sprung me from the hole and put me in the honor dormitory. I went back into the power plant and started organizing—quite successfully so. At that time there were probably about 160 Indian inmates in Stillwater, a majority of them Ojibwe. I got 110 of them to join the Indian Folklore Group.

We started meeting in a classroom with a big blackboard. All of us were in the same boat: We knew we were Indian people, but we didn't know what that meant. We had been raised in the foster system, the boarding school system, the criminal justice system, and by parents who'd had the Indian beaten out of them.

Eddie started us off at square one. He taught us to say "hello" and "thank you" in the Ojibwe language. As people got comfortable with simple words and phrases, Eddie began to teach about our history, about the Great Anishinaabe Migration from the East Coast of the continent, from the St. Lawrence River to where we are today in Minnesota and surrounding areas. Eddie taught that the people knew to stop their migration when they found the food that grows on water. That was what they were told to do in the Anishinaabe prophecy. Of course that food was wild rice or, as we know it in the Ojibwe language, *manoomin*. He introduced us to the Midewiwin Lodge, the Anishinaabe way of spirituality. He drew pictures and diagrams of the Midewiwin Lodge and then discussed all of the different stages and degrees of learning within it. Eddie encouraged us to make a commitment to a traditional way of life. In order to become a full-fledged Midewiwin, he said, you must know your language, culture, ceremonies, prayer songs, and many other things.

Not all of the men in the folklore group were Anishinaabe. We had Dakota, Lakota, and men from many other Indigenous nations. Even though most of the teachings came out of the Anishinaabe tradition, all of the men found commonality and drew strength from the learning we did. We found, for example, that all of the tribes represented in our group used and revered the drum. Also, we found a bond in the way we were treated by white society. White people didn't care if we were Ojibwe or Dakota or Omaha. To them we were all Indians.

After a while we had spiritual leaders from many tribes coming to visit. When they came, it made us understand that we weren't forgotten.

We actually got the class accredited out of the University of Minnesota. Warren's *History of the Ojibway Nation* was our primary textbook.

Boy, I really got into it. I really started feeling good about being an Indian. I stopped thinking about killing myself.

I was typical of the other Indians there: spiritually and emotionally bankrupt. We had no way of expressing our feelings, our hopes and fears. Nobody ever asked us; nobody cared. We had nobody to talk to when times got tough, when somebody at home got sick, or had a car accident, or was dealing with divorce or suicide. So we started to depend on our little group there, the Indian Folklore Group. We started conducting ceremonies. The Sacred Pipe, tobacco, and sage came into use. Reliance on spirituality and each other became the foundation of our whole situation. We understood that we couldn't achieve anything unless we developed a strong traditional spiritual base.

The other men took to the lessons as we hoped they would—as if their lives depended on it. As I look back on it, I realize that not only did their lives depend on it, but also the lives of their families and future generations. After all we had been through, all the abuse at the hands of the church, the government, and the education system, it was literally do-or-die time for our people.

We started holding Midewiwin ceremonies inside the prison. We started down a healing path that would lead us places we never could have imagined. The more I learned, the more I yearned to get out of there. I wanted to use this newfound knowledge to help young people get their lives together and stop them from ending up in institutions.

Also, I had a young lady I'd met before I went to Stillwater, when I was in and out of St. Cloud; I met Peggy Sue Holmes, who was only fifteen years old. I was more and more excited about coming out and seeing her again and showing her how I'd changed.

After two or three of these ceremonies, Eddie said our progress would have to come to a screeching halt, at least temporarily. "We can't go any further unless we have a drum," he said.

So we went and saw Dr. Moran and requested a drum. Eddie told him the drum is the center of our universe. No matter where that drum is, wherever that drum is set, that's the heart of our nation. All of our teaching comes from that drum.

"Oh no, we can't do that," Dr. Moran said. "If you get a drum the Black inmates will want a piano and saxophones and all sorts of instruments." He made those kinds of comparisons, not understanding that we weren't trying to start a jazz band. We were trying to send prayers to the Great Spirit.

Eddie said, "There's no way we can go any further. The drum is the center of the universe. It is the heartbeat of Mother Earth."

Dr. Moran was a really nice guy, and as Eddie explained the sacred significance of the drum, he really started listening. "If a drum should show up on my desk someday," he said, "I guess I'd have to give it to you, right?"

So we went to work assembling a drum. Eddie took these old leather welding aprons, and we soaked them in water for about two weeks to make a drumhead. I spent five cartons of cigarettes to buy a big empty ice cream barrel from one of the kitchen workers. I was able to hide this stuff under coal piles and in the dark corners of the power plant. When we had everything together we stretched the leather over the barrel, sewed it on taut, and painted it all up nice. It was really beautiful.

Even though we were in prison, the minute we hit that drum for the first time we were free. It was the first time I had ever been free to stand next to a drum and hear its beat. As a child I had heard drums, but I was never allowed near them. Sometimes, from way back in the woods, I would hear the sound of a drum. I'd peer out the window hoping to catch a glimpse of what was going on, but was always told by my mother to stay away.

After it dried, we placed our drum in a big box. It was now too large for me to keep hidden in the power plant. Dr. Moran started a two-week vacation, so I had to keep it hidden until he returned. It cost me another six cartons of cigarettes to bribe a kitchen worker into keeping it in one of their storage pantries. This was the best place for it because the mail came into the prison through a loading dock at the back of the kitchen. When Dr. Moran returned from vacation, we addressed the box to the Indian Folklore Group, care of Eddie Benton-Banai. I bribed one of the mailroom workers with several packs of cigarettes. He carted that box through three locked gates and placed it on Dr. Moran's desk.

About a week later Dr. Moran sent Eddie and me a kite, a written message, saying that he wanted to meet with us in his office. We went up there, and he had this big box open on his desk, and here's this beautiful drum inside of it.

He said, "I don't know who this came from. There's no return address—somebody sent you guys a drum anonymously. As promised, I'm going to give it to you."

We pretended like this was all a great surprise. Eddie acted all excited. He took one of the sticks we had made, hit the drum four times, and then sang a round dance song. As Eddie sang I was just feeling the drum, and just happy, and free.

3. CONFRONTATION POLITICS

DR. MORAN TURNED THE DRUM OVER TO US, and we started learning powwow and ceremonial songs. Just a few months after a group of us started practicing together, we put on a performance for the rest of the institution. Everyone was really impressed by our progress; after that things started to improve rapidly for the Indian prisoners.

But we weren't the only ones to benefit. Sure enough, just as Dr. Moran predicted, the Black prisoners asked for a saxophone and other instruments; they got them, too. These were the things they needed to start healing their incarcerated men. Every group within the prison benefited from our example.

We continued to push Dr. Moran to help us get what we needed for our community, and for our families. Eddie told him the next thing we needed would be a powwow within the walls of the penitentiary.

"I don't know about that," he said. "How are we going to pull that off?"

Eddie had a plan, of course. He called an elder he knew in Minneapolis named Emily Peak, who arranged everything. She brought in a group of traditional dancers. Many of us arranged to get our hands on dance regalia, and we held our first prison powwow.

Next we told Dr. Moran we had to have a wild rice celebration in the fall. Soon we had a big feast, and our families were all there with us.

We pushed Dr. Moran's comfort zone again. We told him about the sweat lodge, our purification ritual, and said we would need to have a sweat lodge in order to continue moving forward.

He said, "I think you all are going a little too far now. You would need wood and rocks and heavy-duty canvas to cover it. And who's going to build it?"

A week or two later some friends came with willow branches and canvas tarps and helped us build a sweat lodge. As far as we knew, this was the first sweat lodge built in any correctional institution in America.

There was an Indian renaissance going on in that prison. Our powwow became an annual event, as did the wild rice feast. Our purification ceremony was held weekly. Now we had friends, family, and community members coming into Stillwater to celebrate our culture and spirituality.

Those experiences not only changed my life; they changed the lives of many of the Indian inmates. Dr. Moran was very pleased, too, because he saw the Indians bettering themselves. The members of our group started going to Alcoholics Anonymous, to Narcotics Anonymous, and taking advantage of educational opportunities. Guys were studying for careers as dental assistants, X-ray technicians, and small business owners.

Eddie and I continued to engage in self-improvement as well. We joined the Dale Carnegie course on public relations. It was in that course that I learned how to debate, how to change minds, and how to speak in front of large groups. I owe all of my oratory skill to what I learned in that course. I learned techniques on how to win friends and influence people. Eddie and I both learned to become excellent public speakers.

We held a prison-wide speech competition in which Eddie and I competed against professionals—members of the state legislature and the mayor of Minneapolis even came in to compete. And guess what? I won. I mean, not only did I win, I beat their asses. I won the top speaking award by discussing what I was going to do when I got out of prison. I spoke about everything we had achieved, and how we could duplicate our approach on the outside to heal the lives of Indian people.

We started getting all kinds of recognition. People in the prison administration, in the community, and in government credited Eddie and me for the changes the Indian brothers were making. There was a monthly newspaper in Stillwater that sent a reporter to interview us and write about our culture program, how it was advancing the lives of Indian men and how it could be used in other institutions across the country.

Our ideas would soon catch fire. You might say that we established one of the first Native American studies programs in the United States.

Today, there are whole departments in many colleges and universities; prisons everywhere are offering the kind of programs we started in Stillwater.

As time went by, we had more than anecdotal evidence to back up our claims that the cultural restoration program was working. You can't get out of prison without a parole plan. Before we started the folklore group, our men were passive about the things they needed to do to make a plan, such as find a job, a sponsor, and a place to live when they got out. Our men suddenly became proactive; they wanted to get out. We saw the average time an Indian inmate spent behind bars decline from six years down to three years. The Indian brothers were making it happen, dealing with their addictions, learning how to make presentations, increasing their personal confidence, and caring about themselves.

Through the Dale Carnegie course, we were able to make contacts in the corporate world—executives came in from the leading businesses in the area and presented to us. We made many positive impressions on these leaders; they started to see the potential of the Indian brothers and offered many of them employment. Dennis Banks, who would later become famous as an American Indian Movement leader, was hired out of Stillwater as a public relations man for the Honeywell Corporation.

Eddie and I started planning for our release. We would transpose our Native American studies program to the streets of Minneapolis, catch young people before they got into trouble, and keep them from going to prison.

Eddie was released in 1967, a few months before me. He moved to Minneapolis, where there were only two programs for Indian people: the Upper Midwest American Indian Center and the Twin Cities Chippewa Tribal Council. These entities would give out used clothing and food baskets, and that was about it. Nobody was dealing with police brutality in the Indian community, unemployment, poor housing, health disparities, lack of quality education—at that time the average Indian adult in Minneapolis had a fourth-grade education.

Eddie started talking about cultural enrichment in the Minneapolis Indian community, about all the good it could do, restoring pride to our youth. He didn't know many people in Minneapolis, and most of the people he spoke to weren't open to his message. He'd make presentations before all these old-timers, and they'd just grumble: "Goddamn ex-convict gonna come out here and tell us what to do?"

He soon became frustrated and returned to his former job as an ironworker. He moved to Gary, Indiana, where he was hired as the foreman of an iron erection crew that built bridges and buildings.

I got out of prison a few months after Eddie and came back to Minneapolis, where I lived in a halfway house run by a Thomas Kondrak, a Catholic layperson known as Brother DePaul. In short order, I got in trouble again and ended up going to the Minneapolis workhouse. They were going to send me back to Stillwater, but I talked the judge into giving me another chance, and this Catholic brother allowed me to return to his halfway house.

I arrived at the halfway house on a very cold day in 1968, as they were in the midst of a gathering. They were celebrating the house's anniversary and toasting its success in helping men return to society. They had arranged to bring in a speaker—the priest who started one of the first halfway houses in America. But there was a big blizzard that night, and the guy was stranded at the airport.

This Catholic brother approached me and asked if I would give the keynote address. Here I was facing more time in Stillwater. I couldn't get a job. Everywhere I went, if I told them I was an ex-convict, nobody would hire me. Yet I found myself standing before this room full of church officials, business leaders, and dignitaries telling my life story.

I told them how I came from the reservation, all the racism I'd experienced, how I went to jail, the bad experiences I had in Red Wing, getting framed at St. Cloud, going on a hunger strike at Stillwater, and here I am today just trying to make it. I told them I had a first-class engineering license but couldn't even get a job.

When I finished speaking, it was desperately quiet in the house. Just then my probation officer, who was one of the invited guests, got up and said that because of my honesty and the power of my personal story, he was going to see to it that I didn't get sent back to Stillwater. Another guy stood up, an executive from Northern States Power Company, and told me to come down and see him. He said he thought they would have a job for me. I was absolutely stunned. That had to be one of the most surprising days of my life.

I think I realized then the power that a personal story has to transform people's understanding of what it means to be Indigenous in America. There were so many stereotypes about us. Most people thought Indians were extinct. Here I was telling the raw truth about my life, and people were blown away.

So I went down to Northern States Power (NSP), put in an application, and waited for a call. In the meantime, Peggy got pregnant. We had been together for almost five years by this time, dating while I was in and out of prison. If you count those years, we've now been together for more than sixty years. We had a Catholic wedding, held at St. Stephen's Church in south Minneapolis. We held the reception at Brother DePaul's halfway house, where I was living, and had a big feast there. Peggy's family from the Lac Courte Oreilles Ojibwe Reservation in Wisconsin came down for the wedding.

Spring broke, and we had a big flood. One of the NSP power plants flooded out. They had to reopen this old plant at Twenty-Eighth and Marshall Avenue along the Mississippi. Northern States Power called me to work to help with the sandbagging and heavy labor. I told the management there that I knew how to run those old boilers, and they put me to work full-time. As far as anyone knew, I was the first Indian, and the first felon, ever to work for that company.

I spent several months in Brother DePaul's halfway house. I was doing pretty good, holding down a steady job. When I was finally released, Peggy and I moved into a little apartment in Northeast Minneapolis and started raising a family together. I was not drinking, running around, or doing any drugs.

As my life stabilized, I could pay attention to other things, and around 1968 I started organizing. Unlike Eddie, who wasn't from

Minneapolis, I had friends and allies in the city to work with, but it was still difficult. We didn't have a meeting space, and so did all of our work in bars and restaurants. We couldn't get hardly anybody involved. I started hearing about these meetings that were taking place with Dennis Banks, George Mitchell, Harold Goodsky, and Annette Oshie. Other Indian people were getting together, too, and they invited me and my group to join them. At first I'd go sit in on them, you know, just listen to what they had to say. They were talking about the deplorable conditions that Minneapolis's Indian people lived with.

Dennis Banks was a natural leader and a very charismatic speaker, but he ran into some of the same roadblocks as Eddie had; the elders weren't listening to him, either. Dennis and I, and the others at those early meetings, decided we had to join forces, start a new organization to tackle issues like unemployment, poor housing and education, and police brutality.

Although we had both spent time in Stillwater and were both Anishinaabe, Dennis and I came from different backgrounds. He went through the boarding school system, spent something like eleven years separated from his family, most of those in Pipestone, Minnesota, hundreds of miles from his home on the Leech Lake Reservation. Afterward he enlisted in the air force and spent a lot of time stationed in Japan, where he fell in love, had a baby, and came to despise the US military.

Dennis and I disagreed about some things, but on the important issues, we were on the same page. We both knew that if we didn't do anything, we Indians were going to vanish as a people.

We decided to call ourselves the Concerned Indian American Coalition. That's all we were, just a little group that had no meeting place. Nevertheless, we started to raise eyebrows within our community. We would not have a meeting without a prayer. Today, it is expected, whenever our people meet, that we will begin whatever we're doing with a prayer, an offering of tobacco, smudging with sage, putting out a spirit plate. But back then, everybody kind of laughed at us.

These were people who had come through the boarding schools

and prisons and had the Indian beaten right out of them. They were scared. They associated their culture, their language, and their spirituality with pain and suffering. Our people didn't remember that, before the white man's intervention, these were sources of immeasurable pride, power, and pleasure for our people.

I argued with community members. I'd say, "If we forget about our past we'll never have a future. People have to know who they are. They must be proud of who they are. They have to get rid of this John Wayne syndrome that causes our community to not want to be Indians; they prefer to be cowboys."

Although we couldn't explain it at the time, our people were suffering from historical trauma. They were hurting and scared because of the things that had been done to them—and carrying the pain from the suffering of their parents, grandparents, and ancestors. We now understand historical trauma, a form of post-traumatic stress disorder, as the cause of much of what ails our people.

After six months of organizing, we called a meeting at 1212 Plymouth Avenue in north Minneapolis. This was our first meeting in the space that would come to be known as the first AIM headquarters. We estimated that fifteen thousand Indian people lived in the Twin Cities area. But only eighty-six of them came to that meeting, mostly women and children.

They say a people will never be defeated until the hearts of its women are on the ground. The men in our community were defeated by unemployment and alcohol. The men didn't see a future. The women were raising the kids; they looked the future in the eye every day. It was always the women who stood up first for the Movement, even though many of them never received credit for their contributions. The Anishinaabe and many other Indigenous cultures recognize the women as the true leaders, the ones who select our leaders.

On the agenda was leadership elections. Dennis Banks was nominated first. He got up and gave a short talk. I liked his ideas, but I didn't agree with his lack of urgency. I thought we had to take immediate action, that there was no time to lose.

Somebody nominated me, and I got up and started telling them about the issues we had to deal with. When I stood to speak that day to advocate for my election as chairman of the Concerned Indian American Coalition, I had not prepared any remarks. I spoke from the heart, and because I gave voice to my heart, I said the right things.

I had gained a lot of confidence through my prison experiences, and due to the success I was having in my career. I told them about my personal success and the success we'd had with Indian inmates. I said my first priority as chairman would be to deal with the Minneapolis police, the mayor, and the city council regarding the issues of poor housing, unemployment, and racial discrimination in the Indian community.

Someone asked me how I intended to do that.

I don't even know where the hell it came from, but on the spot I coined a phrase: I told them I'm going to do it through "confrontation politics." I didn't know what I was talking about; the phrase just flew out of my mouth.

Someone asked, "What does that mean?"

I said, that means you go knock on the door of the mayor's office, and if he doesn't let you in, you knock a little louder. If he doesn't hear you, I said, you kick the damn door down. But when you go in there, you better have your shit together. You got to know exactly what you want, and why you want it, and be able to prove to the mayor, the chief of police, the city council, the superintendent of schools, the Bureau of Indian Affairs that discrimination is occurring.

When I talked about confrontation politics, about half the people started tripping over each other to get out the damn door. The response from the people who stayed, however, was overwhelming. People stood and spoke about how their kids were beaten up in school. Someone said Indian people weren't being served in certain restaurants. Someone else complained that police were rounding up Indian people in Franklin Avenue bars and forcing them to clean up the city parks.

I told the people that as chairman I would confront the three worst enemies of Indian people: white European education, organized religion, and the Bureau of Indian Affairs. These institutions sought to destroy our language, our culture, our traditional way of life and relocate us into large urban areas, where so many Indians are stuck yet today.

When talking about religion, I was talking specifically about organized religion. In no way would I attack Christianity. There's nothing wrong with Christianity when people practice it and live it on a daily basis. I'm talking about organized religion, you know, where they solicit billions of dollars based on the conditions of poor people around the world, and all we see being done by these massive institutions is construction of glass cathedrals and ever-higher steeples.

In my speech I said that 80 percent of all the natural resources left in America were on Indian land. I told those community members that we should never give up another inch or another ounce without a struggle, even if that meant giving our lives.

I talked about the children and the unborn generations to come. Because that's what Black Elk, Sitting Bull, and all of our great leaders talked about whenever they signed treaties. They always asked: How is this going to affect our children seven generations from now?

What I said that day became the blueprint for our long-term struggle. Myself, and many others, would spend the rest of our lives fighting white European education, the BIA, and organized religion.

I was elected with 99 percent of the vote, and I was eager to get to work but was immediately sidetracked by criticism coming from within the Indian community. People heard me speak and discounted my message, saying we were just trying to walk in the footsteps of the Black Panthers. While I had done a lot of work in the Black community and wholeheartedly supported the Panthers' struggle for equality, we were after something much different. I responded angrily to the comparison. Our Indigenous nations had fought the United States and had signed nation-to-nation agreements. These agreements were the law of the land—equal in stature to the Constitution. The treaties contained language ensuring our civil and human rights, but also much more. We had the rights to large tracts of land on and off reservation. We also were guaranteed education, health care, housing, and access to traditional hunting, gathering, and fishing areas—yet many of our people were hungry, sick, poorly educated, and homeless.

Back then race relations in America were seen strictly as a Black and white issue. Nobody cared about Indigenous people. Most Americans, I think, weren't even aware that Indians still existed. America was busy creating all these civil rights organizations for African Americans. Corporations here in the Minneapolis area stepped up and released their Black employees who were community leaders, with pay, so they could devote themselves to developing groups like the Urban Coalition. But the same corporations were doing nothing to help Indians.

So I went after them.

I went to an Urban Coalition meeting downtown with a young Black militant named Matthew Eubanks. He was a Panther who would come in to town from down South and stir people up. He and I became really good friends.

Eubanks organized boycotts of Dayton's department stores and other businesses that wouldn't hire Blacks. He'd get about a hundred people to go down to these coffee shops, stores, and big corporations and occupy them for hours. That affected their bottom line; that's when they started taking notice.

Because I was chairman of this new Concerned Indian Americans group, people in the community thought I should be released from work, like the Black leaders, so I could devote myself full-time to fighting for my people. I had a good job and an opportunity to study for the next five years to be a nuclear engineer. At the time, NSP was just starting to build the Prairie Island and Monticello nuclear power plants near Minneapolis on the Mississippi. But I had to put my career on the back burner to follow my heart.

The Urban Coalition meeting Eubanks and I attended just happened to be in the basement of Northern States Power's office building. We had a plan. We brought chains and padlocks with us. We chained the doors of the meeting hall, trapping these big bankers, executive directors, and heads of all these huge companies. We demanded that I be released from work with pay for a year to carry out the objectives of the Concerned Indian Americans.

At first they were angry and demanded to know what we thought we were doing. But after hearing us out, they agreed to our demands.

Northern States Power released me from work with pay for a year. They even arranged office space for me. I was supposed to work out of the Urban Coalition at Seventh Street and First Avenue North in downtown Minneapolis, where the Minnesota Twins built their baseball stadium a few years ago.

I spent about five minutes in that building. I said to my friend Harry Davis, who was then the head of the Urban Coalition, "With all due respect, I'm not going to sit at a goddamn desk and answer phones all day. My work is going to be out in the streets. That's what I do, that's what I know best. I'm going to be a community organizer." Harry gave me his blessing to go out on the streets and fight for my people.

We weren't happy with the name of our organization, of course, Concerned Indian Americans, because that's CIA, like the Central Intelligence Agency—folks you wouldn't want to be confused with. So we asked our people to come up with a better name. An older woman named Alberta Downwind came up with the idea.

"Call yourselves AIM," she said.

"AIM?" I said. "What does that mean?"

"American Indian Movement," she replied. "You're always aiming to do this or that. We should call the group AIM."

"Well, I want to drop that word Indian," I argued. "We are finally through with that word. We're not from India."

Alberta grabbed me by the arm and said, "Listen, *Indian* is the word that they used to oppress us. *Indian* is the word we'll use to gain our freedom."

I said, "Right on."

We called a big meeting. We discussed it for several hours and finally agreed to make the change. Dennis Banks and Clyde Bellecourt

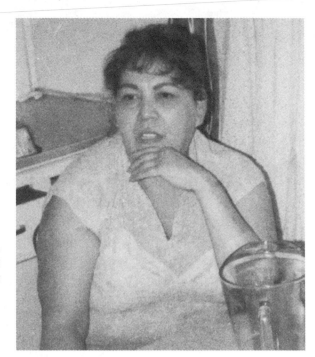

Alberta Downwind,
date unknown. *Courtesy
Downwind family*

had nothing to do with it. It was the idea of one young woman that was
adopted after it had achieved consensus from the community. And so
we became the American Indian Movement.

AIM meetings in those days never had an ending time. Often,
we'd start a meeting at six o'clock in the evening and be there still at
four in the morning. The decision-making process seemed to define
itself. Once we hammered out an issue and decided to go with it—had
achieved a consensus with the majority of folks—no matter how we in
the leadership felt, that's what we had to do. The Movement has operated that way ever since. We always go to the people and ask what they
want us to do, and then we go through ceremonies and seek spiritual
guidance before we move ahead.

At the time, AIM was only concerned about what was happening
in Minneapolis. Until we cleaned up our own backyard, we decided,
we couldn't even think about taking on a national or international

platform. We set down our goals and published them in AIM's first annual report, in February of 1970.

Objectives of the American Indian Movement (A.I.M.)

We the Concerned Indian Americans, residents of the Minneapolis area, organize to upgrade the conditions in which the urban Indian lives, and to improve the image of the urban Indian.

We the Concerned Indian Americans, to be known as the American Indian Movement (A.I.M.), residents of the Minneapolis and greater Minneapolis area, do hereby adopt the following goals:

Our main objective is to solicit and broaden opportunities for the urban Indian in order that he may enjoy his full rights as a citizen of the United States.

SHORT-RANGE OBJECTIVES

A. Establish a program to better the Indian housing problem.
B. Establish a program directed toward Indian youth.
C. Establish a positive program for employment of American Indians.
D. Establish a program to educate industry in the area of Indian culture and its effect on the Indian.
E. Establish a program to improve the communications between the Indian and the community.
F. Establish a program to educate the Indian citizen in his responsibility to his community.

LONG-RANGE OBJECTIVES

A. To generate unification within the Indian people.
B. To inform all Indian Americans of community and local affairs.
C. To encourage Indian Americans to become active in community affairs.
D. To bring the economic status of Indian Americans up to that of the general community.

As one of its first acts, the newly branded American Indian Movement established a street patrol in Minneapolis. At first we called it the Indian Patrol, and then the AIM Patrol. We had our people out keeping an eye on the cops who had long been known as a brutal and oppressive occupying force in our neighborhoods.

Most of our Patrol members were young Indian men and women. We wore red T-shirts emblazoned with the AIM logo so that people could identify us and know we were there to help. We advertised for volunteers and donations for things we needed, like radios and uniforms. Soon we had all sorts of people showing up to help, many non-Indians among them. We had nuns, neighborhood people, and even young law students, like Larry Leventhal, now a very well-known attorney, but then just a bushy-haired kid who was passionate about justice. The Minneapolis Black community had their Soul Patrol on the north side. We merged our efforts and worked as a unified protective force in our communities.

In order to gain legitimacy, AIM had to be out on the streets. We had to show our people we were going to be there with them when they were getting beat up and harassed. We were going to take pictures. We were going to get them lawyers. We were going to follow them down to the courthouse and get them bailed out. We were going to go to court as witnesses. That was our plan, and that was what we did.

Back in those days it was almost a seasonal sport to arrest Indian people. If the City of Minneapolis needed extra help cleaning up the parks in the spring, they arrested a lot of Indian people, because they knew we could be trusted to care for the land. And when they needed people to work their gardens in the fall, they rounded us up and sentenced us to community service. So we started focusing attention on that.

We also joined forces with the Black community on the issue of police misconduct. We made up our mind that no Indian and no Black person would ever plead guilty again, regardless of the charge, regardless if they were guilty. Doug Hall, a prominent civil rights attorney in town, started taking our cases. He also worked to get other attorneys involved. We would go to court and demand jury trials. We'd demand that they furnish us all the information pertaining to the crime. In

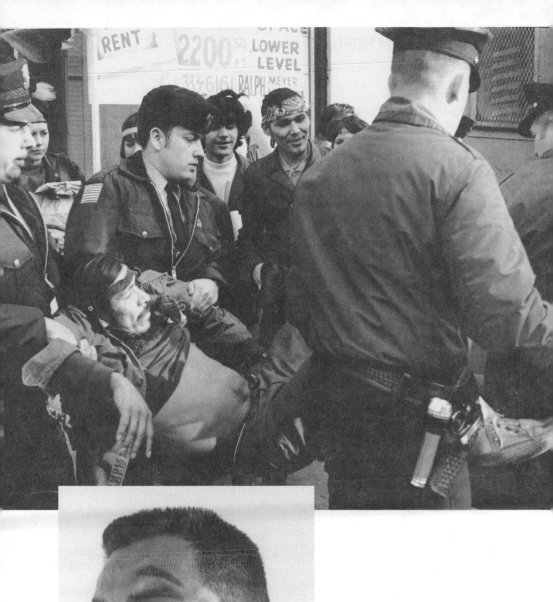

We took pictures while people were being arrested—above, of Tom LeBlanc—and other pictures of people who had been beaten up by the cops—left, Royce Sayers— so we could show them to the court. *Courtesy AIM Interpretive Center*

short order, we backed up the whole criminal system so that there wasn't an open court date for a year. We went before judges demanding that they release people awaiting trial to the Movement—whether or not they had bail money, or a job, or the other things the court demanded. We promised to see that they returned when required. Pretty soon, the judges and prosecutors were negotiating with AIM, making deals with us. That was a good start, but we had to keep pressure on the system that had oppressed us for so long.

We implemented additional strategies to expose those who were misusing their power. Say we knew the police were doing something wrong; we'd go and talk to them and they wouldn't listen. We'd go to the Office of Civil Rights, Human Rights, go to the governor, go to our congressman, and nobody would listen. This is what Indians in the 1960s felt every time they were harassed and brutalized on the streets of Minneapolis. No one would listen to us.

I held a meeting with our lawyers, and we decided that there was something we could do to take justice into our own hands. We implemented our own kind of court. We called it the Red Ribbon Grand Jury System. Our all-Indian juries investigated the Minneapolis Public Schools system, how they were spending money meant for Indian education on everything but Indian education. We convened our own hearings on police brutality. Witnesses would come in, and we'd take affidavits and record testimony. We had lawyers and paralegals helping us. We used the affidavits to press charges against the police department through the Minneapolis Civil Rights Commission. We conducted several of these over a span of about three years beginning in 1969. These Red Ribbon Grand Juries took place in the AIM office. We'd set up a big conference table with the names of all the commission members, witnesses, and community elders arranged on nameplates. We'd also have a nameplate for the police chief, the superintendent of schools, or whatever government or church official we had subpoenaed. In the beginning, of course, they wouldn't show up. We'd drape that chair with a big black sheet and put their name on it. And then we'd go ahead and hold the tribunal without them.

Once the media started showing up, we were able to send a wider message. We presented photographs, evidence of Indian people who had been beaten by the police. We had some horrible cases over the years: Indians stuffed into the trunk of a squad car; Indians thrown into snowbanks and pissed on by the police; an Indian woman taken down by the river and raped by police officers. As soon as these photographs appeared on television and in the newspapers, the goddamn chief of police started showing up as we had requested. All these officials started to see that it was better for them to face the music than try to sweep the allegations under the rug.

A woman who worked for the Minneapolis Civil Rights Department testifies before our Red Ribbon Grand Jury. *Courtesy AIM Interpretive Center*

Our intention was to reveal the truth, so that we could change these oppressive institutions and make a better life for our people. We had a fair, orderly process. First, the accused would be read the charges against them, and they would have the opportunity to respond with a statement. We would present all the evidence we had collected to the media and then turn it over to the grand jury; they'd go down to the basement of the AIM office to deliberate for an hour or two. They'd come up with an indictment against the chief of police or the superintendent of schools. We started developing powerful evidence against the government, the education system, and the churches that would serve as the foundation of AIM's future actions.

After addressing police abuse and educational abuse, the Red Ribbon Grand Jury moved against an organization called the Minnesota Council of Churches' Division of Indian Work. This group had been pulling in funds since 1952 for the benefit of the urban Indian community. But they had no Indian programming. There wasn't one single Indian working there. There were no Indians on their board. All they were doing was facilitating the adoption of Indian babies by non-Indian families.

We demanded that the Division of Indian Work create a new board that would be at least 75 percent Indian controlled, and that the chairman, the vice-chair, the treasurer would all have to be Indian. The executive director, we said, also had to be Indian. We demanded that they change; they could no longer solicit millions of dollars on behalf of Indian people and then fail to administer any services.

We went after them hard; we changed the Division of Indian Work completely within a three-month period. They agreed to all of our demands.

We immediately accepted the resignation of the executive director and hired one of our own for the position, a White Earth Band member named Emmanuel Gustav Holstein, known as Hap. He was an old organizer from the days when they had all these Teamster Union riots here, when the police killed striking truck drivers from Local 574 on the streets of Minneapolis. He was one of the chief union organizers way back in 1934. He was an old guy when we hired him, gray hair and all, but boy he was militant; he was radical. He would never forget those brutal cops; he got hit so hard—police clubbed him in the head, split him open. So we hired Hap Holstein to be the first executive director under the new regime.

Next we went after the Archdiocese of St. Paul and Minneapolis.

We had an ally inside the local Catholic hierarchy, a priest named Father Frank Kenny. He was, at that time, priest at St. Stephen's church in the heart of our urban Indian community. When we marched on city hall against police brutality, Father Frank came and marched by our side. When we protested at the Bureau of Indian Affairs, he was there fighting with us.

He was well known and trusted within the city government. So when all of these things were happening in the late sixties and early seventies, the mayor of Minneapolis would call him for advice. "Well, Frank, what do you think of what the American Indian Movement is claiming?"

He would say, "It's not what I think, it's what the Indian people think. I'm here to support them." He was that kind of guy.

He wrote a paper critical of the archdiocese, blasting leaders for their mistreatment of Indian people and demanding that the church issue an apology.

Because the archdiocese never had Indians in their leadership, he called for me to be placed on their Urban Affairs Commission. That's how I became the first Indigenous person in the history of the archdiocese to be placed on one of their governing councils, even though I opposed everything about the church.

Father Frank wrote a beautiful proposal in which, I think, he embarrassed the church. He demanded they free up $5,000 to help AIM get off the ground, a first step in undoing some of the harm that had been done to Indian people within the archdiocese. I think they just wanted us to go away, and so finally the church granted the money. But the only way they would release the check was if Father Frank agreed to remove all accusatory language from his paper, because that paper would be tied to the money and would eventually become part of the church record with the Vatican. They didn't want this to become an admission of guilt that could lead to further settlements.

But Frank Kenny was a man of honor, and he refused to remove the contentious language. So the church held up our funding for three months. One day me and Dennis went and saw him and said, "Frank you made your point. We need this money now." Still, he refused to give in. He wanted the abuses of the church against Indian people to finally become part of the official record.

One day he called us over to the rectory at St. Stephen's church. Dennis and I went. He said, "You guys really want that money, don't you?"

I said, "Yeah."

"Goddamn it," he was cussing and swearing. "I'll go take that language out of there then," he said, "but I'll never give up on what I'm trying to do."

A few days later he took me to the offices of the archdiocese, where he agreed to take the language out of his paper. They handed me a check for $5,000, at which point Father Frank announced that he would be with St. Stephen's for only six more weeks. He planned to marry.

After that, while on patrol, I'd see Father Frank cruising around the neighborhood in his car. I'd say, "Frank, it's pretty quiet on the streets, we're gonna take a break." The whole AIM Patrol would go over to Stardust Lanes after our shift to bowl and have a meal.

He'd tell me, "Oh no, we got a few more house calls to make." He'd wink at me and smile and drive off.

Father Frank's girlfriend was a Catholic school teacher. When he stepped away from the priesthood, she quit her job, and they went off to Seattle, Washington, where they got married and had three children.

I remember the $5,000 check we received from the archdiocese as the first official donation AIM ever received. That was the kind of effect the Movement had on men of conscience like Father Frank; they started finding out the truth of what the church was doing to Indian people, and they demanded something be done about it.

4. PEGGY SUE

WHEN I THINK BACK ON MY LIFE with Peggy Sue Holmes, it really is insepara-
ble from the Movement. Our relationship grew as the Movement did;
her strength and support made my work in the Movement possible.
I met my future wife back in the early sixties. Peggy's mom, Florence
Holmes, became real involved with the Movement. She was a very
strong-willed woman. A lot of our early planning took place at their
house before AIM had a space of its own. Peggy and I talked a lot and
liked each other. We started going together.

Peggy was—and is—a very beautiful woman, and unlike just about
everyone else in those early days, she didn't drink. She was against
alcohol and drugs and all those things people were into in the early
sixties. I wanted to surround myself with positive people like her. I
had been in and out of detention facilities for years, and I planned
never to return.

Peggy and I shared similar politics when it came to the antiwar
movement. She was really angry about the use of napalm and the
carpet bombing of innocent people in Southeast Asia, the burning
down of their forests and their villages. We started attending demonstrations together. We met a lot of people involved in the antiwar
movement: Black Panthers, radical white activists, and people like
that. When we finally got around to starting our own Indian movement, she was right beside me, working for everything we were trying to do.

Peggy and I talked a lot about her family history. Her mother was
Ojibwe with heritage from Bad River and Lac Courte Oreilles. Her
father was Japanese American, a soldier stationed at the local airbase,
out here where the Minneapolis–St. Paul International Airport is today. He was a patriot, but when the Japanese bombed Pearl Harbor in
1941, the government built concentration camps and started rounding
up all the people of Japanese descent on the West Coast, including
American citizens.

Peggy's mother and father separated, her mother always explained,
to protect them from being locked in those camps. Peggy was just a
baby then. She was born with her father's last name—Hakida—but

soon after, her mother changed her name to Peggy Sue Holmes, to protect her. She never really knew her father.

Several years after we started dating, Peggy tracked her father down and worked hard to establish the missing bond between them. She wrote to him, saying she loved me very much, and that we were serious about our relationship. Like any father would, he asked lots of questions about the man his daughter intended to marry. She told him I was working at Northern States Power Company—and he was pretty happy about that—and that I was the leader of an organization called the American Indian Movement. She told him that we were taking over government buildings and demonstrating against the police. She told him I had been in prison.

He completely rejected the idea of me being in his daughter's life.

He was an ex-military man, and although he had been held in an American concentration camp, he maintained a fierce loyalty to the US government. He would later see me on the news during the Trail of Broken Treaties and Wounded Knee—my antigovernment positions completely turned him off.

One day Peggy received a letter from her father. It explained his feelings about me and said she would have to choose between having him or me in her life. She chose to break off relations with him. Even though they never saw each other, they did exchange letters, and she always kept a picture of him close. Eventually, they stopped writing to each other altogether. But she still talked about him all the time. Even now she often thinks out loud, "I wonder what happened to my dad."

I wanted to help. I told her I would track her father down and try to arrange a meeting with him. But she didn't want me to do that. She was turned off to him because of the way he felt about me. When we got married, Peggy didn't seek out her father to be part of the wedding, or our family life.

In her first pregnancy, Peggy had toxemia, a condition that sent her blood pressure through the roof. She had a very hard time again when our daughter Susan was born. The doctors told Peggy she shouldn't have any more kids. Five years later came our second daughter, Tanya, and this time, again, Peggy went through a very hard time. Peggy started to think, five years after Tanya was born, that she could no longer get pregnant. That summer we were at a Sun Dance, and Crow Dog walked by and kind of tapped Peggy around the stomach. He asked to know how that little boy was doing. Peggy said to him, "What are you talking about? I can't have any more children."

Crow Dog just laughed and walked away. It bothered her so much that when she returned home she went to a clinic, got tested, and found out she was pregnant.

When our son Crow was finally born, we gave Eddie Benton-Banai tobacco to name him. Two or three weeks later Eddie dreamed that he died and went into the spirit world. When he arrived there, all of the animals and all of his relatives came out to greet him and just crowded around. Eddie said hello to them in English. Suddenly, everyone around him scattered and went away. Eddie was all alone and thinking, here I am in the spirit world; my elders told me that when I would get here all my family was going to be here to greet me, but here I am, and I never felt so lonely. Just then he heard a noise; a little crow flew out of a tree and sat down next to him on a log. That bird started talking to him in Ojibwe.

The little crow said, "What's bothering you, brother?"

Eddie said to him in Indian, "Well, here I am in the spirit world, and all my relatives come here, and I said hello to them, and they all took off."

The little crow told him, "They got scared because they didn't know that language you were speaking. You were speaking English." Eddie was grateful to the little crow for speaking with him and making him feel less lonely. He woke up and knew my son's name would be Little Crow, Aandegoons.

Five years after that, Wolf, our youngest child, was born. He was a breech baby, coming out backward, and presented a lot of complications. When Peggy went into labor, she was in a great deal of distress. An ambulance rushed her to the nearest south Minneapolis hospital—

Deaconess Lutheran. It was a horrible hospital. This was a place infamous for malpractice: they had amputated the wrong foot from a diabetic patient; they sewed people up after surgery with surgical tools left inside of them.

I was on my way into town from a trip when they took her in. I arrived to the hospital at about two in the morning, and she was in just terrible pain.

I asked the doctor, "What are you doing for her?"

And he said, "Well, we're going to have to operate. She's going to need a cesarean section to get the baby out." He warned me that there was a possibility that both Peggy and the baby could die during the procedure.

I said, "I'm telling you right now, I'm taking my wife out of here, whether you like it or not. Please get her ready."

They refused. They said not only would they not get her ready, but they would not allow her to leave.

I called an ambulance from Hennepin County General Hospital to come and get her.

The doctor finally came in with a piece of paper for me to sign releasing them of any responsibility. They rushed Peggy downtown in the ambulance. She nearly died on the way. At Hennepin County they quickly examined her and decided they needed to get that baby out immediately.

Mary Jane Wilson, the longtime AIM activist and leader, was with me. I had already asked Mary Jane's mother, Irene Bellanger, to give this child an Ojibwe name when he was born. She had agreed to do that. But as Peggy went into labor, Irene was in Denver, Colorado—she had a daughter that got sick out there.

So I told Mary Jane, "You go call your mother and you tell her to get back here right now." So she went and called her mother.

Meanwhile, the doctors came in and said, "We can't wait any longer," and they wheeled Peggy out. A young man I knew who was a pipe carrier came down, and we held a pipe ceremony within the hospital while Peggy was in the operating room.

Mary Jane returned after calling her mother in Denver. It must have been two or three in the morning. Mary Jane look stunned.

I asked, "What is it? When's your mom coming?"

She told us how the phone call went.

Mary Jane said, "Mom, what are you laughing about?"

And her mother replied, "Well, that baby is born already, and he's a little boy."

"Mom, no!" Mary Jane said. "Peggy's still in the operating room."

"Oh yes," she said. "That baby was born."

And Mary Jane said, "What do you mean?"

Speaking in the Ojibwe language, she told Mary Jane that a little wolf came in her room early that morning. He told that old lady he'd been traveling through space for a long time, and he was having a hard time getting here, but he was here now.

"I'm here now," he said. "My name is Ma'iigaans." Little Wolf.

Mary Jane's mother told her that the little wolf turned around and ran out the door. And as he ran out the door he turned into a little naked baby boy.

And I said, "Mary Jane, our little boy is here."

I had been in the room with Peggy when he was born. They cut her open and they took that little boy out. He started crying and pinked up right away. He was a month and a half premature.

Mary Jane ran down to the nursery. Our boy was in a basket in there, smiling at her.

Mary Jane's mom came back two weeks later, and we had a big feast at her house. She told the story of the little wolf who turned into a boy and said that our son would carry the name Ma'iigaans until he would be about eight years old. She said, "Whenever you think he's starting to become a young warrior, a young man, you will drop the 'Little' and he'll become just Wolf, Ma'iingaan."

My wife was very strong from the beginning of our relationship and through the decades of our marriage. She has had to be. People around town admire her fortitude because they know that anytime I'm needed elsewhere, I will pick up and go.

The only thing I really regret as far as the Movement is concerned is that I didn't spend enough time with my family, taking care of my children.

Today my children, whose ages range from twenty-eight to forty-seven, say they don't resent me for being away so much. Their mother still worries that they suffered, growing up so much without a father in the home. Whenever Peggy brings up the subject of my absence, the children tell their mother: "We knew what Dad was doing. We knew it was important. We're proud of what he did."

So it's been hard, you know, but I feel it was worth it. My whole family sacrificed for all the other Indigenous families out there who have seen so much suffering and separation, and I'm proud of them. As a family, we helped restore Indian family life.

I'm also very proud of the way my children were raised, and the adults they've become. They were provided a really strong traditional and spiritual base to work from, and they have embodied Anishinaabe values and are passing those on to the next generation.

Living in a white-dominated society always presents challenges as we work to revive and renew our Indian way of life. Sometimes these challenges translate into conflicts that we must work to resolve within our families. Take my son Crow, for example—his mother used to get after him. "You got to go to school," she'd say. "Go to college, get a degree! You need an education."

Finally, Scotty Brown Eyes and some of the old-timers that have been around for years, teaching Anishinaabe ways to our young people, stepped in and said, "Just leave that boy alone, Peggy. If it wasn't for young men like Crow our traditions wouldn't be carried on. Our traditional music wouldn't be with us today. What would we do without young people willing to dedicate their lives to preserving our ways? We would lose our songs. We would lose everything."

So Peggy listened, and she encouraged Crow to follow his passion. Today our son is a champion traditional singer, and he performs all over the world. Peggy is really proud of all that Crow has accomplished and happy that he has thrived while keeping alive the spirit of our people.

All of my kids are involved in the Sun Dance and the Midewiwin way of life. They have a spiritual base, a culture I never had when I was growing up, and my wife never had when she was growing up. That's what the American Indian Movement has been able to provide them. It was their own willingness to stick with me, and to believe in the work I was doing, that made it possible for them to have these opportunities.

Men who are experiencing difficulty in their marriage often come to me for advice. They ask me to give them the secret of my long marriage to Peggy. They know that ours is one of very few marriages to survive the upheaval of the Movement.

When I sit down and speak with them, and find out what's going wrong with their relationships, it usually comes down to one thing: they always want to be right, and so they create conflict with their spouse where there should be peace and understanding. Peggy and I argue, sure, but in the end, even when I feel sure that I'm right, I always bow to her. I have found that the ability to utter one simple phrase has kept our long marriage alive. Our arguments most often end with this phrase: "Yes, you're right." I say this not to be condescending but because, when I lay my ego aside, I see it is usually true.

Sometimes it really bothers Peggy that we have no privacy. I can pick a restaurant we've never been to before, and without fail, in the middle of dinner, somebody will come up to me. They'll often say they're having a problem in the community and need the help of the American Indian Movement. They'll say they've talked to everybody—politicians, police, bureaucrats, tribal leaders—nobody would help them. Almost fifty years after we began, the Movement is still seen in the Indian community as the court of last resort. When everything else has failed, our people come to the American Indian Movement.

I have the responsibility to see to it that something is done, that they don't go away saying, "What do you mean, you can't help?"

I almost invariably say, "The Movement can help you. I know we can."

5. THE INDIAN IN WHITE AMERICA

IN 1969, AIM WAS GOING full speed ahead, devising ways to protect our people from police and judicial abuse in Minneapolis. Peggy and I joined with several others and conceived an organization to support Indian people, for low or no cost, who were caught up in the criminal system.

We met in downtown Minneapolis with judges from the city and county courts, and representatives of the big local law firms, to propose the idea for a legal rights center. Notably, around that planning table were Doug Hall and Peter Dorsey, both talented and influential attorneys; Syl Davis, a Black community leader from north Minneapolis; and University of Minnesota professor Gwen Jones Davis, who was married to Syl.

In 1963 the US Supreme Court had ruled that if someone who was accused of a crime couldn't afford a lawyer, the court had to appoint one. That meant that big law firms, heavy hitters, were suddenly doing a lot of pro bono work, defending petty crimes. The way they saw it, they were wasting millions defending people on driving charges, simple assaults, and custody hearings, when they could be working on lucrative corporate lawsuits. These law firms saw that they could actually unburden themselves of all this pro bono work if they pitched in and funded our idea. So after forming the AIM Patrol, the second thing we did was form the Legal Rights Center of Minneapolis. Since 1970, we've served thousands of low-income clients—Indians and people of many other races.

With legal help finally available to our people, one of the most urgent areas we addressed was what the system called "parental determination of rights," which was the polite term they used when stealing Indian kids from their homes. I called it "parental termination of rights" because that's what the government was doing. Simply put, they were stealing our children. It could also rightly be called genocide. For many years the government took Indian siblings from their families and sent them to different families. One might become a Catholic, one might become a Lutheran, and one might end up in

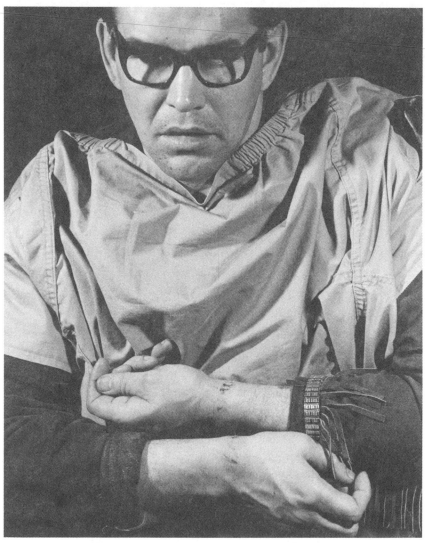

With all the protesting that we did, I was charged forty-four times between 1968 and 1974, but I was never convicted. Cops had dragged me by the handcuffs before this photo was taken. *Courtesy AIM Interpretive Center*

Utah and become a Mormon—never to see one another again or have any contact with their parents.

When AIM started, our friend Dr. Paul Boe, who was the head of the Division of Social Services for the American Lutheran Church, told us his organization alone was handling fourteen hundred Indian adoptions a year. We started meeting in Dr. Boe's church with real church leaders, real Christian people who walk in the footsteps of Jesus Christ. One of these real Christians was a young Indian guy, a Red Lake Ojibwe named Al Wennsmen, who worked for Lutheran Social Services. He brought us information about their adoption program, which he and others in the organization felt needed to be stopped. We also learned from Dr. Boe about a committee they operated called Lutheran Church and Indian People (LUCHIP) that would meet in Sioux Falls every two years.

Representatives of the Lutheran synods would come together and talk about all the "good work" they were doing with Indian people. They would pat themselves on the back, Al said, for all of the Indian souls they'd saved. Their method of saving souls was stealing Indian children away from their families. They would reinvent, at these semiannual meetings, guidelines for what constituted a safe Indian home. These rules were arbitrary and subject to change—you know, you can't have six children living in a two-bedroom home, or you had to have a certain number of bathrooms. Boys and girls can't share a room, and this kind of thing. They would use these guidelines in court, and because they were the church, the courts considered them experts and went along with them.

The government would take Indian families to court and after just one hearing—boom—they would be torn apart. Three of my brother's children were stolen away in this manner, so this issue is very personal. This destruction was almost always carried out on the word of missionaries who served as agents for the government in their campaign to annihilate Indian people.

In 1969, AIM issued our "Challenge to the Churches," confronting Christians with the evil they'd perpetrated on Indian people and pressing them to repent and to live up to their professed ideals. We met with Lutheran, Evangelical, and Catholic congregants and leaders, the Minnesota Council of Churches, and many others.

On July 29 of that year we met with the Lutheran Council of the U.S.A. and presented our case against them. We issued a list of demands that day, similar to those we asked of every other denomination operating within American Indian communities:

1. That a National Board of Lutheran Churches be set up, with 75 percent of its members American Indians, and that the chairman of this board be Indian.
2. That this National Board commit itself in supporting Indian groups in their efforts to determine their own needs, priorities, and actions.
3. That this National Board assume a positive role in influencing legislation created or supported by Indians and beneficial to the welfare of all American Indians.
4. That this board condemn the criminal actions of the practices and policies of the B.I.A. wholly, and that it be abolished.
5. That this board demand that their churches employ their influence as an organized body in meeting the urgent need for adequate housing available to Indians and that they support the efforts of Indian groups and individual families to provide themselves with more adequate housing.
6. That this board commit itself to spend $1,000 per year on every Indian American for the next ten years.
7. That this board make available without charge all church properties for use by all minorities; further, that all church properties be shared equally by all minority groups.

While we didn't get everything we wanted from the churches, we did start a new kind of relationship with them, particularly when it came to the obliteration of American Indian families. We were very pleased—shocked—by the forceful response to our Challenge by the

National Council of Lutheran Churches. The following is the statement they issued at the conclusion of their 1969 gathering:

> In that race is a gift of God that we have tragically abused, we would
> ask forgiveness of our Indian brothers and sisters and hereby publi-
> cally acknowledge our personal and corporate sins of racism, greed,
> insensitivity, dehumanization, robbery, assault, haughtiness, apathy,
> and other overt and covert injustices and inhumanities.
>
> We have been repeatedly reminded and confronted by the realities
> of Indian fragmentation, starvation, and confinement. Our declara-
> tions of "freedom for all," and "love thy neighbor," have been hollow
> words lacking integrity of positive life actions. Voices of protest with-
> in the Indian community have been largely silenced by inattention,
> organizational hang-ups, and tactics which promise action later on.
> Our political and ecclesiastical systems have fostered second-class
> citizenship where rules are written to play a white man's game. The
> beauty, depth, and sensitivity to the rhythm and wholeness of life in
> the Indian community have been methodically obliterated from the
> American scene. We are less human; our nation is poorer; the family
> of God in Jesus Christ is hurting because of the continuing anguish
> which is carried by Indian people.
>
> The Lutheran Churches have been firmly confronted by certain
> "Challenges" which will require a major reordering of existing prior-
> ities in these three bodies. The "Challenges" have been offered in a
> serious, open manner. They represent a solid opportunity for the Lu-
> theran Church to earnestly re-examine its theology, practices, sense of
> mission and public posture. They are anchored in the comprehensive
> "Goals for the Indian Ministry" authored through the Division of Chris-
> tian Life and Mission of the National Council of Churches in the U.S.A.

"Recognizing that the gifts and needs of Indian and non-Indian
Americans are significantly different, and massive effort is required
to enable the free and creative use of these gifts across demonic and
man-imposed boundaries of race," the council endorsed our Challenge
and decided it would be presented to the church presidents and boards
involved; results would be reported at their conference the next year.

The damage caused by all those adoptions, however, continues even now. I get calls almost every day from people who say they were adopted out; they suspect they're Native American and are hoping to find their way back to their families of origin.

I'd like to tell you a story about how I became reunited with my long-lost relatives. It starts out tragically, with the murder of my fifteen-year-old nephew, Evan Denny, who worked at the Metrodome, cleaning the stadium after Minnesota Vikings football games. He was on his way to work one afternoon in 1995, driving with his girlfriend, when they stopped to get some gas at the SuperAmerica on Eleventh and Franklin. These other Indian kids drove up, rolled down tinted windows, and called him over to their car by name. His girlfriend said Evan was chatting and laughing with them. He told his girlfriend she could go home; he would get a ride to work from these guys. He got into the other car, and they all drove away.

That night Evan Denny failed to show up for work. His body was found along the tracks on the west bank of the Mississippi near the University of Minnesota. The guys he got into the car with, we later learned, were out that night to prove their allegiance to a Black gang they were trying to join. In order to gain acceptance into the gang, they had to kill one of their own. They shot Evan four times in the knees and killed him. It was a very sad time for our family. My sister, his mother, was devastated, of course, and asked me to help her handle the arrangements. I reserved the Catholic Charities building on Thirty-First and Park Avenue for the wake and funeral.

I was sitting at my traditional altar during the wake, praying with my family, when I felt a bitter cold breeze sweep into the room. I looked up at the man who had just come through the door. I almost couldn't believe my eyes. There stood my oldest nephew, Chuckie, with his wife and children, and their children's children. I hadn't seen him since he was three, when he was taken from my sister and our community. He was now fifty-four years old, yet I knew who he was the minute I laid eyes on him. He and his siblings had been taken from my brother Charles during a time when Charles was drinking and unemployed. This had happened to almost every Indian family in America.

We just grabbed one another and wept.

He told me he was living in Northeast Minneapolis. He had a Polish last name, like his adoptive family. He thought he was Polish. He told me he used to see me in the news all the time, and he'd tell his adopted dad, "That guy has got a lot of guts demonstrating against the police all the time."

Finally, the father broke down and told him, "That guy you admire on television, Clyde Bellecourt, that's your uncle."

"No way," he said. "Where does he live?"

And he said, "I heard he's running that housing project in south Minneapolis, Little Earth of United Tribes."

After that our family started coming back together. We found each other in every way you can imagine. Chuckie and his sister Heidi—my niece—were actually going to Edison High School over in Northeast Minneapolis and didn't even know they were related.

It's amazing how this niece found out who she really was. She used to go to a mom-and-pop store down on the corner of Park and Franklin. One afternoon, while shopping, she bumped into this woman she didn't know. For whatever reason they started walking around together, talking and joking. This woman had a light complexion, didn't look Indian.

They bought their groceries, walked across the street, and hung out for a while, chatting on a park bench. They really hit it off, so they agreed to meet again the following week.

When they met again this lady, whose name was Helen, naturally asked my niece to talk about her past.

My niece said, "I'm from White Earth."

"What? I'm from White Earth, the town of Mahnomen," Helen said.

My niece asked Helen about her maiden name. Helen said it was Green.

That girl looked at her like she'd seen a ghost. "Green? Helen?"

"Yeah."

"Who are you married to?"

Helen said, "I used to be married to Charles Bellecourt."

My niece started crying. This woman, Helen Green, was her mother.

They were both so happy.

One day I heard a knock on the door, and here's this strange girl. I let her inside, and she told me she had just met her mother, Helen Green, and that she was my niece. She started crying and hugging me. We sat down, and she told me she was looking for her sisters. I happened to know exactly where one of them was—five doors down the street. So we walked over and knocked on the door, and the crying and hugging played out again as they were reunited.

I asked around a little and found her other sister. She was in the process of divorcing her husband and had just moved to Minneapolis from their home in San Francisco. So the two of them reconnected as well.

Within a period of about three years, my whole family came together as if drawn by a magnet.

There are thousands of Indian people separated from their families during early childhood, wandering the earth today not even knowing where they come from; not even knowing they are Indian.

AIM, with the help of some brilliant young lawyers at the Legal Rights Center, let the world know about the genocidal practice of splitting up Indian families. We started attacking the government and the major Christian denominations for their complicity in destroying Indian families.

The Legal Rights Center has helped to boost the early careers of some fantastic legal minds, attorneys of color who came to work with us for the early part of their careers and went on to achieve great things.

Pamela G. Alexander, for example, sits on the Hennepin County bench in Minneapolis today. Keith Ellison was the first Muslim elected to Congress and the first African American from Minnesota to be elected to Congress. Keith and Pamela worked for our Legal Rights Center early in their careers.

Michael J. Davis is another example. Mike, who is African American and counts Native American people among his ancestors, was a US district court judge for twenty-one years. He handled several very high-profile Indian treaty rights cases. He was well educated by the American Indian Movement.

I recently had the pleasure of visiting Mike Davis in his chambers on the thirteenth floor of the federal courthouse in Minneapolis. From where we sat we would see the Mississippi River in the distance. Mike and I reminisced about the bad old days when the Minneapolis cops used to speed past the jail with their Black and Native prisoners, drive down to the river, and beat the crap out of them with rubber hoses. We discussed the early years of the Legal Rights Center and our efforts to put an end to such barbaric police tactics.

Mike recalled how the Center was led by community workers, like Willie Mae Dixon and Mary Jane Wilson, and not lawyers. Many of the lawyers thought this was backward, but we knew the grassroots people had to lead the push for justice.

I knew Mike's days at the Center had been life-changing, but I was deeply moved when he said that, along with his mother, I was one of the most influential people in his life.

Mike was nominated to the federal bench with the backing of Senator Paul Wellstone and attorney Ken Tilsen, and appointed in 1993 by President Bill Clinton. In 2008 he became the first African American chief judge of the District of Minnesota. And in 1999, United States Supreme Court chief justice William Rehnquist appointed Judge Davis to a seven-year term on the United States Foreign Intelligence Surveillance Court. I am so proud of everything Mike has accomplished.

Mike also expressed his pride in me. One thing he said I will never forget as long as I live. We were talking recently about how his experience at the Legal Rights Center influenced his long, distinguished career. Judge Davis looked at me. "Brother, I want you to understand," he said, "I am a foot soldier for you. Always have been."

The Movement has a tremendous track record of helping our people navigate a legal system that has long been too confusing, too expensive, and too biased against Indians. Long after Wounded Knee, when many people thought AIM's usefulness had ended, we were just getting going. Indian people took notice of that and recognized, *hey, these guys are still working hard for this community. These guys aren't going away.* Our longevity in the community has made a tremendous difference in thousands of lives.

Because of the attention our work in Minneapolis was receiving, Vice President Spiro Agnew asked Dennis Banks and me to participate as investigators in a national study on the condition of Indian America. Shortly after he was elected as Nixon's running mate, Agnew invited Dennis and me to a meeting at the White House, where he chaired a meeting of the National Council on Indian Opportunity, an advisory group created in the wake of the publication of a groundbreaking book called *Our Brother's Keeper: The Indian in White America* (edited by Edgar S. Cahn). This must have been about 1970.

Let me say a few words about this book before moving on. For several hundred years, Indian people in America had been reeling, under tremendous pressure from the government and the church to assimilate. The processes used against us were tremendously successful, creating near-total confusion among Indian people about our true selves. Slowly, our people were waking up and asking questions. This book, researched by such esteemed scholars as Vine Deloria, Alvin Josephy, and many others, showed where Indian people stood after the long period of cultural obliteration.

The cover had a picture of an Indian with an upside-down US flag draped around him. This gesture is known internationally as a sign of distress. Many within the Movement adopted this notion; the upside-down flag came to be associated as an iconic symbol of the Movement. Out of respect for my father and brother, and other Indian veterans who fought to protect that flag, I never really agreed with that.

Our Brother's Keeper helped to raise the consciousness of Indian people to a level where they could finally comprehend the rapid, confusing, and devastating changes that had taken place in their families and communities over the past few generations. It also became a sort of bible for the Movement, a catalog of many of the areas of American Indian life that needed to be addressed.

Agnew explained that the whole project was going to be carried out by Indians. He said, "This is what we want you to do—go out to Indian Country and find out everything you can about how Indian people are doing." Then he asked us: "Does this sound like something you'd like to do?"

It was exactly what we wanted to do. This was information the Movement needed to know in order to back our arguments when we confronted the government and the church.

"Go and do the work that must be done," Agnew said, "and we'll support you."

Dennis and I recognized Agnew's offer as a tremendous opportunity. What we found out about the condition of Indian America, from our own research and from that reported in *Our Brother's Keeper*, would help form the basis of everything we did in the Movement.

We traveled coast to coast and back again, going into boarding schools, public health services, reservations, public schools—any place that received federal money for Indian people. We also studied treaty rights. We saw that the services being delivered to our people did not in any way match the language of the treaties our grandfathers had made with the United States.

We found out that Indian people lived to be an average of forty-four years old. In 1968, for white Americans, life expectancy was sixty-four.

Indian people on the Pine Ridge Reservation in South Dakota had a gross annual income of $1,910. By government standards, in those days, if you lived on $4,500 a year, you were in poverty. The book reported that there was "one bureaucrat for each and every family on the reservation," so $8,040 a year was spent per family to help the Oglala people out of poverty. Over 60 percent of the reservation's workforce was unemployed. People talk about a recession today when unemployment gets up around seven percent. By those standards, Indian people had been in a recession for two hundred years.

We found out that 90 percent of Indian housing in America was substandard. Seventy percent of our people didn't have indoor running water, or if there was, it was often contaminated by industrial toxins.

We found that Native adults had an average 5.5 grade level education, nationwide.

We looked into the dropout rate of Indian children in public schools. Right here in Minneapolis, 85 percent of our kids entering public high school were not earning a diploma. We found places, communities like Cumberland, Wisconsin, where 100 percent of the Indian children going into high school never made it through because of racism, ignorance, and brutality—kids getting beaten up by white classmates, having their hair cut off on school buses, and finally refusing to go to school.

We learned that Indians had the highest infant mortality rate in the United States. "On some reservations," the book reported, "the rate ranges to 100 deaths per 1,000 births—roughly twice as many as in the worst Negro ghettos in the nation, and four times the death rate among white babies."

Suicide was virtually unknown before Columbus. We don't hear about suicide in our oral history. In 1968, Indigenous people in the United States had a suicide rate many times the national average. On some reservations the suicide rate among teens was ten times the national average.

We found out that of every dollar appropriated by the United States government—by that I mean money generated by the government from the sale of coal, gold, silver, oil, and timber taken from Indian lands, money transferred to the Bureau of Indian Affairs to serve Indian people—of that, ninety cents out of every dollar was used in administrative costs by the Bureau of Indian Affairs. Only ten cents were trickling down to the Indian community.

The book reported that Indian people suffered more pervasively from hunger and malnutrition than any other group in the United States.

But the most drastic statistics that were pointed out in *Our Brother's Keeper* showed what alcohol and other intoxicants had done to us. When Indian people signed treaties, there were built-in guarantees that they would never allow alcohol on the reservations. Every treaty was written that way. Our grandfathers, our leaders, our chiefs looked at alcohol as a poison. They called it the firewater.

"If you drink that," the elders said, "you will end up just like the person that gave it to you. You will go home and beat up your wife, and start stealing, and lying." And sure enough, that's exactly what happened. We saw the devastating effects of this everywhere we went.

Our Brother's Keeper reported that Indian people suffered from mental illness and addiction at alarming rates: "Suicide, alcoholism, glue, paint, and gasoline sniffing, delinquency, and broken homes all are considerably more common among Indians than among the general population. Accidents, cirrhosis of the liver (attributable to excessive drinking), homicide and suicide accounted for 222 deaths per 100,000 population among Indians in 1964, nearly triple the national rate."

After Dennis and I concluded our research, we testified before the National Council on Indian Opportunity, who ultimately published a final report. I was disappointed in the way they presented the information we had provided; it was too narrow. It only concerned itself with the money that was stolen from us. It didn't deal with health disparities, dropout rates, police brutality, the dual system of justice, environmental racism, or racism in the schools.

Of all we learned from that study, and from *Our Brother's Keeper*, the greatest takeaway for me was that we needed a different kind of organization to help Indian people, one that would stand up and fight.

The information we uncovered was shocking, even to those of us who had lived it. The research helped motivate the Movement; it

showed us we weren't alone, and that what was happening in Minneapolis was happening all over the country. We came to the conclusion
that we must expand into a national activist organization. We had to
be prepared to give our lives if we hoped to create a better world for
our people.

One of the places we visited during that time was Alcatraz Island, the
old federal prison in San Francisco harbor. The takeover of Alcatraz
by a group of young Native people, mostly Indian students from the
Bay Area, informed our work, energized and mobilized Indians everywhere, and influenced the direction of the Movement. Seventy-eight
Indians made it to Alcatraz Island on November 20, 1969, in small
boats. Calling themselves "Indians of All Tribes," they would soon be
joined by hundreds of Native people from across North America. They
wanted to take control of the island and turn the infamous former
maximum security prison into an Indian cultural and spiritual center.
They cited as legal justification the 1868 Treaty of Fort Laramie, which
declared that all retired, abandoned, or out-of-use federal land would
be returned to the Native people from whom it had been embezzled.
Since Alcatraz penitentiary was closed on March 21, 1963, and the
island had been declared surplus federal property in 1964, the Indians
felt the island qualified for reclamation.

Organizers like Richard Oakes and Adam Fortunate Eagle also
sought to protest the federal government's policy of removal of Indians off their lands, a policy which had begun with the Indian Relocation Act of 1956. Ironically, it was this very act that brought so many
Indians together in the Bay Area. Adam Fortunate Eagle, for example,
was from the Red Lake Indian Reservation in Minnesota, and Richard Oakes was a Mohawk from Akwesasne, New York. Like so many
others, they ended up in urban areas, far from their traditional lands
and communities.

In an earlier landing attempt on November 9, fourteen occupiers
had issued the Alcatraz Proclamation, a statement of context and pur-

pose for their actions that still speaks to the conditions many Indigenous people around the world live in today. It was written by Adam Fortunate Eagle on behalf of the group.

To the Great White Father and All His People:
We, the Native Americans, re-claim the land known as Alcatraz Island in the name of all American Indians by right of discovery. We wish to be fair and honorable in our dealings with the Caucasian inhabitants of this land, and hereby offer the following treaty: We will purchase said Alcatraz Island for 24 dollars in glass beads and red cloth, a precedent set by the white man's purchase of a similar island about 300 years ago. We know that 24 dollars in trade goods for these sixteen acres is more than was paid when Manhattan Island was sold, but we know that land values have risen over the years. Our offer of $1.24 per acre is greater than the 47 cents per acre the white men are now paying the California Indians for their land. We will give to the inhabitants of this land a portion of that land for their own, to be held in trust by the American Indian Government for as long as the sun shall rise and the rivers go down to the sea—to be administered by the Bureau of Caucasian Affairs (BCA). We will further guide the inhabitants in the proper way of living. We will offer them our religion, our education, our life-ways, in order to help them achieve our level of civilization and thus raise them and all their white brothers up from their savage and unhappy state. We offer this treaty in good faith and wish to be fair and honorable in our dealings with all white men.

We feel that this so-called Alcatraz Island is more than suitable as an Indian Reservation, as determined by the white man's own standards. By this we mean that this place resembles most Indian reservations, in that:

1. It is isolated from modern facilities, and without adequate means of transportation.
2. It has no fresh running water.
3. The sanitation facilities are inadequate.
4. There are no oil or mineral rights.
5. There is no industry and so unemployment is very great.
6. There are no health care facilities.

7. The soil is rocky and non-productive and the land does not support game.
8. There are no educational facilities.
9. The population has always been held as prisoners and kept dependent upon others.

Further, it would be fitting and symbolic that ships from all over the world, entering the Golden Gate, would first see Indian land, and thus be reminded of the true history of this nation. This tiny island would be a symbol of the great lands once ruled by free and noble Indians.

AIM was in total solidarity with the Alcatraz takeover and stood ready to provide support. Since this was not specifically an AIM action—even though we were excited about what was happening out there—we waited respectfully for a request from the organizers before making any moves. Shortly following the takeover, we received a phone call from Oakes asking for AIM's support and inviting us to Alcatraz. He looked at us as fresh new leadership that might be able to come in and help unify the people.

The effectiveness of our AIM Patrol in protecting Indians on the streets of Minneapolis was now recognized throughout Indian Country. Having reintroduced traditional methods of peacemaking, we knew how to protect our Indian community from external threats and resolve internal differences. We had also developed a survival school, and a legal rights center, so the folks on Alcatraz were looking to us for guidance.

My wife, Peggy, Mary Jane Wilson, Dennis Banks, George Mitchell, Annette Oshie, and others that were on AIM's original governing board traveled out to the coast and stayed on Alcatraz for a few days. There were well over a hundred Native people staying there when we arrived. A lot of them would come out during the day, and then some of the people who lived in the Bay Area would go home at night. Different tribes would come from their homelands, spend a few days, and then go back home.

AIM made suggestions regarding the establishment of a security patrol on The Rock, much like the one we had going on the streets of Minneapolis. There were dozens of people coming and going every day, and every one of them had to be oriented and vetted. Tourists also continued to land on the island on certain days, depending upon what was going on. Most days, however, the tourists stayed in their boats and gawked at us through binoculars.

In addition to security threats coming from the outside, there was all sorts of tension among the Indians on the island that constantly needed to be dealt with. There were all kinds of people claiming that they took Alcatraz. Unlike here in Minneapolis, where the Indian community is made up of people of many tribes but is predominantly Dakota/Lakota and Anishinaabe, the Bay Area has sixty or seventy tribes, each with its own opinions on how things should be done.

They had a governing board which should have provided some structure, but the rules established for membership led to more instability. For example, if you missed two meetings in a row, you were immediately eliminated from the board. But sometimes there were two or three meetings a day; if board members were off the island, attending meetings at the San Francisco Indian Center—as was often the case—they were kicked off the governing board. We suggested changes to the organizational structure that ended that practice and led to greater continuity.

A system for receiving donations had to be established to keep the Alcatraz Indian community going. People from all over wanted to help. They started bringing food, clothing, and monetary donations to a drop-off center that we helped establish on a San Francisco pier.

We made all sorts of practical suggestions to the leadership there which were based on our experience in Minneapolis. AIM felt a survival school should be established on the island for the many families whose children were missing school during the occupation.

The legacies of Alcatraz are many, but I think the opportunity for Indians from everywhere to gather and visit, and share our cultures and experiences with one another, was vital, especially considering the long fight ahead. For so long the government had kept us divided. Now we had a space, an island in that beautiful harbor, where we could all come together and be ourselves. That's where many of the networks were established that would later be used to mobilize our people for the Trail of Broken Treaties and Wounded Knee.

Some very concrete examples of the Alcatraz legacy can be seen and heard throughout the country today. John Trudell, who would later gain prominence as an actor, poet, and performer, started a little radio station on The Rock. It was the first Indian radio station in America. It didn't have much reach at first, but with several million people living in the Bay Area, it didn't have to. As the occupation continued, radio stations across the country and around the world started picking up the broadcasts and replaying them. At the time, there were hardly any Indian newspapers, so you might say that little Alcatraz radio station represented the birth of Native media.

As our AIM delegation prepared to leave Alcatraz, we held a conversation about the importance of Native media. We decided radio was the most effective form of communication in places like Indian reservations where families and communities are spread out across wide areas. After Wounded Knee, AIM would be instrumental in establishing KILI FM Radio, "The Voice of the Lakota Nation," on the Pine Ridge Reservation. The hundred-thousand-watt station covers thirty thousand square miles and puts out news, talk, and music that support Lakota communities and the Lakota way of life. It only grew. Now there are some fifty-five Indian radio stations across the country, as well as scores of newspapers, websites, blogs representing just about every point of view in Indian Country, a Native American Journalists Association, Native youth journalism programs, and Native American journalism fellowships.

The island never became the American Indian cultural center envisioned by those who seized it. The occupation had sort of lost steam, and by the time the Coast Guard raided the island nineteen months after the takeover, only fifteen Indians remained. But the example of Alcatraz did inspire the 1970 takeover of Fort Lawton, a surplus air force base in Seattle, part of which was eventually converted into Daybreak Star Cultural Center, an American Indian gathering place. That occupation included a bloody confrontation between about a hundred Indians and a platoon of military police.

6. OCCUPATIONS

WHEN WE STARTED THE MOVEMENT, our first instinct was to go after the Bureau of Indian Affairs, the branch of government that belongs to Native people, and which had been oppressing us for so long.

We got our first opportunity to take on the BIA in March of 1970. I received a call from a woman named Tillie Walker, who was well known in Indian circles as an advocate for Indian self-determination. She told us that they were having a demonstration outside of the Bureau of Indian Affairs Central Office in Littleton and asked if the American Indian Movement would send somebody down there to help them, to support them. They had heard about the things we were doing in Minneapolis, and they wanted our support.

Tillie said the protest against anti-Indian employment practices was sparked by a local incident where a Native woman applied for a position as school counselor working with Indian children and was turned down despite her qualifications for the job. At the time, 95 percent of workers at the BIA were non-Indian.

AIM was broke. We had no resources to send a big group to Denver. We could barely afford to send a package. But we didn't want to ignore their cry for help. Somehow Dennis Banks scraped together the money to put me on a plane to Denver.

I was picked up at Stapleton International Airport early in the morning and driven out to Littleton, Colorado. When I arrived at the BIA headquarters, there was a group of fifteen or twenty older ladies, and kids, out there protesting. There were no men. It was cold and windy, snow whipping around. I stood among them and gave a talk about the Movement. I told them we would do whatever we could to support their protest.

I said, "If this federal agency is going to be called the Bureau of Indian Affairs, it ought to be controlled and run by Indian people. Why do they call themselves the BIA when 95 percent of the people working there are non-Indian?"

I looked up at the building and saw BIA bureaucrats standing in the windows pointing at us and laughing.

My blood started to boil, you know. It occurred to me what we had to do. "We got to take over this building," I said. "It belongs to us."

The building was called "Indians of the Prairies."

"Indians of Prairies," I said to the group. "That's us!"

About an hour before closing time we all went into the building, to the office of the associate superintendent. We filed in and refused to leave until he met our demands: We wanted to meet with the secretary of the interior about the Indian Preference Act. We wanted Indian people running the BIA.

"Well," the associate superintendent said, "I'm going to have to call the police."

We said, "You can do whatever you want, we're not leaving."

He called Washington, DC, and they told him to stay there while they worked on sending the BIA superintendent out to meet with us.

Around 6:00 p.m. I excused myself to use the restroom. As I sat there in a stall, the assistant superintendent and his assistant came in. They didn't know I was there. I listened to their conversation. They were hungry for dinner. The one guy said, "I'll tell you what, here's some money. You go and get some food; I'll babysit while you're gone."

Oh, it pissed me off when I heard the word "babysit." I thought, that's what them sons of bitches have been doing to us since they got here—taking us into custody and stealing our land.

I returned to the office and spoke to the group. By this time some young men had arrived, and I told them what I heard in the restroom.

I said, "In order to get them to take us seriously, we have to take control of this building."

They asked how I was planning to do that.

I said, "First of all, we need three six-foot chains and several padlocks. We'll lock the back entrance, the side door, and the front entrance." We pooled our money and sent one young guy to the hardware store. He came back with equipment.

I said, "We have to evict the superintendent and his assistant."

We called them into the office, and I told them, "I was in the toilet when you said you were babysitting us. We don't need your babysitting no more. It's over. You got to leave."

"We are the only thing standing between you and the cops," they said. "If we leave here, you're not going to be protected. The cops are going to come in and have you all arrested."

"I don't care," I said. "You got to leave."

We escorted them out and chained the doors.

If we were going to stay inside the building for long, we would have to arrange support from the outside. Without outside help, we would have lasted only hours. I knew we might need to be there for days, even weeks, to get what we wanted.

I thought about calling my brother Vernon for help. He lived in the Denver area. We were close, but this was about three months after he took that swing at me over our mother's heart condition and my involvement in the Movement. I wasn't sure I could count on him to back us up.

The next time I saw Vernon, several hours after we took the building, he was standing outside a window of the Littleton BIA headquarters. The police had us surrounded, but he was able to approach the building under the guise that he was going to negotiate our exit. We pried the window open, and he started loading in bags of groceries. The next time he came he was with a group of community members, arms full of food and supplies. All night long we were loading food and supplies through that window.

I had not called Vernon, and I was surprised to see him there. I think he had come to understand, since he took a swing at me in Minneapolis, that by doing nothing he was part of the problem. He would become one of the main spokesmen for the Movement. He had a real talent for diplomacy. It was good to have my brother on my side again. Looking back, that day was important for many reasons. Never again would Vernon question my dedication to the Movement. It was also the day he joined us in the struggle to which he would dedicate himself for the rest of his life.

Two weeks after the Colorado occupation, Vernon would contact me to say he was in the process of developing one of the first chapters of the American Indian Movement outside of Minneapolis: Denver AIM. Vernon, who had been so angry about my involvement, would eventually give everything to the Movement, including his marriage. His wife, a non-Indian, didn't support his activities for Indian self-determination. She was living a high lifestyle, with cars, vacations, and parties, and she didn't want to give it up. He divorced her and returned to Minneapolis. He also gave up a career that had taken a lifetime to establish. I can't account for his complete change of heart. Probably, like most everyone else, he was scared at first to step out of line. Once he realized the necessity of our struggle, he joined with his whole heart. He died on October 13, 2007, at age seventy-five. To his very last days he was working to improve the lives of Indian people.

Today, Vernon is remembered as a strong leader, willing to take risks to force the dominant culture to recognize what had been done to Indian people. One of the actions he's widely remembered for happened on May 29, 1992, at the Science Museum of Minnesota in St. Paul.

I remember stopping by his house the day before that. There was a nurse with him, and she had a needle stuck in his arm. I said, "Vernon, what the hell are you doing?" He told me this was his third session with this nurse. That she had accumulated two pints of his blood. He told me he planned to use it at a protest the following day. A traveling exhibit called "First Encounters: Spanish Exploration in the Caribbean and the United States, 1492–1570," which featured a replica of the *Niña*, Christopher Columbus's ship, was in town. AIM led a demonstration to focus attention on the mass genocide of Indigenous people which accompanied the lost pirate's arrival. Vernon splattered his blood on the ship's sail, then picked up and threw a mannequin representing Columbus from the ship. He said, "This is symbolic of the blood spilled by Indian people."

Museum officials declined to prosecute Vernon. They left the bloody sail on the ship for the duration of the exhibit and added a videotaped message by Vernon explaining the infamy with which Indian people regard Columbus.

Vernon Bellecourt, in Washington, DC, at the conclusion of the Longest Walk, 1978. *Dick Bancroft photo*

Vernon's emerging activist spirit proved vital to those of us inside the Denver BIA. As we settled into the Indians of the Prairies Building for the long haul, the associate superintendent we had kicked out was on the phone, talking to journalists all over the country. By four the next afternoon we were national news. They were calling us militants and radicals, a bunch of ex-cons, and dope addicts. They said we were under the command of the Black Panthers. They dug up all the Indian people they could find to badmouth us. They reported that the National Congress of American Indians was condemning us.

Despite the negative coverage, it didn't take long before the BIA superintendent agreed to meet with us and hear our demands. He had one condition: he didn't want me in the meeting because, in his words, I was an outsider, an agitator, a militant, and a radical. If they thought I was militant and radical at that time, boy, they hadn't seen nothing yet.

I met with the people, and we agreed I didn't need to be there; they could handle it without me. I told them not to leave that meeting until the BIA agreed to follow the law, to let Indian people have preference for BIA jobs.

That night, as they were gathering, I snuck out of the building and went to work organizing on the outside. I got on the phone and mobilized Indian people all over the country. One of the unintended effects of Indian relocation programs was that our families were scattered across the country; we knew people everywhere. I called Russell Means in Cleveland, and John Trudell in San Francisco. By the next day we had succeeded, through demonstration and occupation, in shutting down eight of the twelve BIA headquarters nationwide: Chicago, Alameda, Minneapolis, Philadelphia, Cleveland, Dallas, Los Angeles, and Albuquerque. We became a national movement overnight, although one that had been years in the making. The newspapers were reporting an "Indian uprising."

That same month, Fort Lawton in Seattle was taken by a group called Indians of All Nations—some of the same folks who had initiated the Alcatraz takeover.

The takeovers would force the BIA to start hiring Indian people. Not long thereafter we would start seeing Indian faces in all positions within the BIA, all the way up the chain of command.

Four months after the BIA takeovers, we heard about this situation over in Wisconsin on land that had been occupied for generations by the Lac Courte Oreilles (LCO) Anishinaabe. Eddie Benton-Banai called me and said his AIM group up in northern Wisconsin was planning to take over Winter Dam.

He quickly brought me up to speed on the situation there.

Since the 1740s the Lac Courte Oreilles people had occupied the village of Pahquahwong. The Wisconsin-Minnesota Light and Power Company, in 1914, proposed a hydroelectric dam whose reservoir would flood the town under twenty-five feet of water. For years the LCO tribe fought the plan. The US Congress, however, went around the Lac Courte Oreilles people and passed the Federal Water Power Act of 1920. This made it legal for the government to approve dam projects on tribal lands without tribal permission.

With the completion of the dam and the flooding of the reservoir, many Lac Courte Oreilles lost their homes, ancestral burial sites, fishing areas, and ricing beds. Wisconsin-Minnesota Power and Light agreed to build a town to replace Pahquahwong but never completed it—except for constructing a BIA office and a Catholic church. It also did not make good on its promises to stock the lake and replant ricing beds.

In 1971, as the power company's fifty-year lease of the dam came up for renewal, new battle lines were drawn. Eddie pressed the tribal council to resist the BIA and refuse renewal, and the company positioned armed guards around the dam.

A group of AIM people traveled up to LCO to support Eddie and the Indians who were ready to fight to take back their land. AIM and Lac Courte Oreilles supporters held a powwow on the reservation on the night of July 31, 1971. We made a decision to take the dam.

Dennis Banks smashed the locked gate with his car, and the guards fled the area without a fight.

We had thirty thousand acres of liquid negotiating leverage behind that dam. We never threatened to use it, but they were scared all the way to Milwaukee—three hundred miles away—due to frantic news reports that we might blow up the dam. That was the first really big news AIM made.

The Winter Dam occupation ended three days later, when Wisconsin governor Patrick Lucey expressed sympathy with the tribe and agreed to sponsor negotiations. By the terms of the agreement, concluded fourteen years later in October 1984, Northern States Power, the dam's new owner, made a large cash payment to the tribe and returned forty-five hundred acres of land.

The LCO people had won that all back. But the graves of their ancestors are still underwater. You can go up there and look down on a clear day and see those gravestones. In the spring of the year when the ice goes out, skeletal remains still float up to the surface. Turtles have been coming up with human bones in their mouths for many years.

Winter Dam and the many other takeovers empowered Indian people across North America. It made them see they could do something to improve their lives; they could take action, take back the things that belonged to them, and that were being used illegally to oppress us. Native people saw that confrontation politics was the only way we could get things done. We had to take control, occupy, and fight—whatever it took to bring our grievances to the forefront.

We held a press conference at Winter Dam. Eddie Benton-Banai, wearing a beaded vest, is speaking, and I'm to the left of him. *Dick Bancroft photo*

7. SPIRITUAL REBIRTH

WE HAD SWEAT LODGES IN PRISON, but we didn't have them on the outside. Why not? All people—not just those who are incarcerated—need to pray, need to connect with the Creator, need to ask the Creator for help. I certainly needed the help. I had big ambitions. I wanted to change everything for Indian people. Most Indian people had forgotten how to talk to the Creator. It was vital to our continued survival that we remember, and reestablish that relationship.

One of the first things I did following the first AIM leadership election was start developing sweat lodges. I set about looking for a suitable place to build a lodge somewhere near south Minneapolis. It would have to be a quiet place where people could gather, and where a fire could burn for hours, heating piles of rocks until they burn so hot you can almost see through them.

But first it was important for me to go into a sweat lodge and pray about it. I had to travel all the way to the Rosebud Reservation in South Dakota—425 miles southwest of Minneapolis—in order to sweat. I had heard about a man there by the name of Leonard Crow Dog, a young medicine man in his early twenties. I heard he was doing healing ceremonies, achieving results that would be considered miracles in the non-Indian community. People told me Crow Dog had a lot of power.

Eddie Benton-Banai and I journeyed out to Rosebud to meet him in the dead cold of winter. When we got there, Leonard was nowhere around. Someone on the property—they call the place Crow Dog's Paradise—said he was out of town. We were directed to visit one of his uncles by the name of Bill Schwegmann. They called him Eagle Deer.

Eddie and I dug an old sweat lodge out of a snowdrift. We dug for hours. We cleaned it out, pried the frozen rocks off of the ground and into the fire as dark set in. We covered the lodge frame with green canvas tarps and tied them down so that no light could come in, and no heat could escape.

A few hours later, I experienced my first sweat lodge outside of prison. I crawled on the frozen earth wearing just my shorts and entered through a flap in the tarps. The rocks were brought in and set in a pit in the center of the circle. Soon the pile was about up to my chin as I sat facing them. Some unbelievable things happened in there.

First, the old man, Eagle Deer, spoke as we sat in that dark lodge. He said he knew we were coming. He knew exactly what kind of car we would be driving. He knew how we would be dressed. He knew we represented the Movement. Way out in Rosebud, he heard about Indians standing up for themselves in Minneapolis. He knew about AIM Patrol and the other ways we were helping people.

As we prayed, an eagle came right into the sweat lodge and brushed me with its wings. I could feel its feathers beating against my body. It was scary because I had never come into actual physical contact with a spirit before.

That night we went into a Yuwipi ceremony and, once again, the spirits came and blessed us. The spiritual energy in that dark room was like nothing I'd ever known, and the things I saw, felt, and heard taught me about the true nature of our existence, that it is richer and more complex than I could have imagined. That night changed my view of everything. I understood that the only way we were going to succeed in the Movement was to place healing and spirituality at the center of everything we did.

The spirits in the ceremony told us that we were to continue on our journey, that we had to bring back the spirit of the Indian people. They gave us instructions, which we carried out from that day forth. We returned to Minnesota and built our own sweat lodge.

That visit motivated me. I wanted to Sun Dance. I had been thinking about the Sun Dance since I'd dreamed about it in prison. I wanted to Sun Dance in order to help show our Indian people a way back to themselves.

Finally, in 1971, I was invited to Pine Ridge, South Dakota, for a Sun Dance. This was the first Sun Dance held publicly since Native American spiritual practices were banned generations earlier. I had been asked by Ed McGaa, an Oglala Lakota Vietnam veteran, to act as his primary supporter, or sponsor.

The Sun Dance is a four-day event. Dancers fast from food and water. The fourth day, we believe you're like a little baby again, and they pierce you by making two small incisions in your chest or back and slide a finger-length peg made of willow or buffalo bone under the skin. Then they tie you to the cottonwood tree.

The cottonwood tree represents the umbilical cord of Mother Earth. So when they tie you to that tree, you're completely purified, like a little baby going back into the womb of Mother Earth. With the help of the spirits, dancers break from the tree by leaning back to tear the pegs out from under the skin of their chest or back.

When I got to the Sun Dance grounds early that first morning I had no idea what I was in for. Here was something I had dreamed about in prison after reading *Black Elk Speaks*. I dreamed about all these beautiful things. I saw horses dancing, tipis magnificently painted, people praying, and faces illuminated by the Sun, blowing eagle bone whistles.

When I got there the Sun Dance was already under way, and I couldn't believe my eyes. The scene was nothing like my dreams. It was more like a carnival, with food trucks and vendors set up around the perimeter of the arbor. They had merry-go-rounds and Ferris wheels. They had a rodeo going on. It was just a ridiculous atmosphere.

Dennis Banks and Russell Means came up and greeted me. They were two of the four Sun Dancers taking part, but Dennis was licking a snow cone, and Russell was eating what they were then calling a "squaw burger," a hamburger with a deep-fried bun.

I was in shock. This scene in no way resembled my awe-inspiring dreams. I asked Dennis and Russell what the hell was going on. "This is a sacred ceremony," I said. "We're supposed to be fasting. Why are you eating that?"

They told me the Sun Dance was no longer conducted as it had been described by Black Elk. Now the Catholic Church had control over our ceremonies. The Bureau of Indian Affairs would allow us to conduct our ceremonies as long as we first obtained the church's blessing.

It would be another seven years before the American Indian Religious Freedom Act would legalize outlawed Indigenous spiritual practices.

Dennis and Russell said the church stopped the Sun Dance ceremony every afternoon at two. At that time the Sun Dance drum was removed and replaced with the powwow drum. For the remainder of the day, a powwow was held there—a party that welcomed all the drunks and bootleggers into what was supposed to be a sacred circle.

As the dance began that morning, I stood under the arbor and watched. Because the church wouldn't allow the dancers to pierce, Russell and Dennis and the others were out there wearing horse harnesses, and dragging buffalo skulls attached to them with ropes clipped to their skin. One of the dancers was so weakened—even from this bit of effort—that he repeatedly collapsed into the dirt right in front of me.

That was all I could take. I started shaking my head. I broke down and started crying.

Leonard Crow Dog came up to me and said, "My brother, what is wrong?" He gave me a big hug.

I told him, "I've been dreaming about the Great Sioux Nation and the Sun Dance. I've been reading all these books like *Black Elk Speaks*, and here I am, finally. What a mockery they've made of our way of life." I said, "Today, Leonard, I'm ashamed, ashamed to be Indian."

Leonard Crow Dog said, "Brother, if you take this ceremony back from the church, AIM must come to Rosebud next year. We're going to dance in the old traditional way, and we're going to pierce."

I felt so happy. I just said, "All right! We'll be there."

I found out from Leonard that on Sunday, the final day of the Sun Dance, a Catholic priest would come into the arbor and administer communion to all of the dancers and supporters. That would be the final closing ceremony. I was really disgusted when I heard that. I didn't know what to do. Leonard Crow Dog didn't know either.

I talked to Dennis and Russell, and I pointed my comments particularly at Russell, because Pine Ridge was his home. I said, "I thought I was involved in a movement of warriors here. Why are you letting this happen? Why don't you put a stop to that? The church has no right to come in here and desecrate our sacred ways."

They acted like they couldn't do anything about it.

I said, "I'm going to stop this from happening on Sunday."

They said, "Well, you better go talk to Fools Crow. He's the traditional chief. We'll do what he says."

Frank Fools Crow, the grand chief of the Lakota Nation, was seated nearby, under the arbor. He spoke no English, only Lakota, and so I spoke with him through his interpreter, Severt Young Bear. He told me it was time now in the history of the Indian people to claim the things that belonged to them; that we weren't going to move forth as a strong nation until we developed a spiritual base. Fools Crow said, though, that he could not change the arrangement he had made with the church; the priest had offered him tobacco, and he was obligated to honor the gesture.

"However," he said, "whatever the warriors want, I'll abide by it."

I was confused. I asked, "Who are the warriors?"

"The Sun Dancers are the warriors," Fools Crow said.

Warriors, I thought, *don't drag buffalo skulls attached to horse harnesses.*

I went across the arbor to where the supposed warriors were resting and conveyed Fools Crow's message. The Sun Dancers agreed with me. They said, "Whatever you have to do to stop that priest, go ahead and do it."

So me and Lehman Brightman, a Lakota/Creek Berkeley professor and head of the activist group United Native Americans, went back and talked to Fools Crow. Brightman was the only man among the Sun Dancers willing to help me remove the priest. We went and told Fools Crow we were going to put a stop to church interference in the Sun Dance. He gave us some tobacco, and we walked away determined to do what we must to restore dignity to the Sun Dance.

The next morning, right before noon as promised, this Catholic priest, Father Stanislaw, drove up to the arbor and stepped out of his car. The arbor was packed with people from across the reservation who had heard AIM was in town from Minneapolis, planning to do something at the Sun Dance.

Father Stanislaw was dressed in ornately beaded vestments and carried a Sacred Pipe in a bundle. Two altar boys trailing behind him carried a loaf of bread and a chalice filled with wine. Father Stanislaw took the microphone to announce that people should line up to receive communion. Lehman Brightman and I walked out into the arbor and interrupted him.

I said gently, "Father, it's over. The Sun Dancers don't want you here."

He pulled away from us and said, "The Sun Dance can't go on without me."

We said, "Father, with all due respect, please leave. If you don't leave here, we're going to have to take you out of here."

He said, "Well, you'll have to take me out of here. The people aren't going to stand for it."

Lehman and I each took one of his arms, put it around our necks, and carried Father Stanislaw outside the arbor. I could hear sirens closing in from all directions. Many in the crowd started throwing sandwiches and pop at us, and spitting at us, condemning us, calling us outsiders, yelling that we had no business coming there and doing that.

I told Lehman not to let this upset him. He wanted to fight. But I said, "These people have been terrorized and brainwashed by the American system, and by the church, and don't understand what we're trying to achieve. It will take time for them to understand why this needs to be done."

We placed the priest right at his car and told him to leave.

The BIA police arrived and escorted Lehman and me to the reservation border, called us lousy troublemakers, and told us we'd be arrested for trespassing if we ever stepped foot on Pine Ridge again.

Today, every Indigenous nation across Indian Country is practicing and enjoying their traditional ceremonies, culture, language, and fulfillment of age-old prophecies. During the same period, churches across Indian Country have been closing down. On Pine Ridge alone, since that day, over a dozen churches have packed up and left the reservation.

The following summer, thirty-eight of us from the Movement committed to Sun Dance. We hadn't planned it that way, but when we showed up at Crow Dog's Paradise for the ceremony we thought it was quite significant. Thirty-eight was also the number of Dakota men who were hanged in Mankato, Minnesota, following the War of 1862. That horrible event, sanctioned by Abraham Lincoln himself, remains the largest mass hanging in American history.

We went down by the Little White River to cut a cottonwood tree to stand at the center of our Sun Dance. The Bureau of Indian Affairs and tribal police came and arrested us for violating logging laws and the prohibitions against Indian religions put in place by the federal government in 1884.

They put us in jail. We bailed out, of course, and went right back to that tree. Henry Crow Dog, the renowned medicine man and father to Leonard, said, "You bring that tree down to my place. Nobody's going to bother you there." We carried the tree to Crow Dog's through the Grass Mountain district of the Rosebud Reservation.

We planted that tree and we danced.

A lot of Rosebud Natives drove by on the road tooting their horns, making war whoops at us, making fun of us. Soon, as the power of ceremony took hold of us, we wouldn't notice anything happening outside the arbor surrounding the dance grounds.

I was the first person to pierce. They didn't have scalpels and all the nice modern equipment used today. Henry Crow Dog had an old ice pick that he hammered on an anvil to flatten the tip. He then sharpened his ice pick on a grindstone, and that's what was used to pierce us. He made small incisions in my chest, below my collarbone, and inserted two wooden pegs.

Because I was first to pierce, Henry honored me with the title of "head Sun Dancer." He said I was leading a movement back to our traditional ways after more than a century of assimilation.

Today over three hundred people dance at Crow Dog's annually. Thousands gather to support them. There are dozens of Sun Dances on the Rosebud and Pine Ridge Reservations. The Sun Dance has been revived in Montana and Wyoming, Utah and California, all the way down to Tucson, and to Mexico, and all over Canada. Hundreds and thousands of people are coming back to that spiritual way of life, fulfilling prophecy handed down from Black Elk. Knowing the traditional Sun Dance is once again being practiced by the people makes me so proud to be Indian.

8. THE DAMN HARD WORK

IN 1971 THREE YOUNG INDIAN BOYS were picked up by Minneapolis police for truancy. They had been out of school, homeschooling for six months. Their parents refused to let them go back to class because the boys were getting their hair pulled, were being bullied by the other children, and were discriminated against by the teachers and administrators. At the time the only legal homeschoolers in Minnesota were licensed teachers.

Authorities dragged the parents before a juvenile court judge, who found them guilty for contributing to the delinquency of their minor children. They threatened to take those three young boys away from them, put them in foster care, and split them up from one another.

The terrified parents were looking at six months in the workhouse unless they provided the court with education plans for their children within ten days.

At the time there wasn't one single Indian licensed foster care facility here in Hennepin County, because they had regulations that barred poor people from becoming foster parents. Poor people didn't have enough room in their homes, they said. We didn't have separate beds for every child. We didn't have enough toilets. We didn't have a shower. We didn't have this or that. They had all kinds of rules designed to remove Indian children from their families and communities.

So me and Dennis Banks went down and saw the judge who had heard the case. His name was Lindsay G. Arthur. He would become a very dear friend of ours. When Dennis Banks was married, Lindsay performed the ceremony.

We said, "Your Honor, we're tired of getting our kids taken away from their homes."

I told him about my life, and how I had grown up in correctional institutions. Dennis told his story about the eleven years he spent separated from his family while he was stuck in boarding school at Pipestone. Judge Arthur listened closely. He actually got tears in his eyes.

He said, "The hardest thing in my life is to take children out of a home, out of their community, and put them away somewhere. What am I supposed to do? There's alcoholism. There's physical abuse. There's sexual abuse going on in some of these homes. Many children are not being properly cared for. These kids are better off in foster homes."

"We want them in this community," I said. "There's no Indian licensed foster care facilities here, so we'll start them."

We asked the judge, "If the American Indian Movement comes up with an alternative education program, would you send these kids to us?"

He said, "You bet I would send them to you."

Early in January 1972, without a penny spent, we opened the Heart of the Earth Survival School in an old condemned basement on Franklin Avenue. It had one little lightbulb hanging from the ceiling, cockroaches crawling on the walls, a toilet that wouldn't stop flushing. We had an old blackboard and a piece of chalk, one pencil for the kids to share—but most importantly we had a lady by the name of Ona Kingbird.

Ona hadn't herself graduated from high school, but she knew our Ojibwe language and medicine. Her dad was a well-known medicine man from Red Lake named Dan Raincloud. We asked her to become our teacher of traditional culture. Ona agreed, and we were in business; we opened Heart of the Earth Survival School.

Within one week we had those three boys in our school. They would soon be joined by thirty-three other little Native boys and girls. Too many kids, in fact—the bureaucrats soon shut us down. That started the school's long migration, searching for a home.

Heart of the Earth moved a total of twelve times in two years. Every facility we used, they found a reason to shut us down: didn't have enough toilets, didn't have proper windows, didn't have a playground, didn't have enough windows, didn't have enough desks, and didn't have enough this and that.

We lobbied the National Congress of American Indians and the National Indian Education Association, where we were told, "Oh, it's a good idea to build an Indian school, and have your own curricula, teach your own culture and language." But nobody would step forth and actually fund the idea.

We found our financial footing in the last place we might have expected when, on June 23, 1972, the United States Congress adopted the Indian Education Act. This act allowed Indians to have control over educating our own people. This was a big deal; the Indian Education Act ensured the continued survival of Indian education. It recognized that American Indians have unique, culturally related academic needs. We were able to receive federal funding for each Native child enrolled at our school. The Indian Education Act was an answer to our prayers.

The school's first years, 1972 and 1973, were incredibly busy for the Movement. I was away from Minnesota for huge chunks of time, fighting in places like Washington, DC, and Wounded Knee against the terrible injustices suffered by Indian people. Those stories appear below. But through it all, AIM members continued the damn hard work to protect and preserve the Minneapolis Indian community, and that's what I returned to after things calmed down from Wounded Knee.

We finally found a permanent facility for Heart of the Earth Survival School in Dinkytown, a neighborhood adjacent to the University of Minnesota in Minneapolis. We launched our program there in 1975 on what was then the campus of a United Methodist church. We scraped together a down payment and bought an old building for $300,000.

Elaine Martin Salinas is one of the most respected Indian women in this community. She is an Indian educator, a woman that graduated from Moorhead State Teachers College and came to work for the American Indian Movement. She never went into the mainstream educational system. She ran our Heart of the Earth school and developed numerous programs and initiatives to help young people both in Minnesota and nationwide. She was tough, and savvy, which allowed her to go into places like Stillwater State Prison and teach classes to the Indian inmates there.

Over the years of our existence, Heart of the Earth graduated more Indian students than the whole Minneapolis public school system combined. Our secret to success was this: every Monday morning, without fail, we would bring the drum. Every Monday morning, without fail, we would pray together with the pipe. Every Friday, before our kids would go home, we prayed again. We taught kids how to sing and dance in their traditional ways. We sent our kids all over the state demonstrating their cultural achievements and abilities. Everything that we did in our school—even math and science—used Indian-based curriculum, which made our young people feel good about their culture.

I knew the power of Indian studies from my own experience at Stillwater State Prison, learning with Eddie Benton-Banai. And now by opening this school, AIM was caring for our Native children, which means we were following the path of the true warrior, as the old chiefs, like Tatanka Iyotanka (Sitting Bull), defined the term.

Tatanka Iyotanka said: "Warriors are not what you think of as warriors. The warrior is not someone who fights, because no one has the right to take another life. The warrior, for us, is one who sacrifices himself for the good of others. His task is to take care of the elderly, the defenseless, those who cannot provide for themselves, and above all, the children, the future of humanity."

Today, we have hundreds of Indian licensed foster care facilities. Through the advocacy of our Legal Rights Center, and with the help through the years of allies like Judge Lindsay Arthur and other juvenile court judges, we have been able to accomplish our goal of keeping our children within our community.

Our passion for improving the lives of our people naturally led AIM into health care. When AIM formed, we were tired of seeing our people languishing in the hallways of local hospitals, dying of heart attacks, sitting there with broken arms and legs, and bleeding to death—not being served because they didn't have the right insurance. We went down and started raising hell with the directors of University of Minnesota, Lutheran Deaconess, and Hennepin County hospitals. Pretty soon, they had Indian advocates working in every one of these facilities. We started having medicine men coming into the hospitals—which they had never allowed before—started having healing ceremonies, helping people obtain the spiritual resources they needed to heal.

The first urban Indian Health Board in America was created by the American Indian Movement in 1971. At the time, our people were afraid to seek treatment within the federal government's Indian Health Service system. One of the major factors driving the fear and distrust Native people had of IHS doctors was the widespread practice of involuntary sterilization of our women. In those days, we had only anecdotal evidence to back our suspicions. In 1976, however, the

I spoke to students at a school in Dublin run by Sinn Fein. The children here learned to speak their native Gaelic language. We brought a drum from Heart of the Earth Survival School.
Dick Bancroft photo

US government would finally admit to its complicity with these horrific crimes. A study released by the General Accounting Office found that between 1973 and 1976, Indian Health Service offices in Phoenix, Oklahoma City, Albuquerque, and Aberdeen, South Dakota, had sterilized three thousand Indian women of childbearing age without their permission. Thirty-six women under the age of twenty-one had been sterilized, even though there was a court-ordered moratorium against that. We were convinced that full-blooded Indian women were singled out for sterilization procedures.

Today, in our community, we have culturally specific mental health programs. We have an AIDS project. We have Indian AIDS housing— special housing set aside for families dealing with AIDS. We have the Native American Community Clinic and a dental clinic. We have special programs for diabetics. We have public health workers going out in the community teaching about nutrition and preventative care.

Much of the hard work that AIM took on was the direct result of the devastation that resulted from the Indian Relocation Act of 1956. The federal government, in its lust to terminate the tribes, sought to move Indian people off the reservations so they could come in and claim our land and natural resources. Those who chose to participate in the program soon found they had been duped. In the city they had to deal with low-wage jobs, unemployment, a lack of quality housing, and discrimination in schools and workplaces. All told, the Indian Relocation Act enticed some 750,000 Natives off their reservations.

When AIM began, we had entire Indian families living on the streets. Many of our people were sleeping in alleyways and in bushes along Franklin Avenue, or crammed into squalid, overcrowded housing projects. These were people who had left their reservations, believing the government's false promises of a better life in the cities. When they arrived, however, they found the same poverty and deprivation they had left behind. In many ways the cities were worse. In addition to all of the other hardships, they found themselves socially isolated in white man's society.

I would venture to say there's probably thirty thousand to forty

We organized some programs for young people that celebrated positive things. In about 1970, at the Café di Napoli in Minneapolis, I'm surrounded by candidates for the annual Indian Princess competition. *Courtesy AIM Interpretive Center*

thousand Indian people here in the Twin Cities area. There are differing opinions, however, as to the exact Native American population of Minneapolis and St. Paul. It seems that every ten years, when the census rolls around, we only get about 40 percent of the Indian people participating. Our people are hard to count for a number of reasons: homelessness, distrust of the government, a transient population that moves back and forth between urban areas and the reservations, and a disdain for the way the census counts us.

I think the American Indian Movement could only have started in the Twin Cities. It could never have started in San Francisco or Los Angeles or Milwaukee, because those towns are designated relocation towns and they have maybe a hundred and some tribes living there. They've got these intertribal fights that go on constantly. It's very difficult to organize Natives in those places. Minneapolis and St. Paul have residents from dozens of tribes, certainly, but the great majority of our Native people are either Anishinaabe or Dakota/Lakota.

This area is the center of Indian activism and development. We've got every kind of program you can think of here that deals with every aspect of Indian life. In order to help our people gain shelter and stability, AIM built an Indian housing program—a home ownership program and a large rental complex. The homeowners' program has allowed families to get into single-family homes with fixed interest set at a very low rate—closing costs and insurance included.

We initiated the development of a 212-unit housing complex in the heart of the Minneapolis urban Indian community. It's called Little Earth of United Tribes, and it provides all manner of rental units, from five-bedroom townhomes to single-occupancy studios. Little Earth, along with all of AIM's programs and projects, lies within about forty square blocks of a south Minneapolis neighborhood called Phillips, which boasts the largest urban concentration of Native people in America.

Little Earth of United Tribes housing opened its doors in 1972. It was supposed to be an all-Indian project, but the makeup turned out to be about 45 percent Black, 35 percent Indian, and the rest of the residents white, Asian, and Hispanic. This was an issue we would have to deal with over time. There was so much work to be done. We had to turn our attention for the time being to the national level, where Congress was hard at work trying to eliminate all of the arrangements and protections our ancestors fought for.

9. THE TRAIL OF BROKEN TREATIES

IN 1972, AIM DECIDED TO LAUNCH a major campaign directed at the Bureau of Indian Affairs. It was called the Trail of Broken Treaties. Its goal was to draw Americans' attention to the truth about their government's bad-faith dealings with the Native nations of this land. We would accomplish this by sending several caravans of Indian people across the United States, starting in San Francisco, Los Angeles, and Seattle, that would move eastward, visiting communities, reservations, and sacred sites, while recruiting Indian people for a massive demonstration in Washington, DC.

We would meet along the way with tribal governments and traditional leaders to gather ideas for a document we planned to present to Congress. We were very careful to make sure the thoughts of the more than three hundred tribal citizens who contributed ideas to the paper had a voice. This was not just an AIM thing. This paper would represent all Indian people in the United States.

The document would be boiled down to twenty principles for new nation-to-nation understandings that would govern all dealings between the federal government and Indian people. We would ask Congress to recognize and respect treaties they had made with Native nations. We would demand that Indian people be allowed to exercise total control over their lives and over their destiny, and have opportunities to create a better way of life for the unborn generations to come.

In early October the caravans, composed of activists and representatives from the American Indian Movement, National Indian Brotherhood of Canada, National Indian Youth Council, Native American Rights Fund, American Indian Commission on Alcohol and Drug Abuse, and other organizations, began winding their way across the United States. The plan was to converge on Washington during the final week of the 1972 presidential campaign between George McGovern and Richard Nixon.

One of the caravans arrived in Minneapolis in mid-October. We spent two solid weeks here drafting what we called the "Twenty-Point Position Paper," which was twenty pieces of legislation that we wanted enacted by the Congress of the United States in support of Indigenous treaty rights. We wanted to change our nation-to-nation relationship with the federal government so that they would finally respect Indian sovereignty. We were tired of not having our voices heard, even after the colonizers had almost completely ruined our country. We could not leave it up to them to fix it. If Indian people were going to heal, going to be made whole, we had to develop our own Indigenous solutions. Here's a summary—written by AIM activist Hank Adams—of what we came up with:

1. The president and Congress should repeal the component of the 1871 Indian Appropriations Act that eliminated the power of the Indian Nations to contract constitutionally bound treaties with the U.S. government.
2. The government should establish a Treaty Commission that will have the power to contract new treaties to ensure the future of the Indian Nations. In addition, it should be established that no terms of existing treaties can be violated.
3. The president and congressional leadership should pledge that they will, together with four American Indian representatives who have been selected by Indian people, address a joint session of Congress before June 2, 1974, in order to discuss the future of the Indian Nations. The national media should be present for this meeting.
4. The president of the United States should establish a commission consisting of both Indians and non-Indians to examine treaty commitments and violations and to write legislation to protect existing rights and eliminate the unending patterns of prohibitively complex lawsuits.
5. Treaties that have not been ratified should be presented to the Senate, and the Senate should certify prior de facto ratification.
6. All American Indian peoples should be considered to be in treaty relations with the federal government.
7. The Congress and federal courts should ensure that there is judi-

cial enforcement and protection of the treaty rights of American Indians.

8. The Congress should provide a new system of federal court jurisdiction through which American Indians can address treaty or tribal rights. This system of jurisdiction must apply both in cases between American Indians and between American Indians and non-Indians. Leaders of the Indian Nations are to take part in the process of interpreting treaties.

9. The Congress should withdraw control over Indian Affairs from current committees and create a joint House-Senate Committee on Reconstruction of Indian Relations and Programs.

10. By July 4, 1976, the federal government should restore a permanent Native American land area of no less than 110 million acres (about 172,000 square miles). This area should be perpetually non-taxable by the federal government. Sub-points address issues in how landless Indian nations were to be given priority, consolidation of resources, methods to re-secure Indian ownership of alienated lands within reservation boundaries, and immediate repeal of the Termination Acts of the 1950s and 1960s.

11. There should be a revision of 25 U.S.C. 163, restoring Indian rights to individuals that have lost them due to issues with enrollment. In addition, American Indians must be able to qualify for membership in more than one tribe and not be prohibited from receiving dual benefits.

12. Congress must repeal state laws passed under Public Law 280, which robs Indian communities of the core of their governing authority by transferring jurisdiction over law enforcement from federal to state authority.

13. All violent offenses against Indians, on or off reservations, should be treated as federal crimes and the persons committing the crimes must face penalties under federal prosecution. Sub-points call for creation of a national federal Indian grand jury made up of Indians; elimination of immunity of non-Indians on reservations; and acceleration of release of Indian prisoners.

14. The Bureau of Indian Affairs should be dismantled by 1976 and a new government structure that maintains Indian-federal relations should be established.
15. The new structure that will replace the Bureau of Indian Affairs will be called the Office of Federal Indian Relations and Community Reconstruction.
16. The Office of Federal Indian Relations and Community Reconstruction will promote equality between the Indian Nations and the federal government and seek to remedy the wrongdoings of the federal government against the American Indians.
17. Congress should enact a statute that allows for trade, commerce, and transportation of Indians to remain outside the jurisdiction of state governments. American Indians within reservation areas should have immunity from state taxation.
18. The Congress shall protect the religious freedom and cultural integrity of Indian people and provide that Indian religion and culture shall not be interfered with, disrespected, or denied.
19. The Indian population should be able to vote in local and national referendums; the number of Indian and Indian-interest organizations and Indian advisory boards, controlled by those who seem to accept any viewpoint or proposal from an official source, should be restricted.
20. The Congress, president, and proposed Indian Community Reconstruction Office should focus on the improvement and creation of better housing, education, employment and economic development for the American Indians.

On November 1, 1972, right before the election, the caravans began arriving in Washington, DC. We had established a local office several months before we got there. We'd had all sorts of meetings with government officials. Commitments had been made by all these different federal agencies that we would be accommodated upon arrival, that serious meetings would be held, the Twenty-Point Position Paper would be presented, and there would be hearings on it. We planned, after that, to turn around and go back home. But when we arrived we found all doors closed to us.

We later found out (from FBI testimony at the 1974 Wounded Knee trial of Dennis Banks and Russell Means) that, while we were traveling across the country, FBI director J. Edgar Hoover had labeled the American Indian Movement a dangerous, radical organization that had to be obliterated from the face of America. Hoover was successful in turning the federal government, as well as some of our own Indian people, against us. He persuaded all of these various sellout tribal chairmen, notably Wendell Chino from the Mescalero Apache in New Mexico, Roger Jourdain of the Red Lake Anishinaabe in Minnesota, and Joe DeLaCruz from the Quinault Salish in Washington, to put out press releases condemning AIM as a militant organization. The Bureau of Indian Affairs used them to launch a media campaign to discredit the Movement and the Trail of Broken Treaties.

So when we got to Washington we were not welcome. There was no place to stay. We ended up at a little place called St. Stephen and the Incarnation Episcopal Church, which housed a lot of civil rights demonstrators and other activist groups who came to protest. I arrived at the church early in the morning, after some of our people had already settled in. On the way down to the basement to have breakfast, I thought there was a cat lying on the stairwell. I tapped it with my foot, but it didn't move. It was a huge dead rat. The squalid state of this place really got me angry. There were little kids and elders sleeping in that church.

I told everybody: "This is bullshit. Gather all your belongings. We're going to the Bureau of Indian Affairs. The Bureau of Indian Affairs belongs to Indian people. It was established by taking our money. We're going there to stay until they provide us with decent housing, and until they listen to the demands of this Twenty-Point Position Paper."

I was really angry. AIM had an advance team in place in DC, and they had arranged accommodations for us. When we arrived, however, everyone turned their backs on us. I think they were intimidated by the Nixon administration, didn't want to be seen helping AIM.

Everybody packed up, and we went over to the Bureau of Indian Affairs building.

When we arrived on November 3, 1972, we were about five hundred strong, and that number would grow during the occupation to over a thousand. Then at the end of the day, we called a big meeting in their auditorium where BIA officials tried to get us to leave, to move to another building. Instead, we evicted them and chained the doors shut, just like we had at BIA offices in Colorado, Minneapolis, Cleveland, San Francisco, and so forth. Here we were, finally in the belly of the beast, and here we would remain until the president of the United States, Richard Nixon himself, met with us. We also demanded that a congressional committee be established to look into our Twenty-Point Position Paper and give us a timetable on when and how those things would be implemented. We understood that what had taken centuries to destroy would not be fixed overnight.

We let them know that we were serious, that we were not going to leave.

When we took over the building, I sat at the desk of Owen Morken, who was the BIA's area director for Minneapolis. *Courtesy AIM Interpretive Center*

We didn't have any guns, but many guns were soon pointed at us. In no time the government overreacted, of course, and we were surrounded by police from multiple law enforcement agencies.

Our non-Indian supporters countered the government's move. Human rights protesters pushed inside the police lines. These were mostly white people who were willing to put their lives down in support of us. People in the antiwar movement came to our aid. We watched this take place out the windows of the building and on television news reports with a great deal of satisfaction. We knew we were not alone in this struggle.

Even without guns, we had a good plan for defending the building. We placed all the heavy metal typewriters in the upstairs windows. We were ready to drop them on the police if they started raiding us. We took lightbulbs and filled them up with gasoline. Crow Dog was the one who figured out how to do that. We were ready to start setting these lightbulbs off and burning the building to the ground if we were invaded. We thought no matter what happened, if we had to give our lives, one thing we could do for sure is destroy the building that served those who oppressed us, where those responsible for so many deaths of Indian people, and the theft of our land and resources, spent their days.

In response to the occupation, the DIA flew in some of the tribal leaders they had in their back pockets. These were members of the National Tribal Chairmen's Association. They put these men up in luxury, in the Hyatt Regency Hotel—wined and dined them—when we were lying on floors, had nothing to eat, and were cold. Soon after the takeover, the building's heat and electricity were cut off.

The AIM leadership went over to the hotel and met with these sellout tribal leaders. They told us the association was going to have a press conference and they were going to condemn the American Indian Movement. It was all orchestrated by the Bureau of Indian Affairs, the FBI, and J. Edgar Hoover to promote the fallacy that we were just a bunch of militants, criminals, and drug addicts. They hoped to build public outrage against AIM so they could come in and murder

us. We pleaded with the tribal leadership to join us. We showed them the Twenty-Point Position Paper. Even though they agreed it was good we were doing this, they said that they were the "legitimate" tribal leadership, and what happened to Indian people, they said, was up to them, and not us.

We had a bumper sticker that said "AIM for Sovereignty." Everybody in the Movement had it on their cars. Most of these tribal chairmen didn't even know how to spell the word "sovereignty" when AIM started using it. We went to the press conference. There Roger Jourdain, Wendell Chino, and Joe DeLaCruz held that bumper sticker up in front of the world press, and they said, "This is what we think of AIM for sovereignty," and they cut that bumper sticker in half, and it fell to the ground. Of course, at that point, we spoke up and condemned them as well. We left the press conference and returned to the BIA building.

It was unbelievable what happened next. Support came from all over the country. Indians came in from every direction. We had a delegation of Lumbees from North Carolina, people who had been oppressed two hundred years before the colonizers ever reached the Anishinaabe people. We had Dakota people come to our defense from the impoverished reservations of Nebraska and South Dakota. From the Six Nations Confederacy, all of the chiefs came and joined us. Traditional people that had long suffered all across America came and joined, and they brought with them letters of solidarity from their tribes.

Non-Indian supporters came and held big demonstrations on the streets outside the building. People were carrying picket signs saying it was time for the American government to live up to its treaty obligations with Indian people.

With the election coming up, Nixon and his people wanted us gone in the worst way. US government officials started coming into the building to negotiate a settlement.

AIM security at the BIA takeover. Young Horse (Floyd Condon) is at center, with two unidentified men. *Dick Bancroft photo*

At one meeting we held with Nixon's representatives, one by one, the American Indian Movement leadership and others got up and talked about the rapes and murders that were happening on the reservations and in urban communities, the violations of treaties and hunting and fishing rights, and the poverty-stricken condition of Indian people. We told them we were putting our foot down; we refused to live like that anymore.

These words, as desperate, heartfelt, and genuine as any I've heard, did not seem to move the president's men. They really didn't care what we had to say. They just wanted us gone. We were embarrassing the administration before the election.

After the initial failure to negotiate some type of settlement, we put together a delegation of elders—they would have the foresight and wisdom to succeed where the AIM leadership had not. Our elders went into meetings with White House staffers; they secured a commitment that the president would, in fact, send an official delegation to meet with them.

The FBI during the Nixon administration was out of control, but in some ways Nixon was the friendliest president to Indian people in history. When he came into office, he had inherited the Eisenhower administration's Indian Termination Policy. Eisenhower offered cash to tribes if they would give up their sovereign status, and some, like the Menominee in Wisconsin, were accepting it. Richard Nixon came along and said he didn't believe in termination, he believed in self-determination. His policy was self-determination without termination. He negotiated on a nation-to-nation basis with some tribal governments and ended up returning more land to Indian people than any other president in history. But, as we all know, Nixon wasn't perfect. He had a few tricks up his sleeve.

So after we occupied the BIA building, who did Nixon send in to negotiate? He sent none other than John Ehrlichman, a top administration aide, and H. R. Haldeman, the White House chief of staff.

Following Nixon's resignation, both men would be convicted of conspiracy, obstruction of justice, and perjury, and serve eighteen months in prison for helping to cover up Nixon's role in the Watergate scandal. They were joined at the talks by the whole group of cronies that were later responsible for the break-in at the Democratic National Headquarters in the Watergate Hotel.

We should never have trusted them, but we did. Finally, after a weeklong standoff, a deal was made. We thought we had accomplished what we went there for. The administration promised that a presidential task force would be established to look into our Twenty-Point Position Paper, and that they would respond to us in a very short period of time.

The election took place on November 7. Richard Nixon won by a landslide over George McGovern. Two days later, we ended the action and made plans to disperse.

We had a new problem now: how to get all these people back home. We were broke. So we continued to negotiate with the president's men, telling them we wanted their promise not to prosecute, and cash to help people get home. They asked how much money we would need. We talked about it for a few hours and came up with a figure of $66,650. That amount was agreed upon. The president's men were so eager to have us gone from DC that they pulled some string and got some bank to open on a Sunday morning. They delivered a briefcase full of cash, which was received by me and John Trudell. John and I were responsible for distributing that money.

Of course, I never had $66,650 that I could just hand out. If somebody came up and said they needed $350 and I only had hundred-dollar bills left, I'd give them $400. People needed a few more dollars for baby diapers, or to put an elder relative in a hotel on the way home, and I gave it to them. Before I even got through a fraction of the crowd, I'd already given away most of the money.

As I was doing that, U-Haul trucks rented by AIM pulled into the loading docks, and we filled them with tons of Bureau of Indian Affairs records. No one asked what we were doing, and no one tried to stop us. In fact, the DC police escorted us out of town with thousands of records which proved all our accusations of corruption within the BIA: missing money, stolen land, and the systematic violations of Indigenous peoples' rights. In the last few years it's been made public that billions in royalties off our timber rights and minerals and resources are missing, trust funds that they were supposed to be taking care of for us. They're missing. We knew that back in 1972.

The feds searched desperately for those documents, focusing their search on the Pine Ridge Reservation. But they were never hidden there. We stored them in unlikely places, like backyards in North Carolina.

We had brokered a promise with the feds that nobody would be arrested or prosecuted for the takeover of the Bureau of Indian Affairs. Several days after we left there, the government selected an Indian delegation to come to Washington and inspect the damage that was done to the Bureau of Indian Affairs building, which they estimated to be in the range of $2.2 million. Navajo leader Peter MacDonald was among them. As he was walking through the hallways, he later told us, he saw graffiti painted on the wall: *Fuck the BIA. Fuck the president.* We didn't graffiti walls; if we had, I guarantee we would have done so more eloquently. McDonald thought something about it didn't seem right. He walked up to that wall and ran his finger down it. The paint, which would have been dry by then had we done it, was still dripping wet, as if it had been sprayed that day.

There was a lot of stuff broken and damaged within that building that we never did. This deception was part of the FBI's campaign to demonize the American Indian Movement and set us up for prosecution. A month after we vacated the BIA building a grand jury met and handed down fourteen indictments against the leaders of the American Indian Movement. But to this day they still have never issued a single warrant.

They couldn't prosecute us, because Nixon too would have been implicated.

Shortly after we left the BIA, *Washington Post* reporters Bob Woodward and Carl Bernstein discovered that the Committee to Re-elect the President had carried out the Watergate break-ins. Had they indicted us and served warrants for our arrests, I'm convinced that these reporters would have found out that the $65,500 given to AIM by Nixon's cronies was an illegal use of official funds.

We returned home armed with boxes and boxes of evidence that could be used against the government in a court of law, and I think that also frightened them away from prosecuting us.

Following the BIA takeover, the feds did everything they could to turn Indian people and the general public against us. They were successful in getting corrupt tribal governments across America, particularly where support for AIM was strong, to pass resolutions prohibiting peaceful assembly of Indian people. All of these resolutions were similar. They decreed that if more than three Indian people gathered in any location—on the Pine Ridge Reservation where Dick Wilson was tribal chairman, for instance, or Red Lake Reservation where Roger Jourdain was chairman, or down on the San Carlos Reservation where Wendell Chino was chairman—that they could be arrested for inciting a riot. These resolutions, particularly the one issued by Dick Wilson on Pine Ridge, would set the stage for the biggest AIM action of them all—the 1973 occupation of Wounded Knee.

But the feds weren't interested in arresting the AIM leadership; they wanted to kill us. They didn't want a bunch of trials. They planned to entice AIM into doing something where the government would have an excuse to bring in the military and do away with us. As we were departing Washington, DC, the FBI was on the Pine Ridge Reservation, distributing weapons to supporters of tribal chairman Dick Wilson. These FBI-sponsored vigilantes called themselves the GOONs (Guardians of the Oglala Nation), and they took their shiny automatic assault weapons and started what is known to history as the Reign of Terror. The GOONs went after the traditional people who opposed Wilson for signing away one-third of the mineral-rich reservation to the federal government, for distributing federal funds meant for the Oglala people to his family, and for cracking down on his opponents with an iron fist. Many traditional people were raped, injured, and killed. The FBI knew, of course, that AIM would respond.

As AIM considered its response, the FBI started arming the GOONs. One of their leaders, an Oglala tribal member named Duane Brewer, did an interview with journalist Kevin McKiernan in which he admitted the FBI armed Wilson's hit men for their war against AIM. The ammunition the GOONs received included armor-piercing .357 magnum bullets.

"Them were expensive rounds," Brewer said. "You don't get them anymore. They only go to law enforcement people. But, you know, we had them. We had all that stuff."

This interview appeared in the 1990 Frontline documentary *The Spirit of Crazy Horse*. The film tells the story of how the Lakota suffered as white men came onto their lands, chased the Indian people all over the plains, murdered them, and stole their Black Hills. It talks about Wounded Knee and the continuing resistance.

McKiernan asked why the GOONs needed armor-piercing rounds; AIM didn't have no armor.

"In case they're in a brick building or something," Brewer said. He added that the FBI gave the GOONs everything they needed "to do a job." That job was to assassinate the AIM leadership. In my case, they would nearly succeed.

10. CEDAR PASS

WE WERE BUSY IN 1972. In the months following the Trail of Broken Treaties, we had a whole series of actions around the Lakota reservations in South Dakota and Nebraska, where bad things were happening. We were hearing about a lot of abuse and killings of Indian people.

We got word in February 1972 that Raymond Yellow Thunder was taken off the street and forced into a VFW club in Gordon, Nebraska—a cowboy town south of the Pine Ridge Reservation—and wound up dying early the next morning. We couldn't get any information from the police that made sense, so we initiated our own investigation.

From all over the continent, the American Indian Movement gathered in Gordon to protest racist attacks on Indian people in the region. Severt Young Bear came into our meeting and told us about the way Yellow Thunder, a Lakota man in his fifties who was Young Bear's uncle, had been assaulted. We'd already been investigating several murders of Indian people. We'd held marches in these little towns and met with sheriffs, judges, and mayors to try to put a stop to the racist attacks. But when we learned about the killing of Raymond Yellow Thunder—that one really got our attention. Everybody there got really upset.

We were successful in getting a pathologist from Denver to come in, and we exhumed the body. The first autopsy had claimed that he died of exposure, passed out from drinking. The second autopsy found out that Raymond Yellow Thunder, brutalized and beaten badly, died of a head injury.

We took over the town without opposition. Many of the townspeople had fled in fear when they heard we were coming. We occupied the town hall and the mayor's office, and held a press conference on a truck bed for a few reporters and a small number of residents who dared to come out and hear our grievances. We held meetings with Gordon's mayor and sheriff and other local and state leaders; we convened a Red Ribbon Grand Jury to shine a light on all the harm that the white power structure in the area had inflicted on local Indians. We found, through some of the testimony that was presented, that one racist cop was well known to force Indian women into his squad car, drive them out of town, and abuse them.

We saw results quickly from our confrontational approach. The mayor agreed to fire that racist, sadistic cop. We got local officials to agree to set up a Gordon Human Relations Council on which local whites and Indians would be equally represented. We got them to agree to no longer place young Indians who had been charged with minor offenses in jail with adult prisoners. All parties signed onto an agreement which promised that a federal grand jury would investigate Raymond Yellow Thunder's murder. We got everything we asked for. It was a major victory for the Movement. Finally, our long-standing grievances were being heard and taken seriously.

The Hare brothers were tried for the killing of Raymond Yellow Thunder in Alliance, Nebraska. They were found guilty of manslaughter. Leslie Hare was sentenced to six years, and Melvin Hare to two years. Some said their punishment should have been harsher, ten years apiece. But we knew that without the Movement coming in and calling attention to the corrupt power structure in Gordon, those brothers would have gotten off altogether.

When that information spread throughout Indian Country, the Movement started getting requests from all over South Dakota and Nebraska; they called from places like White Clay, Rapid City, and Custer, places where Indian people were being brutalized, raped, and murdered. These were towns surrounding the Lakota reservations where discrimination had long been the norm for Indian people. We were done putting up with that sort of treatment.

In January 1973, we went to a conference in Scottsbluff, Nebraska, where local Chicano people were facing similar racist abuse and wanted to talk about how to deal with police brutality. Russell got set up by local cops and arrested, as did some others, but the Mexican-American Legal Defense Fund bailed them out. From Scottsbluff we drove up into Rapid City, South Dakota. We held nightly meetings where everybody started showing up and talking about the abuse they had endured in these border towns and, increasingly, on their own reservation.

Many people told us their relatives were being held in terrible conditions in small-town jails where they were not allowed visits from family members. We started organizing caravans to take family members to the jails and demand they be allowed to see their son or daughter, father or mother. Wherever injustices were happening against Indian people, we went there en masse.

At that time we heard about the murder of Wesley Bad Heart Bull. The Lakota man had gotten into an argument outside one of these little reservation border-town bars and ended up getting stabbed to death. We decided we needed to really put the heat on these racist towns. Again, Indian people started coming from all over the country to help.

Sarah Bad Heart Bull, Wesley's mother, told us she was with her son in a saloon at Buffalo Gap, South Dakota, on the night he was killed. That area sits between Rapid City—with its large white population—and the Pine Ridge Reservation, and was known as a place where Indians were often mistreated. In those days, it was not uncommon to see signs on the outside of bars and shops in that part of the country that read, "No Dogs or Indians Allowed."

A reporter named Terry Devine from the Associated Press did an investigation of the crime. I like how he captured the feel of that bar, and many others like it, in those days. I have the article here, from February 12, 1973. It says: "It was a jovial crowd, cowboy hats on tables and atop booths. The band played the Western music loud enough to muffle the stamp of high-heeled boots on the bare, wooden floors. From the outside, the bar with its fancy front looks like something from the Old West. Inside, it's a small-town bar typical of most in the crossroads villages of this plains state."

But on the morning of January 21, 1973, Sarah Bad Heart Bull's twenty-year-old son was "flat out murdered" by a white man named Darrell Schmitz outside of Bill's Bar.

Schmitz was jailed, but released almost immediately on a measly $5,000 bond. When our people were jailed for minor violations, bail was regularly twice that. This guy killed someone, but that someone he killed was an Indian, and in that time and place the life of an Indian wasn't worth dirt.

We sent a group of AIM members and leaders from the Pine Ridge Reservation to Custer, South Dakota, to meet with the prosecutor. The Custer situation quickly got out of hand. Our people tried to force their way into the courthouse, demanding to see the city council and the mayor. They were stopped by police and state troopers who had surrounded the building in anticipation of our arrival. The police agreed to let only four people into the building, but our AIM members were angry and demanded to be heard. A major riot broke out after Sarah Bad Heart Bull was brutally attacked by the police—they started beating her on the Custer Courthouse steps when she demanded to go inside to seek justice for her son. When our warriors saw that happening, they lost their composure. Someone threw firebombs, and several buildings were damaged or burned.

Sarah Bad Heart Bull, Dennis Banks, and Russell Means, along with about twenty other Indians, were arrested. Many were beaten by police wielding clubs in the streets and while in custody.

AIM people set fire to the courthouse, torched the chamber of commerce building across the street, and destroyed two police cars.

They said the Custer Courthouse riot cost the town, named after mass murderer George Armstrong Custer, $2 million in damages. I don't condone violence or destruction of property, but I'll tell you something, nothing gets the white man's attention like losing money. After Custer, the government decided they had enough of the American Indian Movement. They put plans into action designed to eradicate us. We were just weeks away from walking into the trap they were setting for us on the Pine Ridge Reservation.

I was in Minneapolis handling some business when the Custer riot happened. I kept close track of those events. It was all over the news. Twenty-two people, including Wesley Bad Heart Bull's mother, were arrested and would serve five months in prison for "riot with arson." Her son's murderer would be tried by an all-white jury and found not guilty.

Custer was a very serious situation, so I headed immediately back to South Dakota. I felt bad that I hadn't been there when everything was going down.

I went to Rapid City, and AIM started meeting at night at a place called Mother Butler Center. It was run by the churches, kind of a community place, where you could cook food and have crowds gather. We started having caravans every day. We'd drive out of Rapid City in a line, thirty or forty cars long, and make sure the local people understood the old racist ways would have to end. This was a new era. The American Indian Movement was the new sheriff in town.

Over a period of about two weeks we continued to meet in Rapid City and hear the stories of horrific abuses suffered by our people. We called on the media for support. Soon all the major news outlets—NBC, CBS, ABC—came in with these big trailers, cars full of cameras, and newspeople.

In response to all that was happening, at the request of tribal chairman Dick Wilson a restraining order was put out that said if me, Dennis Banks, Russell Means, and other leaders set foot on the Pine Ridge Reservation, we'd be arrested and jailed.

I thought we might even be killed. We had heard rumors of the GOON squad. A group calling themselves Guardians of the Oglala Nation were terrorizing traditional Indian people on Pine Ridge. The GOONs were supporting the Dick Wilson regime and enjoying a cut of that federal money. It's fair to say the oppression inflicted by Wilson and his GOONs was as bad as anything experienced by the Oglala Lakota people at the hands of border-town whites. There are dozens of unsolved murders from those times that we believe were committed by the GOONs, with the cooperation of the FBI, who supplied them with automatic weapons and tactical support. These murders were swept under the rug by tribal and civil authorities.

The GOONs were mostly mixed-bloods from the families that were known as "hang around the fort Indians," people who had given up their traditional ways and embraced white values. They controlled all politics, business, and government money on Pine Ridge. Meanwhile, the traditional people, who were our heroes for keeping the old ways alive, were suffering under 90 percent unemployment and the worst poverty in the United States.

When the Movement and our lawyers later investigated those murders, it was clear the FBI—by the admission of the GOON leaders—was bankrolling the small army whose mission was to terrorize the traditional Lakota people. They had various goals in so doing, but one thing they wanted was to lure AIM onto the reservation, where they would invent an excuse to round us up and kill us, as they had done to Big Foot's band at Wounded Knee in 1890.

When we later put the whole picture together, we came to see what had happened on Pine Ridge as a proxy war, where the United States had propped up Dick Wilson's administration in exchange for federal support, which came in the form of money and weapons.

Wilson's payment for this support was nearly two hundred thousand acres of reservation land, the Sheep Mountain Gunnery Range, which was supposed to revert to the tribe after a World War II agreement ended. He signed it away to the federal government. What AIM didn't know at the time was that beneath the bombing range lay a huge deposit of uranium and other valuable minerals. Nor did we know the extremes the government would go to have it.

The founders of the Movement had formed an alliance with the traditional Lakota and Dakota people of South Dakota early on. History always depicted the Anishinaabe and Dakota peoples as being enemies. But we Anishinaabe people were not their enemies. Sure, when the Anishinaabe moved into Minnesota in the 1700s, there was tension and conflict over territory. But we didn't take the Black Hills. We didn't massacre Dakota or Lakota people. We were not firing cannons at them at Wounded Knee in 1890. We didn't oppress them and take away their freedom. It was the American Indian Movement that joined hands with the Lakota people: the Means brothers—Bill and Russell, and the Fools Crows, and the Crow Dogs, and especially the traditional women among the Oglalas. It was the American Indian Movement that brought about solidarity between us. This alliance, which would enhance the power of two nations that never considered themselves conquered, scared the hell out of the federal government.

After two weeks of meetings in Rapid City I returned to my family in Minneapolis. Almost as soon as I returned, I received a phone call from Gladys Bissonette, an elder woman from Pine Ridge. Gladys was one of the founders of the Oglala Sioux Civil Rights Organization, the group that had tried to impeach Wilson. She told me she was representing the traditional people of Pine Ridge, and the other OSCRO leaders such as Ellen Moves Camp, Geraldine Janis, and Pedro Bissonette. She asked if the American Indian Movement would come out there and help. She described the reign of terror being carried out against the traditional people. They were being shot at in their homes and beaten up at roadblocks by the GOONs.

Gladys Bissonette, 1973. *Courtesy AIM Interpretive Center*

I asked, "What's wrong with Russell Means? How come Russell's not dealing with this stuff?" He was out there—an AIM leader and Pine Ridge tribal member—and had plenty of AIM supporters to back him up.

I didn't know Gladys, but she impressed me as a no-nonsense, serious person. She said she was fed up with Russell. She said he was out drinking and having a good time while all these terrible things were happening.

I said to her, "Well, you know, I have a restraining order against me there. I can't go onto Pine Ridge—but we're going to come anyway. I promise you we're going to come." So I got together with Dennis Banks and a few other people, and we drove out to Rosebud, out to Crow Dog's Paradise, and we started having meetings there.

One of the warriors who participated in those meetings was a young man named George Whirlwind Soldier. He was the kind of young person whose courage and anger fueled the Movement in those days. An example of his dedication to his people happened in February 1972, when he was graduating as a physician's assistant from the University of North Dakota in Grand Forks. The university had a big winter carnival, and a fraternity erected a racist ice sculpture depicting a bare-breasted Indian woman, to promote their mascot, the Fighting Sioux. George and his friends demolished the sculpture, and he got into a fight with some fraternity members. He was arrested, of course, and went to jail.

The president of the university bailed George out of prison, and charges were dropped. Today he is recognized as one of the earliest opponents of racist mascots in sports. His activities would fuel AIM's involvement in the effort to rid sports of these harmful images.

George was at the meetings at Crow Dog's, discussing how we were going to get into Pine Ridge. It was suggested that everyone we needed to connect with would be at the funeral of a common friend of ours named Ben Black Elk. So we sent George over there. We told him to find Russell and others at the wake and tell them we were waiting in Rosebud and needed to meet.

George returned with the message that they had agreed to meet the next day at a place called Cedar Pass in the Badlands—an area considered a national park by the federal government, but which is actually part of the Pine Ridge Reservation. So we drove over to Cedar Pass and walked deep into the Badlands. The day was sunny but cold, so we cleared away some snow, built a little fire, and sat around it. Leonard Crow Dog, Russell Means, Dennis Banks, Pedro Bissonette, myself, and two or three others were present. We offered tobacco, prayed, and deliberated on what to do next.

Russell and the others from Pine Ridge told us everything that was going on there. What they described sounded like all-out civil war. They told us that something big was about to happen. The feds were amassing there—FBI, Justice Department, military, US Marshals.

I am convinced the feds knew the AIM leadership was on Pine Ridge. They knew most of what we were up to because we had been infiltrated by federal agents. This was shortly after the occupation of the BIA and the Custer riot, so they were watching us very closely. We had, after all, been branded a terrorist organization.

Russell and Dennis insisted we go into Pine Ridge and take over the police department and the BIA office.

I was against that. I told them, "Hey, we've done all those things. We've had all these occupations and demonstrations all over the country. Where have they gotten us? We're not getting anything done. We should be taking back land that belongs to us." I told them we should go to Wounded Knee.

"Why Wounded Knee?" they asked. "What the hell you want to go there for?"

I told them about the vision I had about Wounded Knee in prison. I reminded them that *Bury My Heart at Wounded Knee*, written by Dee Brown, was not only on the best-seller list in America at the time, it was on best-seller lists all over Europe. People were reading about Wounded Knee, about the genocide of Native American peoples. I told them I believed Wounded Knee was one of the most exploited places on earth. Over three hundred peaceful Lakota people, mostly old people, women, and children, were massacred there on December 29, 1890. It was the last act of mass murder carried out by the United States during the so-called Indian Wars, and now had become a big tourist attraction. Wounded Knee, I said, that's where we should go to make our stand. We would be occupying Indian land, where we would be protected by the 1868 Fort Laramie Treaty.

I said that everybody in the Movement knows that the three worst enemies of Indian people—the BIA, organized religion, and white European education—are all there stripping our people of their language and culture. There are five churches in Wounded Knee, I said, for only fifty-four families.

They finally agreed. Crow Dog got out his pipe. He filled his pipe, and we smoked.

Russell started organizing the traditional people on Pine Ridge. It was my job to put out the Red Alert; I put out calls to friends all over the continent. I told them to spread the message that all AIM members, and all freedom-loving people, should come to Wounded Knee. I said, we expect this to be a peaceful protest, but be prepared. We had heard all sorts of rumors of heavy weapons and armored personnel carriers being stashed around on area farms. We hoped whatever happened would be peaceful, but we expected the feds were gearing up for a major confrontation.

We decided, before we went to Wounded Knee, to go to the Oglala community, because Oglala was very traditional, home to many full-bloods. We needed to hold hearings to gauge whether we had the support of the traditional people. We also had to document the complaints of the Lakota people so we could present their case to the world when the time came to back up our actions. Among those people who responded to the Red Alert were AIM supporters who had worked in the court systems and could help document these complaints of vicious GOON violence.

From Rosebud we drove through Pine Ridge at eighty miles an hour. BIA police and state troopers chased us, but we just kept right on going. About a quarter mile outside Oglala, all those squad cars stopped. They had gotten word that the Movement was there and heavily armed.

Dennis, Russell, and I called a meeting as our supporters streamed into the area. We told everybody we had to get affidavits. We had to document the abuses that the people of Pine Ridge were suffering. We had to have a good reason to go into Wounded Knee. We had to be able to show the world what Indian people were enduring.

So we moved into a little place called Calico Hall, a little community gathering place no bigger than forty feet wide and sixty feet long. We called on our friends in the legal profession for help, and within a day or two we had court reporters, lawyers, and law clerks—most of them non-Indians—descending upon Oglala.

Within a forty-eight-hour period, we collected testimony documenting over fifteen hundred individual human and civil rights abuses: murders, rapes, arsons, thefts—just a whole litany of charges. Everybody that brought a complaint had to have witnesses, and had to sign their name to it. The families of Raymond Yellow Thunder and Wesley Bad Heart Bull came to tell their stories. In large numbers the people documented their grievances and asked for help.

We started getting phone calls from all over the country. Not only were Indian people calling, a lot of non-Indians wanted to join in the effort. We heard from activists and organizations like the Weather Underground, Black Panthers—former members of Students for a Democratic Society and Freedom Riders.

We had at Calico common people, lawyers, hardened activists, Indian people who had spent their whole lives struggling for their rights, struggling to be treated with dignity. These were Indian people who had seen their children stolen from their homes by the white boarding school system, who themselves had been held prisoner by the boarding schools, who had seen their sacred lands flooded by hydroelectric dams, who had seen the graves of their ancestors washed away, who had developed diabetes after years of living on government-issued foods, who had struggled with poverty for generations, who lived on reservations like prisoners of war, who had been beaten and shot for being Indian, who lived in crumbling homes with no running water, who had been persecuted for speaking their own language and practicing their ceremonies, who had seen their relatives lose all hope and commit suicide at the highest rates in the country, who were sick and tired and hitting a brick wall every time they tried to help themselves and weren't going to take it anymore.

These people all gathered in that little community center in Oglala ready to make a stand. Their expressions seemed to ask a single question: What next?

11. FOOLS CROW

OUR FINAL NIGHT AT CALICO HALL, the place was so jammed you could not have fit in another person. We kept the doors open so the people outside could hear what was going on. I was chairing the meeting when this little elderly woman stood up in the back of the room and confronted me.

She said, "Haven't you heard enough? Our people are suffering, our women are being beat and raped. Our kids are getting shot; they don't even have basements to hide in—they crawl under beds to hide from the drive-by shootings and firebombings. What are you going to do now?" she demanded. "Are you going to go back to Minneapolis? Back to Milwaukee? Back to Denver?" She started naming off all the places AIM people came from. "Or are you going to make a stand here with the women and children?"

I asked, "Who are you?"

She said, "I'm Gladys Bissonette."

Of course, I knew who Gladys was from phone conversations. She was one of the major leaders of the Oglala Sioux Civil Rights Organization, a grassroots organization on Pine Ridge fighting for the rights of the traditional people. If it hadn't been for Gladys, and other brave OSCRO leaders like Ellen Moves Camp, Agnes Lamont, Lou Bean, Pedro Bissonette, and Vernon Long, AIM may never have been asked to come to Pine Ridge.

This was the first time I was able to look Gladys Bissonette in the eye, where I could see all the suffering the Lakota people had endured.

Gladys told a winding story of all that had happened to her as a little girl in boarding school. She described all the anger that had built up in her. She rolled up her sleeve and held up her arm; you could see the veins all up and down her limb.

"See these arms?" she said. "See these veins? The same blood that flows in these veins is the blood that flows in your veins. It's the blood of Crazy Horse and Sitting Bull." She started naming off all of the great Lakota chiefs from the past, the leaders responsible for our survival through the bad times.

That's when she confronted the AIM leadership. "What are you going to do now? Go back to Minneapolis feeling sorry for us? Or are you going to stand here with the women and children?" She said, "Maybe they'll find you strung up in some cell someday, committed suicide, feeling sorry for yourself, feeling sorry because you didn't do nothing. What are you going to do? Are you going to go leave us, or are you going to stand up and be warriors?"

It stung me. I didn't have to hear more. I said, "I want all the traditional chiefs and headmen, and all the leaders of the chapters of the American Indian Movement, and I want you all to come with me. We're going to go across the street to the church and decide on our next steps."

We told the people, "We'll make a decision. Just wait for us."

Everybody followed us and waited outside while we went into the church basement. Fools Crow loaded his pipe as he sat facing the rest of us—the AIM leadership and representatives of the traditional Lakota people: Crow Dogs, He Dogs, American Horse, Iron Cloud, and the descendants of Crazy Horse.

I addressed the chief. I told Fools Crow we wanted to go to Wounded Knee. I told him there was a best seller out called *Bury My Heart at Wounded Knee*. That Wounded Knee is the site of the last major massacre of Indian people, and that's where we should make our stand. I said, "We'll take back the land that has been stolen from us, and we'll expose the exploitation of Indian people. We'll stay there until we get satisfaction."

Fools Crow recited a long list of injustices which had occurred to the Oglala Lakota people since he was a kid. He spoke about the devastating effects of alcohol, how it had turned Indian people against one another, leading to what was happening on Pine Ridge with shootings and killings every night—traditional people versus those Indians who aspired to live like white men.

Fools Crow said, "Just the other night they burned down my barn, killed three of my horses." He said, "Whatever you AIMs boys want to do, I'll support you, but I don't want no more guns. I don't want no more shootings—we've had enough of that." Fools Crow always called us the "AIMs boys."

We told him we would do everything to make sure there was no violence. We all smoked Fools Crow's pipe, finalizing our commitment to do everything we could to move forward nonviolently.

We sent an advance crew into Wounded Knee before we announced our intentions to the people waiting outside the church. About six carloads of AIM brothers went in with these instructions: "Go to every home in the community, go to all the traders, the churches, all the people that live in Wounded Knee. Knock on their doors and tell them we're coming. Tell them it's going to be a peaceful occupation. We're going to close down all four roads going into Wounded Knee. Tell the people of Wounded Knee to be ready for a long haul."

Right after we sent the delegation to Wounded Knee, we went back to Calico Hall and told everybody to get in their cars and follow us. We didn't dare let people know where we were going, because we knew there were federal informants among us.

Everybody got in their cars and followed us. As we drove through the town of Pine Ridge, seventeen miles from Calico Hall, we saw snipers on the rooftops, police and marshals everywhere, everybody was armed. GOON squads were lining the streets waiting for us to come in to take over Pine Ridge, to take over the Bureau of Indian Affairs, to take over the police department and the jail. Our whole caravan sped through town and never stopped.

Ten minutes after passing the town of Pine Ridge, we turned off the highway and headed north to Wounded Knee. As we arrived, someone started shooting at us. It was already dark and we couldn't see who it was. We took over the Sacred Heart Church on top of the hill for use as our main headquarters. We went to the home of Agnes and Clive Gildersleeve—the trading post owners—and told them what we were doing, and that they had nothing to fear.

Clive Gildersleeve, a white man, controlled the entire economy of the Wounded Knee community. He owned the supermarket, post office, filling station, and pawn shop where people gave away their beautiful beadwork, and ended up losing it, because they could never afford to buy it back. The people never saw their monthly checks because they were all in debt to that trader. These were the same sort of desperate conditions that started the US–Dakota War of 1862 in Minnesota. People cannot live with freedom and dignity if they are totally indebted to another.

One of the big mistakes we made was in how we initially treated the Gildersleeves and their property. We treated their general store there like our personal food pantry. It was full of meat and staples, and our people went and cleaned the place out. It was like a holiday; free shopping, you know. The Gildersleeves were nervous about what might happen to them. I stayed with them to reassure them that they would be safe. With the feds looking for any excuse to come in and kill us all, the last thing we needed was to hold people against their will.

Another mistake we made, I soon discovered, was that AIM people had tied up a priest and were holding him hostage. Without the support of many different churches, AIM never would have achieved the gains that it did. I went to where he was being held and ordered his release.

There was all sorts of propaganda that came out later about how AIM was holding the people of Wounded Knee hostage, but the fact was they had been held hostage for a very long time. They welcomed us with open arms, as freedom fighters. Many residents even fought alongside us.

The first morning I awoke to a lot of people running all over. Someone shouted for me to come outside from the church I had slept in. He handed me binoculars. I took a look at the horizon. I never before knew what an armored personnel carrier, an APC, was. I thought what I was seeing out on the surrounding hillsides were tanks. I counted eighteen of what turned out to be armored personnel carriers. I couldn't believe it. You bet this got our attention.

This was only the beginning of a completely excessive federal response. When the United States of America wants to go to war anywhere in the world, it takes them weeks, months, sometimes years, to build public support. They need congressional approval. Sometimes they even ask the United Nations for approval. The president of the

Our negotiations with federal officials took place in a tipi. I'm standing. Seated, from left: Jim Roubideau, Lakota; Hank Wawasik, Pottawatomie; Oglala leader Tom Bad Cob. *Kevin McKiernan photo*

United States must finally sign off on it. It's in all the newspapers all over the world before a move is made. Without a whiff of this to the American people or Congress, the United States military already had us Indians surrounded. I guess when it's Indians involved, all the rules of war, and human rights, and democracy go out the window.

They wanted AIM eliminated in the worst way.

I said, "Holy Christ, these people are serious. They're going to kill us." And just then here come two fighter jets, *shhheewww!* They rumbled the church, and everything was just shaking. It was a very intimidating display.

AIM united the Sioux (Lakota, Dakota, Nakota), Anishinaabe, and people from many other Indigenous nations, bringing us together as warriors who were cooperating in our fight against a government that had waged a war of genocide against all of us. If the government wanted to wipe out this new generation of Indians, this generation that wasn't going to take it anymore, Wounded Knee in February of 1973 was their chance.

It was at this point we started to build bunkers with whatever junk cars were sitting around in the village. We dragged some cars across the highway to stop any flow of traffic to the roads that came in to Wounded Knee. We had promised Fools Crow that we would avoid violence, but with the overwhelming and disproportionate federal response about to take place, we had no choice but to defend ourselves.

Right away we started holding daily meetings. It felt good when some of the old grandmas from Wounded Knee came up and spoke. We had their blessings, they said. We had the community's support. The men in the leadership suggested, when we saw how ugly things could get, that the women and children leave. We were lucky they refused. They turned out to be our salvation, our source of strength.

Luckily for us, also, the CBS news network had a crew inside Wounded Knee. Their van had followed right behind us from Calico Hall, so that by the time the feds arrived at our roadblocks, the media was already inside with us, and there was no way the feds could prevent them from reporting. After a few days, when the feds temporarily withdrew, the other news organizations also sent in big mobile homes with crews. And there was little chance the feds would invade us as long as the media were there.

The feds never cut off our phone lines. That was, of course, because they wanted to know who we were talking to and what we were saying. I started calling all these different movements all over the country asking for support—the Southern Christian Leadership Conference, the Black Panthers—people we'd met over the years. I rang the Six Nations Iroquois Confederacy. They all said they would join us, and they did.

As they arrived, they were allowed to pass the federal roadblocks under the pretext that they'd come to negotiate an end to the dispute.

Soon, many very well-known and powerful people started to arrive and send their support. The Reverend Ralph Abernathy, who took over as head of the Southern Christian Leadership Conference after Martin Luther King was assassinated, came in with a delegation of Black leaders from the Conference. Movie stars like Jane Fonda, Marlon Brando, and Dick Gregory started calling us, sending messages that they were busy working, but would send support. Every time we heard from people like that, it lifted our spirits and just made us feel good.

Eddie Benton-Banai and a lot of our spiritual leaders weren't in there at first, but they all started coming.

We started getting statements of support from all over the world. We were getting telegrams, solidarity statements from groups like the Irish Republican Army, and the Sandinistas in Nicaragua; the Ortega brothers, the Sandinista leaders, sent us a solidarity statement. Media came from Russia and Cuba—countries that didn't like the US government were sending media crews. So we held press conferences every day.

And then, after a couple of weeks, the feds started tightening their grip. They brought in more heavy military equipment. They thought they had us sealed off pretty good. But they were wrong. Incoming supporters would meet at Crow Dog's Paradise on the Rosebud

Reservation. At night they would travel to Porcupine, South Dakota, which was eight miles from Wounded Knee. Severt Young Bear was one of our dear friends there. People bound for Wounded Knee would stay at his house. And then, late at night, we would send out Chris Westerman, one of our warriors. Chris knew the area like the back of his hand. He would slip across all those government checkpoints and go to Porcupine and bring those people in, along with supplies of ammunition, medical equipment, food, and other necessities.

Our daily press conferences allowed us to communicate directly with the outside world about the plight of Indian people. Our words were made more powerful because they were accompanied by images of US military personnel, FBI agents, and vigilante cowboys firing at us. It gave people the opportunity to understand that this was not an isolated incident. The Indian Wars had been going on for five hundred years.

In those days, of course, all video was captured on film. So each night we'd send out these huge newsreels with Chris Westerman or one of the warriors in his group. They would meet in Porcupine with representatives of CBS, who would ship the reels off to New York, where they would air on the evening news. So each night the world was hearing about us, literally. We were on the news in Europe, and Asia, and South and Central America. Our AIM national anthem was heard around the world!

The people who were there still talk about it today, the sense of freedom we had inside Wounded Knee. Even though we were under siege, we were fighting, and it gave us all a sense of liberation to have something to defend. People who had seen family members killed, like the families of Wesley Bad Heart Bull and Raymond Yellow Thunder, just felt really good. For once, someone was standing up for them, someone was listening to them, and someone was working to get the word out about what was happening in Indian Country.

All of this seemed to happen with amazing speed, and it made all of us happy. But there was at least one man at Wounded Knee who was not happy. We had promised Chief Fools Crow that there would be no more violence, and yet here we were engaged in live combat against the forces of the United States.

On the second day of the siege, Fools Crow arrived at Wounded Knee along with his interpreter, a guy named John King. I saw him coming from a long way off, and by the way he was walking I could tell he was angry. All these little kids were happy to see him; they ran up to greet him, but he just went right through them looking very upset.

Fools Crow called a meeting with the leadership. We met in the community hall, and he gave us hell. Man, he was pissed. Through his interpreter, John King, he said, "You promised me there wasn't going to be no guns. People are going to get killed here. You got to put your guns away."

I was first to get up and talk. I told Fools Crow about Minneapolis. How Indian people were being shot in the goddamn back by the police department. How women were taken down by the river and raped instead of taken to jail. Everything they could do to try to destroy the Movement, they did it. But we stood up. I talked about the fifteen million Indian people who had been erased from the face of the earth in the Native American genocide.

Others spoke, too. We reminded him about the American policy of stealing our children, of stripping us of our land and our culture. People talked about Los Angeles and San Francisco and how Native families got relocated to those places from the reservations, and all the racism they were going through, and how it was time now to make a stand.

Fools Crow sat there with his cane, his chin on his hands, listening, shaking his head. He couldn't believe all the stuff he was hearing. He knew things were bad for the traditional Oglalas. He had not known that Indian people were being similarly abused throughout the country.

Finally, I could see his mood change. Fools Crow wasn't angry anymore. He started to get a twinkle in his eyes, and he told this story: Back in 1890, there was a young man on the reservation. He heard these noises in the distance, and he heard there was a war going on at Wounded Knee. So he rode on his horse to see what was happening. He said the young man got to a spot overlooking the valley there at Wounded Knee, and he could see the women and children being butchered with blood all over the snow. He wanted to ride right down there into the battle. The Creator came to him and told him he could do nothing to change what was happening, but that he had the power to heal. He had strong medicine, and he was going to serve his people well. That young man turned out to be Black Elk, Fools Crow's uncle, and he served his people well.

Toward the end of his life, when he was an old man, Black Elk was becoming feeble and forgetful. In 1935, he went up on the hill and he fasted and prayed; he felt pitiful because he thought he was a failure. He told the Creator that in 1890, the sacred hoop was broken at Wounded Knee. In his prayer, he talked about the tree of life withering and dying there at Wounded Knee.

They say that the Creator came to him and told him that he had not failed even though he witnessed Wounded Knee and so many other injustices, such as the taking of the sacred Black Hills. He had never failed.

And when Fools Crow got through talking, he stood up and had kind of a grin on his face. He told the people that now he understood. *Now* he understood. And he talked about Crazy Horse and Gall and all the great Lakota leaders. He said they had fought and died for all of us. And he closed his talk off by telling us he was going to go home.

"I'm going home, and I'm going to put on my war regalia," he said. "And I'm going to get my rifle, and I'll be back in."

Holy God, everybody started clapping—we finally got the grand chief of the Oglala nation on our side.

Lo and behold, the following day here he comes in full regalia—all this beadwork, and a fancy buckskin shirt. He was about seventy and in great shape, still an active dancer. He wore his headdress and came in with his rifle. He looked so powerful, man, like the Great Spirit coming in.

Everybody just started cheering. That's when we really dug in.

12. WOUNDED KNEE

THE EUPHORIA THAT EXISTED during the first few days of the occupation soon gave way to very somber, life-and-death decision making. After about one week at Wounded Knee, the military flew one of them big gunship helicopters over our camp, and a bunch of papers started floating down. A little boy ran out there and picked up one of the papers and brought it to me. The message warned that we had to be out of Wounded Knee by five the next afternoon or they were going to come in and wipe us out.

We called a meeting and told the people we wanted the women and the children, all the families, the elderly, the traders, and the church leaders to leave Wounded Knee. We asked them all to leave while we AIM men were going to stay there and get it on.

During that meeting, Gladys Bissonette got up again, as she had earlier during our meetings at Calico Hall. She walked into the middle of the circle and said, "You AIM boys, you can go home, you've made your point." And she said, "Us women, we're not going anywhere."

Gladys went over to Stan Holder, a former marine and Vietnam veteran who was head of our security. He had a rifle. "Give me that gun!" She grabbed it away from him, and everybody just got quiet.

That's when she really got after us. "We thank you AIM boys for coming here, and if you want to go, now's the time." She said, "Us women are going to stay here. We're never going to get on our knees again and beg this government for anything. This is our land. I'm going to make a stand right here with this rifle."

She embarrassed all of us AIM warriors, this little lady with a face that looked like it had seen it all.

A whole gang of grandmas got up and spoke after that. They spoke in support of making a stand against the centuries of abuse Indian people had suffered. They were the most militant people within Wounded Knee because they were the ones who had suffered the most. They're the ones who carry and deliver the children; they're the ones who feed them; they're the ones who take care of them.

Following the lead of the grandmas, everyone seemed to take heart.

About 70 percent of the people at Wounded Knee were women and children. They all cheered the words of these unbelievable women. Even little boys, seven and eight years old, weren't scared. Everyone was united. We were ready to get it on. Not one single person, not one family left Wounded Knee. Even the white traders and church leaders decided to stay; they were part of that community, and they knew that if they left, the military would come in and wipe us out.

Their example gave me an idea. The more church leaders and white supporters that we could bring in, the safer we would be. So I got on the phone, and the first person I contacted was Dr. Paul Boe, our good friend in the Lutheran Church. Dr. Boe always wanted to be part of the action. He wasn't satisfied to help behind the scenes; he wanted to be on the front lines.

So I called him and said, "Dr. Boe, we need your help. They're threatening to invade. If they do, we'll all be killed. Can you come to Wounded Knee?"

That night I slept in my station wagon. It was cold, and the windows frosted over. In the morning I saw a key sweeping across my windshield, scraping the frost. I got out of the car to see who was there. It was Dr. Boe. I couldn't believe my eyes. He had come all the way from Minneapolis, made his way through FBI checkpoints, and there he was, wearing his red beret.

People were suspicious of this white man. They thought he was an FBI agent. So I introduced him at a big meeting. People expressed their apprehensions about him. I told them who he was, and that he wasn't here to hurt us. I said, "He is here to save us."

I truly believe if it weren't for real Christians like Dr. Boe, who came into Wounded Knee to shield us Indians, we would have been the victims of a second Wounded Knee massacre. I later told Dr. Boe, "You not only walk in the footsteps of Jesus. You also walk in the footsteps of Chief Big Foot."

At first our actions at Wounded Knee were not well publicized in America. The networks and the feds conspired to show us as a bunch of militants and radicals that needed to be contained and eliminated.

This actually felt familiar to us as Indian people. We had been misunderstood ever since that lost pirate Columbus first landed and thought he was in India.

But in Germany, France, Switzerland, and Ireland, in fact all other parts of the world, we were pleasantly surprised. There was full coverage—hours and hours of coverage—where they showed the slum conditions, poor housing, effects of alcohol and drugs that Indian people were dealing with. They showed the sacred lands that were taken from us and exploited. Our story was told around the world, and people expressed an outpouring of sympathy for what we'd lived through. It was reassuring to know the whole world was watching.

The tone and volume of coverage in America began to turn as soon as the Indian journalists came in. They printed sympathetic stories in reservation newspapers all over the country. Native people everywhere understood our struggle because the conditions at Pine Ridge were no different than Indian people were living under everywhere. So they could see in our stand a ray of hope that something was being done to help them.

It was an exciting time, because people were finally understanding the trauma that the Native people on this continent have endured. They were finally listening to us. At night we would gather around televisions and watch the news. Surveys and studies started coming out saying the American public supported us. We were by far more popular than the Nixon administration, which, I believe, is one reason we weren't invaded in those first few days.

As days went by and things became more difficult, you might think we would have lost our resolve and become demoralized. But it seemed the solidarity within our camp only increased with hardship. We ran low on food because we made the big mistake of clearing out the entire grocery store in the first days. Although we ran out of meat and many other foods early on, we never went hungry. We always had staples like potatoes and flour that people brought in with them, or which we received from aerial food drops.

We had about two hundred people inside Wounded Knee at the

beginning, and over the course of the occupation I would guess over a thousand people came and went. During cease-fires, we could move around safely outdoors. Other times the fighting would go on for two or three days straight, and people had to hunker down, while all night long the feds were lighting up the place like daytime with their flares.

We had to have places where people could get away from the gunfire, and also where people could stay warm. The churches and the store served well for that. We were able to keep the heat on the whole time. Out on the reservation they use propane heating, and the feds, even though they shut off the electricity a short time after we took Wounded Knee, were unable to prevent us from keeping warm.

There were many things we did to help the people stay strong as our casualties mounted. We set up an infirmary and staffed it with our people who worked in health care: doctors, nurses, medics. We didn't have all the medical supplies we needed, however, so when somebody got shot, they would give them some alcohol to drink, cut them, and take the bullet out. Those who gave their lives, and those who gave their flesh, and those who took care of us, these were our heroes. They kept us going, kept us fighting. It seems counterintuitive, but within Wounded Knee, while under siege, we had such a sense of freedom. On March 8, we had proclaimed the Independent Oglala Nation, and we were defending it.

We were also held together by our traditional medicine people and the spiritual gifts they shared. Every night we had a ceremony, calling on the spirits for help, health, and strength. We cleared the pews out of one of the churches, made circles in there where our people would gather in the dark to sing, drum, and pray for their loved ones and for what they needed.

We were also sustained by a herd of cows that grazed on the hills above the valley. Every few days I would go and meet with this farmer who was caught inside Wounded Knee. I'd go up and tell him to release a couple cows to us. We'd take them back to Wounded Knee and butcher them; that's the way we ate there. One day I went up to the farm with these brothers and—instead of the usual two—they took fourteen cows back to our camp. I promised that we'd pay him back when this was all over. All the while, as we were negotiating for his cattle, the farmer was convinced I was one of the Wounded Knee attorneys, which put him more at ease. I told him I would make sure he was reimbursed, and he was. Later, when I read the extensive list of charges against me for my involvement in the occupation, I was surprised cattle rustling was not among my alleged crimes.

One night we had a big ceremony, and everybody came. Leonard Crow Dog decided he was going to have a Sun Dance right inside this church. These ceremonies normally take place on large grounds, outdoors, in the summertime. So this was really unusual.

Crow Dog asked me to pierce him. We'd been Sun Dancing at his place, and there was a lot of trust between us. He leaned on that rope until his flesh ripped open. Crow Dog said he was doing that for us, a sacrifice to keep the people going. I felt so good about what he did that I decided to pierce, too. I said I wanted to give my blood, too. Everybody thought I was going to give a flesh offering, a ritual often done alongside the Sun Dance. But I thought, *how can I just give a little flesh out of my shoulder after what Crow Dog had just done?*

I said, "No, I want to be pierced like my brother here."

Before I pierced, about thirty AIM guys lined up behind me. By the time they realized I wasn't just giving a little flesh but actually piercing, they couldn't back down. I could see on their faces that many of them were pissed off at me, but they couldn't get out of the line; they couldn't just sit down, not in front of the people.

Crow Dog pierced me and everyone in that line. He believes it's important to suffer if you want your prayers to be heard. Because we didn't have a tree to tie to, we had men holding the ropes. If someone had trouble breaking free, we put a man on each shoulder and held them while three or four others pulled on the rope like a tug-of-war. I remember that night as fun. We managed to have a lot of fun moments like that within Wounded Knee. It's hard to explain, but we weren't scared. We were liberated.

There was such a strong sense of community; everybody called each other brother and sister. If you were a little older you'd be called uncle. The elders were all referred to as grandma and grandpa.

Later that day we built a big fire down by the tipis and sweat lodges and everyone gathered there. Crow Dog said he wanted to prepare everyone for a long confrontation, the way warriors did when going into battle. I walked up and Crow Dog placed red war paint all the way across my face. Crow Dog started with the warriors, and then the women stood up, and little children too.

Crow Dog then gave an unbelievable speech. He'd never been to school in his life, you know; he was taught by his parents, who insisted he be raised with traditional Lakota values. He speaks fluent Lakota, but his English is a little broken as it's his second language. Yet his talk was so powerful; it was just unbelievable how the people listened to him. He told us we were going to be okay.

He talked about all the things that happened at Wounded Knee on December 29, 1890. He reminded us about the innocent blood that had been spilled on that ground when Big Foot's band was surrounded by the Seventh Cavalry and massacred by American soldiers with Hotchkiss guns. By the time the massacre was over, more than three hundred men, women, and children, he said, lay dead upon the frozen earth along Wounded Knee Creek. He pointed to the graveyard at the top of the hill where those three hundred Lakota people were tossed into a mass grave. By the time he was done, we really understood why we were there. We were there to make sure the victims of Wounded Knee, and all of the other Indigenous victims of the Native American genocide, had not died in vain.

We trusted Crow Dog. We believed in him. He helped us recognize the spiritual power that was there to help us. I remember going in the sweat lodge one night, and while we were praying inside, a firefight broke out that would last about three hours. There was a bunker not far from the sweat lodge, and everybody wanted to get out and run for safety.

Crow Dog told us, "You stay in here."

We had our cars parked in a circle around the lodge for protection. We could hear the bullets zinging off them.

He said, "You just stay in here and you pray, you pray really hard, and the Creator will take care of everyone." We stayed in there for three hours, and not one bullet went through that sweat lodge. Nobody got hurt.

So when things like that happened, it just empowered us. It just felt good. If we were to die, that was the place to die, right there while the world looked on. The sacred power of these ceremonies helped us stay strong.

We later found out that there were so many spirits coming to join us that night that outside it looked like a storm. Lightning was shooting sideways in the skies all around Wounded Knee. One of the US Marshals who came into Wounded Knee for a meeting testified that he was up on one of those armored personnel carriers, and he and others saw Indians on horseback coming at them, jumping right over them.

Crow Dog did much more for us than provide spiritual support. He might have been the smartest person among the whole group. He was always coming up with new ways for keeping us going, and keeping us safe. For example, one day rumors were circulating that a military invasion was imminent; Crow Dog devised a plan to keep them out. In broad daylight, on a nice sunny day, he went out and dug holes all the way around the perimeter of Wounded Knee. He sunk these big buckets down into those holes, then connected them together with concertina wire. Of course, to the feds this must have appeared to be an explosive trip wire, but the fact was there were no explosives in the buckets—they were empty. All day, as he was constructing his dummy land mines, we watched federal agents as they spied him from a distant hill through binoculars. It must have been an effective deterrent, because the expected invasion never took place.

There was a period during Wounded Knee, in March, after we'd been there several weeks, when we were low on supplies. We had hardly any food and medicine. They had a big ring of armed men and military hardware surrounding us. They had United States Marshals around us. They had FBI agents around us. They had the Bureau of Indian Affairs, tribal police, and state troopers, the John Birchers, vigilante ranchers, and the GOON squad all around. We were fully surrounded and sealed off.

We received word that there was a very large contingent of Indian people, several hundred, camped out at Crow Dog's Paradise, trying to come into Wounded Knee. Dennis, Russell, and Crow Dog were confident they could get to Rosebud and lead those people—with their food, medical supplies, weapons, and ammunition—back to Wounded Knee. Grass Mountain, Crow Dog's district, is about one hundred miles due east of Wounded Knee, and it would take a couple days for Russell and Dennis to get over there, organize the people and supplies, and return. They would use the pipeline that Severt Young Bear had set up; this would be the first time we tried to bring in a large group all at once.

We knew, however, that they would only make it back if the media didn't know they were gone. By this time several of us in the AIM leadership had become very well known—we were on TV every night. But Russell Means and Dennis Banks were perhaps the most visible AIM leaders. They were telegenic and were the men the media sought out most often for interviews. As soon as the media caught wind that they had left Wounded Knee, it would be reported, and they would get caught.

We devised a plan to make people think they were still in camp. We got everybody to believe that they were inside a tipi, fasting and praying privately. We put up a tipi near the sweat lodges, placed security around it so that nobody could go in there, and told everyone that Russell, Dennis, and Crow Dog had gone inside overnight, and that they would remain there for four days.

Before they left for Rosebud, they put me in charge of everything.

During this period of time, we had three different meetings, and a group of Indians from Oklahoma, including a guy named Carter Camp, tried to take over. He and his group pushed a plan to draw the armed forces in and then attack them at close range. They brought with them a toxic attitude that was at first confusing.

My brother Vernon and other Movement people had met them in Denver. He said the Camps had been hanging around their meetings dressed in suits and ties. But when they arrived at Wounded Knee they were wearing brand-new western boots, and jean jackets covered with AIM patches. I kept a close eye on them, suspicious that they weren't at all who they claimed to be—Ponca warriors from Oklahoma. I started to suspect they were federal informants.

I'd have to filibuster them because they kept trying to rile the people up, tried to get them to attack the government forces.

I'd step in and say, "Oh, yeah? What you're suggesting is suicide. What the hell is wrong with you?" When I addressed the people I reminded them that we had a Sacred Pipe, and that was all the power we needed to protect our people. We were foremost a spiritual encampment. I'd say, "This is our main weapon right here," and I'd hold the Sacred Pipe in the air.

Everything they tried, I would get up and counter it with common sense, and the people listened to me. As days passed, a deep animosity developed between the Oklahoma group and the AIM leadership. Carter detested me for thwarting his plots.

At the first meeting after Dennis and Russell returned with a massive contingent of supporters and supplies, we told the people they'd been gone and had not been fasting inside the tipi. We admitted that we couldn't have shared that information because we had been infiltrated by federal informants who would have gotten word out to the feds and media. On this point we were not simply paranoid, we were right. A couple years later we were able to get our hands on federal documents that discussed information obtained by informants posing as supporters inside Wounded Knee.

We put all newcomers through a sort of orientation process. It didn't matter who you were, if you came into Wounded Knee for the first time, you would have to go into a sweat lodge right away. When it came to putting our spiritual values and beliefs as Native people above all else, there was no room for compromise. We made sure all newcomers understood the rules: no drugs and no alcohol allowed. Break those rules once, and you were out of there. We could not afford to have anyone on our side whose mind was clouded with pollutants. We had to have our heads absolutely clear. We also let people know how they would fit into the society we had organized there. Everyone was expected to attend the two or three meetings we called every day. There they would learn what needed to be done and how they could contribute to running and defending the camp.

As I look back on those times, we were right to take over Wounded Knee at that moment in history. If we tried to do something like that today, we could never get away with it. Now the government would label us terrorists, send in a drone strike, and drop a laser-guided missile—just like they are doing now to people all over the world.

Don't get me wrong: no one inside Wounded Knee was safe, not for a single moment of those seventy-one days of occupation. In addition to the loss of two of our warriors, we had fourteen people sustain bullet wounds. Of course, when you consider that the feds unleashed upon us some five hundred thousand rounds of ammo from their M16s, it's miraculous that we didn't suffer greater casualties. The government lied about the deadly force they used against us. They put out numbers claiming they had exchanged a few rounds with "AIM militants." But in reality, there were hundreds of thousands of rounds fired at us—men, women, and children. These attacks lasted, sometimes, four or five hours at a stretch.

One afternoon, I very nearly became one of those casualties. I was staying in a trailer with the White Eagle family in the housing community. It was a nice day, beautiful, sunny, when suddenly the feds opened up on us. I dove into a ditch, bullets zinging all around, goddamn gravel hitting me in the face.

I was helpless, but at the same time I wasn't. The spirits were watching over me, protecting me.

I never carried a gun in Wounded Knee—never. I stayed in that ditch there for the nearly three hours they were firing on us, and I prayed—I laid in the damn ditch and just prayed.

Finally, everything stopped.

After about a half hour, nobody was shooting anymore, so I took off running and finally made it back to the house. When I got there I learned that a seventeen-year-old woman named Mary Ellen Moore-Richard— who would one day become Leonard Crow Dog's wife—was in heavy labor inside. That's why I remember the exact date: Friday, April 5, because it was the birthday of the baby born inside Wounded Knee.

I had to use the bathroom, but because Mary needed privacy, I went behind the trailer house. I must have heard some commotion, because I looked up and about fifty yards away three military guys had their rifles pointed at me. I thought, *man this is it, they're going to kill me right here in broad daylight.* But they just laughed at me and walked away. I thought for damn sure I was going to get blasted right there. I finished peeing, turned around, slowly walked into the house, and told everybody what happened. They looked out the window, and those military guys were walking away up the hill.

Every time we experienced another extraordinary event, such as this beautiful birth, or living another day, we would have a ceremony. People got empowered, and they got stronger. The Creator was watching over us. It was a very spiritually powerful time.

I saw extraordinary evidence of the spiritual protection we were given. Crow Dog, like Crazy Horse before him, wore a Ghost Dance shirt during combat. He told us the shirt would protect him from bullets. There were times I saw him walk through a hail of gunfire and come out unharmed.

This was the very best time of my life, and I knew it.

My only regret from that time is the stress my family back in Minneapolis had to go through. I knew I was putting them through hell.

Every chance I'd get I would call my wife, and she'd say, "The FBI was over at the house the other day."

"Oh yeah? What did they want?"

They tried to destabilize my family, and many others, by planting lies in my wife's head. One time they told Peggy that in the days prior to Wounded Knee I was staying at a hotel in Rapid City having drunken orgies. The FBI pulled the same shit on Dr. Martin Luther King and Jesse Jackson, accusing them of drinking and womanizing.

They would ask Peggy what she thought of that. Peggy, who saw through their tired tactics, would say, "When you see my husband, tell him to have a good time." Peggy knew exactly what they were up to. It was well known that the FBI had tapped King's phone before he was shot down in Memphis in 1968. We knew they were doing the same to our home phone in Minneapolis. Peggy and I were very careful about what we said to each other when I called.

The FBI was the driving force behind most of the violence the Lakota people on Pine Ridge endured. They funded the GOONs and supplied their weapons. But the GOONs weren't the only civilian militia the FBI supported. Right-wingers like the John Birch Society did a lot of the FBI's dirty work too. The Birchers let it be known throughout the region that it was open season on AIM and traditional Indian people. They posted signs all over on telephone poles around Pine Ridge and Rosebud. "Clyde Bellecourt Wanted Dead or Alive." They had my picture on there alongside Russell, Dennis, and other Movement leaders. It was like the Wild West all over again.

In April, a Harris poll came out. This was during the heart of the Watergate scandal. The poll on Richard Nixon resulted in only 29 percent of the American public saying they supported him. The rest thought he was a liar and a crook.

At the same time Harris did a poll on the American Indian Movement. Fifty-one percent of the American people supported the American Indian Movement takeover at Wounded Knee. They even supported the use of arms to protect ourselves. So we had more support than the president of the United States at that time.

Senators Edward Kennedy from Massachusetts and James Abourezk of South Dakota interviewed the traders and church people to confirm they were not being held hostage. These white folks said they were part of the Wounded Knee community and intended to stay there, of their own free will, to protect their homes and try and prevent the feds from wiping us out.

But, like I mentioned earlier, this was very serious business. And there were many difficulties. We lost two young men to the fight: Buddy Lamont and Frank Clearwater. No one on the federal side lost their life. Two marshals were wounded by gunfire; as far as we could tell, one was caught in crossfire between his own men.

When Frank Clearwater came into camp, he was not known to any of us. Since we had to vet all newcomers, I questioned him. He said he came up from Tennessee, where he had struggled all his life, where his people were struggling, neglected by the government. He looked like a hillbilly, a young guy with a big cap and beard. He came bearing a shotgun that seemed like it was two yards long, along with his pregnant wife, Morning Star. She was Apache, and he was Cherokee.

The morning after they arrived, April 17, we received a wonderful surprise when three small airplanes, Piper Cherokees flown by our supporters, came flying low over the camp. They dumped one ton of supplies under parachutes—first-aid materials, rice, coffee, tea, flour, antibiotics, cigarettes, baby formula, vitamins. The airdrop took the feds by surprise and apparently made them very angry. Next thing anyone knew a military helicopter flew overhead, and a sniper opened fire on people carrying the supplies into the trading post. Our people shot back, igniting a firefight that lasted over two hours.

During the firefight, Frank Clearwater was sleeping in the church. A stray bullet came through the wall, splitting his head open. We had a line to the feds; we called them and arranged a cease-fire so Clearwater could be taken to a hospital. About ten days later, he died. Crow Dog later honored Clearwater's sacrifice, burying him at Crow Dog's Paradise.

Buddy Lamont returned to Pine Ridge as a hero from the Vietnam War—one of the great warriors of the Oglala Nation. He came home and asked his grandmother, Agnes Lamont, what was going on at Wounded Knee. When she told him we were making a stand, his immediate response was "I got to go out there."

So Buddy spent one day visiting with his family after returning from the war; the next day he came into Wounded Knee to fight for his people. He received an honorable discharge from the marines at about the same time an American bullet killed him. He was shot through the heart and died instantly on April 27, 1973, during a brutal firefight. He was pinned down in an abandoned house next to the community center. A federal sniper apparently had Buddy in his sights, and when he tried after several hours to gain a better fighting position, he ran out of the old house and took a bullet to the chest.

The medics who tried to save Buddy's life were shot at while he lay in the open, bleeding out his wounds. The medics waved white flags and wore red crosses on their arms, but the feds fired at them anyway. They were pinned down for hours, until dark, while the life slowly drained out of Buddy. Then they were held up again as they tried to get through the federal roadblock en route to the hospital. After negotiating with the marshals, a helicopter was brought in. But by the time he arrived at a hospital in Rapid City, it was too late to save him.

Buddy was buried on the hill next to the mass grave containing the victims of the 1890 massacre. He was the only Lakota person killed in the occupation. His headstone carries the inscription: "Two thousand came to Wounded Knee in 1973. One stayed."

13. SPEAKING TO THE WORLD

PEOPLE WERE CONSTANTLY ARRIVING at Wounded Knee, at least until the feds managed to clamp down on our secret routes. We knew there had to be informants. We started hearing news from the outside that some in the media were calling us a bunch of criminals, convicts, and dope addicts. I suspected the Oklahoma guys were the source of these stories, but it didn't matter, the damage was being done.

So we called a meeting with the Oglala Sioux Civil Rights Organization, the traditional chiefs, the AIM leadership, and the leaders among the women—Ellen Moves Camp and Gladys Bissonette. After a discussion of what needed to happen in order for our side of the story to once again reach the public, it was decided that somebody had to leave Wounded Knee. They nominated me.

I said, "No, I'm not going to leave here."

They were adamant. "You have to," they said. "It's important, and we all support you. We need you to go out and speak for us."

Fools Crow stood up with his pipe and addressed me through his interpreter. "This is important work," he said, "and it has to be done." When Fools Crow gave you a mission, there was no refusing.

I was selected because I was known as a good community organizer and an accomplished speaker. I was capable of establishing contact within non-Indian communities nationwide. The Oglala Sioux Civil Rights Organization, all the traditional chiefs, and the American Indian Movement voted unanimously that I'd be the person to go out.

So on the fifty-first day of the occupation, I finally agreed to be the spokesperson for Wounded Knee on the outside.

The following day Ken Tilsen, Douglas Hall, and Larry Leventhal, our attorneys, came and got me. We walked up to the government line, and I surrendered.

The marshals took me into custody and drove me an hour northwest into Rapid City, at the base of the Black Hills. They had me on fourteen criminal counts, all of them conspiracy-type charges: conspiracy to shoot an FBI agent, conspiracy to shoot a marshal, and so on. I was taken into the jail there, fingerprinted, photographed, and released.

A portrait taken just after I left Wounded Knee. *Dick Bancroft photo*

I never spent a single day locked up, due to a woman from New York named Carol Bernstein, who I had never met. She was aware of our story, and sympathetic not only to the struggles of Indigenous people but to liberation movements happening all over the country. She transferred $250,000 from a bank in New York City to a bank in Rapid City to bail me out.

Mrs. Bernstein flew me from Rapid City to Minneapolis to visit my family. Two days later I boarded another airplane for New York City. Mrs. Bernstein had set up a press conference there. And when I got through in New York, she flew me to Texas—Dallas and Fort Worth and all the big cities down there. And then I came up through Albuquerque and Phoenix. And then to Washington, DC, and I was doing press conferences at every stop. I told the American public what was happening at Wounded Knee, how the armed forces had us surrounded, and how the FBI and certain media outlets were trying to demonize us.

Along the way I met with the Southern Christian Leadership Conference and the Six Nations Iroquois Confederacy. They arranged these big press conferences as well, where they stood beside me, in solidarity with our people at Wounded Knee.

I was invited to speak at Jesse Jackson's church in Chicago. I got in to the airport there early one Sunday morning. Jackson sent a limousine out to the airport, and his representatives came to meet me wearing nice black suits. They took me to their church for the morning service.

That place was jam-packed with Black leadership, Black Panthers, congregants, media—everybody came. They had a jazz band in there. And it really made me feel empowered to look out and see Jesse Jackson, and all of these beautiful people, welcoming me. During my talk I started getting loud, beating on the table between every statement: "They have been killing us all these years! We need your support in every way!"

Toward the end of my speech, the jazz band started, and people started getting up out of the pews. They were dancing and hollering,

"Hallelujah!" I got into it even more, shouting out, "We're making our stand!" And by the time I got to the end of my talk, the band was going full blast, and the people were all dancing, putting their fists in the air, and boy I knew we had their support.

I flew out to San Francisco for some press events, and then back to Minneapolis, where I started making phone calls. My top priority now, after weeks on the road, was assembling a legal team. We would have to find excellent attorneys to represent us, and who, at the same time, would put the US government on trial for their despicable history of human rights abuses against Indigenous people. I called attorney Doug Hall, who helped found the Legal Rights Center in Minneapolis.

Hall said, "I'll come out to Wounded Knee. I'll be there."

I called Larry Leventhal. He said, "I'll be there."

I called Ken Tilsen. He agreed to meet at Wounded Knee, too.

Every one of these lawyers were from Minneapolis, some of the best legal minds in the country—men who would make legal history in the coming years for helping to forward the cause of Native American justice.

They all agreed to drop what they were doing and form what I called "The Wounded Knee Legal Defense/Offense Committee" (WKLDOC). I insisted we adopt this name because we were going to put the US government on trial for crimes against humanity.

Then I called Bill Kunstler, the most famous civil rights attorney in America, at his home in New York. His daughter answered the phone, and I said, "I want to speak to Mr. Kunstler."

"That's my dad," she said, and yelled for him.

He got on the phone and said, "I've been waiting for this call, Mr. Bellecourt."

I said, "I want you to come to Wounded Knee."

He said, "Why do you want me involved?"

I said, "Any lawyer that would go to jail for contempt of court has to be a good attorney."

At that time Kunstler was under attack by the federal bench. They were trying to disbar him for his support of the Chicago Seven, and the rioting that happened during the 1968 Democratic Convention in Chicago.

"I'll be out there, Mr. Bellecourt," Kunstler said. "I'll be there."

I called Mark Lane, who has written several books about the CIA's involvement in the assassination of John F. Kennedy. Mark Lane was a terrific attorney who would, five years later, escape from Jonestown, Guyana, where 909 followers of Reverend Jim Jones were poisoned with cyanide and killed. He ran into the jungle; otherwise he'd have been killed, too. He was there trying to help those poor people escape. Mark said he'd meet us at Wounded Knee, too.

None of the attorneys I called turned us down.

We also had aspiring young lawyers that were still going to law school, like Bruce Ellison, who's still with us today, working in Rapid City and handling a lot of Indian cases.

Two days later they all came right into Wounded Knee. We had seven attorneys assembled in all.

I said at our first meeting with our new legal team: "We're not going on the defensive; we're going to prosecute the goddamn government."

Bill Kunstler liked that; he said that's exactly what we should do.

So we had the support of seven top-notch attorneys, most of them Jewish. I used to joke around with them. I'd say, "They got this theory that the Indian people are one of the twelve lost tribes of Israel. But the truth is, Jewish people are one of the lost tribes of the Anishinaabe nation." They liked that.

Of course, their connection with Indian people was no joke. They saw in us a people, like themselves, that had been targeted for extinction, took very deep losses in blood, land, and culture, but managed to survive and even thrive.

With the help of WKLDOC, we did put the goddamn government on trial. For the first time in Native American history, we turned the tables on them.

As the occupation approached its seventieth day, we remained in regular contact with the White House. It had been one of our demands that the White House directly take on the investigation into the GOON squads and the corrupt administration of Dick Wilson.

The White House refused, but promised an independent commission would investigate our claims: the involvement of the FBI in arming the GOON squads, the dozens of unsolved murders. There would be federal grand juries and federal inquiries, they promised, and there would be an independent prosecutor assigned to the cases. These false assurances came directly from the Nixon administration.

We decided that we had won, and that we would de-occupy and leave Wounded Knee. Seventy-one days after taking over that little village on the hill above Wounded Knee Creek, AIM, traditional Lakotas, and supporters from across Indian Country and around the world surrendered to federal authorities. Many of our people were charged and released on bond. We all scattered, back to the cities and reservations from which we'd come.

Not too long after Wounded Knee, I was at the AIM office on Franklin Avenue, and we were really busy dealing with a police brutality case. The phone rang and our secretary said, "Hey, Clyde, someone wants you on the phone."

And I said, "Who is it?"

She said it was a woman, somebody named Coretta Scott. I went and took the phone, still completely distracted by the police brutality issue. The caller wanted to know if I would be willing to fly to Atlanta. She said they had this big march every year to commemorate the Reverend Martin Luther King Jr.'s death. She said they march from uptown Atlanta to the Ebenezer Baptist Church, where they have a memorial ceremony at MLK's grave site.

I said, "Well, I'll think it over and see if I can find some time."

After hanging up the phone I thought, *Coretta Scott, who the hell is that?*

Everyone in the office was curious about who I had just spoken to. I said, "I don't know. Some woman called Coretta Scott."

Our secretary just gasped. "Oh, my God! That's Martin Luther King's wife! What'd you tell her?"

"I told her I would think it over and get back to her."

Everyone got all excited. "You better call her," they told me. "You better call her right back!"

I called right away and played it cool, as if I'd known who she was all along. I couldn't apologize without looking ridiculous; I just told her I'd cleared my schedule and would be honored to come down to Atlanta for the march. A few days later an airplane ticket arrived for me in the mail.

Marching with Coretta Scott King was an unforgettable experience. We walked hand in hand at the front of the largest Black community march I've ever participated in. When we arrived at Ebenezer Baptist Church in Atlanta's Sweet Auburn neighborhood, I followed Mrs. King inside. The place—where Martin Luther King Jr. was baptized in 1934, later started his ministry at age nineteen, and in 1968 was laid to rest—was just packed. There were people spilling out the door, jammed in the hallway, and filling a building next door where the overflow crowd watched the ceremony on closed-circuit television. I entered and stood in the rear of the sanctuary, taking it all in.

Mrs. King was laid-back and soft-spoken. When she talked to you, she kind of called you aside and spoke in private whispers. She approached and asked if I would be willing to give one of the keynote speeches. I agreed, and she took me by the hand.

"Come with me," she said in her gentle, commanding way.

As we found our seats at the front of the church, Mrs. King asked me to address specifically the plight of American Indian people and the need for the civil rights movement to recognize our struggles.

As I stood at the pulpit I could feel the powerful energy of all that had happened in that place. It was a tremendous honor to speak from the same pulpit where Martin Luther King had given many historic speeches.

I've never written a speech in my life, and my talk at Ebenezer Baptist Church was no exception. I shot from the hip and spoke from the heart, as has always been my style. I said, "I support your movement. I support your fight for civil rights. But why have you forgotten about the Indians? You have an organization, the National Association for the Advancement of Colored People, that's supposed to represent people of color. So where are the Indians? Why are we being forgotten?"

I told them about Wounded Knee 1890, and Black Elk's eyewitness testimony of the horror he saw there. I said, "There have been millions upon millions of Indigenous people killed in the Americas. Whole tribes have been decimated, wiped out, extinct. Entire cultures, and entire language families have been lost. So why has the civil rights movement forgotten about us? Have we not suffered enough?"

I recounted the Wounded Knee massacre, a genocidal event that the United States still refers to as a battle. "When Black Elk was a young man," I said, "he heard cannon fire coming from Wounded Knee Creek. He rode out there and saw soldiers running down children, and half-dressed women, and cutting them open with bayonets. He saw babies killed as they lay crying in the snow. The soldiers cut the breasts off the women and used them as pouches for ammunition. They proudly wore these two months later while marching in a military parade in Colorado. The soldiers responsible for this horrific war crime were given medals of honor. It was the policy of military and political leaders, like Ulysses S. Grant and Colonel John Chivington, to kill all of the Indians. They said that 'nits make lice,' so they had to kill the Indian children, too. History says Wounded Knee was the final act of the Indian Wars, of the Indian genocide, but that is not so. The genocide of Indian people continues to this day!"

I said, "Indian people have been through hell in this country, and we deserve the support of the civil rights movement."

The people there gave me so much love. With each remark they were clapping, and verbalizing their support. I just felt they understood what we had been through. After what they too had endured in America, why wouldn't they?

The speech was a tremendous success. Afterward Mrs. King introduced me to her children. The bond I made with them remains to this day. Whenever they come to town, to support Indian month activities or to speak about their father's legacy, we meet and spend time together. Many of the congregants came up to meet me and shake my hand. They told me about the many Indian people they had marched alongside on the famous Selma march.

Later on that year, on November 13, 1973, I addressed the students and faculty at the University of Wisconsin–Madison. With the Wounded Knee trials fast approaching, it was important to drum up support for our legal defense.

I still have the cassette of the talk I gave there, and it's an example of the fund-raising speeches I did all that year. Here is what it sounded like:

I would like to first of all thank all those people who have supported us during the seventy-one-day occupation. I'd like to also thank those people who contacted me or sent telegrams or held sermons in support of the occupation.

A lot of things happened that led up to the occupation of Wounded Knee, South Dakota. Prior to the formation of the American Indian Movement there were many attempts made by Indian people and organizations in the city of Minneapolis, to readdress some of the grievances they had. Groups such as the Upper Midwest American Indian Center, and the Twin Cities Tribal Council were formed to address some of these grievances. But not one of these Indian organizations were controlled by Indian people. In fact, every Native-serving organization in the Twin Cities area prior to the formation of the American Indian Movement was controlled by the Minnesota Education Department, the Minnesota Council of Churches, or the Bureau of Indian Affairs.

Nothing was ever done to deal with the problems that Indian people faced on a daily basis. We had a police problem in the city of Minneapolis. Whenever we went to any of these Indian organizations to try to get a strong resolution passed, such as the establishment of a citizen's patrol, they'd always find some reason not to take action.

When the American Indian Movement came into being we did our research and found out that Indian students have a 65 percent dropout rate from Minneapolis public schools.

We found out that Indian people live to be only forty-four years old. We found out also that on some reservations such as the Pine Ridge

Indian Reservation where the occupation of Wounded Knee took place, the Indian people there have a life expectancy of thirty-two. The life expectancy of a European American is sixty-five-plus.

These conditions are intolerable and have to be addressed.

When we formed the American Indian Movement we decided it had to be totally Indian as far as decision making is concerned—any programs established had to have total Indian control. And this has been the philosophy of the American Indian Movement: total Indian self-determination.

We are well aware of the annihilation that's taken place in this country. The genocide that's taken place in the past, and still taking place today. So we know that when they—and by they I mean the churches— talk about "thou shall not kill," it's a bunch of bullshit.

In the early years of church involvement on this continent, the churches, with their control over the armed forces of European nations, erased forty-seven tribes on the northeastern seaboard.

We know that when they said "thou shall not steal," it was another total lie, because we know today the extent of everything that white America has stolen from American Indians.

When AIM first formed we determined that the Minnesota Council of Churches, who controlled most of the Indian organizations in that state, was one of our greatest enemies. This was true in every state; it's true right here in Wisconsin. This council of churches established what they called the Division of Indian Work. We found out that whites controlled the whole organization, and yet they called themselves the Division of Indian Work.

We discovered that the Division of Indian Work, the DIW, received over $10 million to help raise the conditions of Indian people living in the Twin Cities urban area. We found out that in 1967 only $35,000 was actually allotted in the DIW budget to help the thousands of American Indians in that state who were suffering under horrible economic and social conditions. All the while we kept seeing new churches going up on the reservations.

In 1932 a man by the name of Nicholas Black Elk had a book written about him by author John Neihardt. It's called *Black Elk Speaks*. Before he died in 1950, Black Elk talked a lot about prophecies that had been handed down to his people through the generations. He talked about the foretelling of four races of man being together here in the Western Hemisphere long before the arrival of the first white men. He talked about the prophecy of the churches and the destruction they would bring. Talked about the people coming here from across the ocean seeking religious freedom. He talked about the genocide, annihilation, and the massacres of Indigenous people. He talked about the coming of the Black man, slavery, and that Black man's struggle for freedom. Talked about dark clouds that would cover Mother Earth. He talked about the breakdown of this government that's taking place today.

Some of these prophecies had been handed down to Black Elk; others, such as the rebirth of the Indian nations, were foreseen by him.

Black Elk saw his people massacred at Wounded Knee. He talked about the tree of life that the Great Spirit told him would bloom again someday. He said that when his people were wiped out at Wounded Knee, that tree of life withered and died. He said that beneath the soil of Wounded Knee, the roots of that tree were still alive, and that someday many people, many different tribes and voices of man would return to that place, and they would nourish that tree, and it would grow again. We believe that the occupation of Wounded Knee by the American Indian Movement was the fulfillment of that prophecy.

And I believe that when the Wounded Knee trials start in January in the city of St. Paul, that the American Indian Movement and the people that occupied Wounded Knee are not going to be on trial, but the Nixon administration is going to be on trial. And I'm sure that the conclusion of that trial will be that we as Indian people will be free, free to conduct and run our own affairs.

The total story of Wounded Knee cannot be told by one person. We had a symposium in the city of Minneapolis on September 25 so that our story could be disseminated by those who were there. It was to counteract the government's launching of right-wing symposiums throughout this country. That they are utilizing ex-tribal chairmen and religious leaders from the Pine Ridge Reservation to go across this country and to discredit the occupation and the issues we fought for.

The saddest fact about these false forums is that the brutality, the firebombs, the rapes, and the murders that were taking place on the Pine Ridge Indian Reservation prior to the occupation of Wounded Knee are still taking place today. If this government does not move to relieve the people of Pine Ridge of the violence that is part of daily life there, another occupation could be just weeks away. It doesn't have to take place just at Wounded Knee, South Dakota. It could happen anywhere in the country. It could happen right here in Madison, Wisconsin.

We need your support. Money isn't the only thing needed to help the Wounded Knee legal defense. What we are looking for is lawyers, we are looking for law students, we are looking for clerical help, stenographers, typists, anyone that wants to donate any of their time to come help forward our cause.

What we are certainly trying to say to this government is that they stand in violation of every treaty they've ever made with Indian people. They've never carried out their federal trust responsibilities. And because they never did that, the land still belongs to us. We're not demanding all the land back, but we are telling this administration and this government that we are still the landlords of this country, and it's the end of the month, and the rent is due.

When the Wounded Knee trials start, neither Dennis Banks, Clyde Bellecourt, nor Russell Means will be on trial; it's Nixon and Haldeman and Ehrlichman that will have to answer for their crimes, and for the crimes committed against Indian people throughout the history of the United States.

14. THE THUNDER BEFORE THE STORM

MY INDIAN NAME WAS GIVEN TO ME in a ceremony in 1973, not long after I was shot at point-blank range by what I believe was an FBI infiltrator within the American Indian Movement. A guy by the name of Carter Camp blasted me on the Rosebud Reservation on the morning of August 27, 1973. I was thirty-six years old.

I still remember the beauty of what happened next.

As I lay dying—according to doctors and medicine men, I was dead for a time—I recall coming out of the woods and seeing the river. At first I felt all the suffering I was going through as I bled out the chest wound. The pain faded as I thought of crossing the river. They say once you cross that river you never return.

It was right at daybreak, and I could see the petals opening on the wildflowers, and I could smell their nectar. I was really thirsty. I went over to the banks, splashed my face, and took a big drink. I heard a rustling across the river. I looked to the west, and my father was standing there with a bunch of people. I recognized a couple of my sisters who had died, overdosed on heroin in Chicago. They were standing there with my father. I was really happy to see them, and I hollered at them. But they just walked on as if they couldn't hear me. I started going across the river and here comes this fog; it grabbed me by the knees. I couldn't move.

I shouted, "Pa! Pa!" But he and the others just walked away.

Oh man, I felt so bad.

According to all the stories I've been told, once you meet your family on the other side, you never come back. And here they all just took off. I was just lonesome standing there, and I started to cry.

I came to and, oh man, I could feel that pain again where I was shot. I saw Leonard Crow Dog. I had danced at his Sun Dance two weeks earlier. He was leaning over me, and I must have been in shock because I couldn't hear what he was saying; I knew he was singing.

Next thing I remember he was chewing on something; he started pushing it into my wound. I thought I was at the Sun Dance. Then I thought he was piercing me. I looked around and saw a bunch of people standing around watching me, and there was blood all over the grass.

When I regained consciousness again sometime later that morning, I was laying on a bed in a hallway of the Rosebud Indian Hospital surrounded by American Indian Movement men armed with rifles. My blood was going right through the mattress and pooling on the floor. All of a sudden I heard this woman; she was furious. She turned out to be a surgeon from Los Angeles, an Indian woman who happened to be attending a powwow in the area. She heard I was shot and came to the hospital to help.

She started screaming at all these AIM guys: "Get out of there with those guns right now!" AIM had formed a posse to protect me, and find the guy who shot me, and she was chasing them out of there. "Get out of there! Get out of here with these guns."

I heard the doctor on the phone making arrangements to send me to the hospital in Winner, South Dakota. It was fifty-six miles away, but they had supplies of my blood type. She said to them, "Get ready, he's been shot. We only have two pints of his blood type here in Rosebud. I'll send them with the ambulance."

Crow Dog and his girlfriend got in the ambulance with me. We took off on this old bumpy road and drove to Winner bouncing all over. In the midst of all this, Crow Dog grabbed his girlfriend and started shaking her. "Why didn't you tell me this was going to happen? You knew this was going to happen!"

She had been partying that morning with the group of guys that came after me. She must have known they had a bullet with my name on it. I don't know why she didn't say anything. In those days, following all we had done—taking over the Bureau of Indian Affairs building in Washington, DC, taking over Wounded Knee—we had so many federal informants among us it was often impossible to know who to trust.

I knew something was up that morning. A friend of mine named Sidney and his girlfriend had a little house on the Rosebud, and a large AIM group of about a hundred people were camping out there, partying. People were sleeping in sleeping bags and little pup tents. The next thing I knew, everybody was drinking wine and getting pretty rowdy. Carter Camp and some of the others in his Oklahoma group claimed they had knocked over a liquor store in nearby Valentine, Nebraska. I was suspicious of this immediately; no one robs a liquor store and then takes only wine. You would go for smaller items, like bottles of hard liquor that are easier to carry. You don't start grabbing big wine bottles! In fact, there was never any police or media report of a liquor store robbery that night in Valentine. They made the whole thing up so they would look like outlaws instead of what they were—FBI infiltrators.

It must have been about four in the morning when I noticed a gun being passed around.

After Wounded Knee, none of us were supposed to have guns. We were all out on heavy bail, $200,000 bonds and like that. We were court ordered not to associate with one another, be around alcohol, drugs, guns, or anything that would be a violation of our bond. They could put us all back in jail.

I took Bill and Russell Means aside and told them, "You guys better get your shit together. Somebody's going to get shot here this morning."

Russell said, "Why?"

"Just look," I said, "they're hiding a gun, they have a pistol, they're handing it around." By "they" I meant the members of this suspect Oklahoma delegation who were always causing trouble and making the Movement look bad. They had refused to disarm after Wounded Knee. I could see the gun in the moonlight.

We were inside the house discussing all this when one of those Oklahoma guys came running into the house. "Get out there. Craig Camp is going to shoot Jimmy." Everybody went running outside. Craig had this young brother over the hood of the car and he had a .38 pistol on him ready to shoot.

My natural reflexes kicked in. I ran up and said, "What the hell is going on here?" I grabbed him by the shoulders and pulled him back.

He wheeled around and he put that gun in my face. It actually hit my nose. He put that gun right in the middle by my eyes and started smiling. I threw my arm up, hit his arm, the gun went flying. He tried to take a couple swings at me, but he was drunk and caught nothing but air. I smacked him a couple times and took him down. Everybody was hollering, "Let him up!"

I said, "I'm going to let you up. You know there's not supposed to be any guns here. We're not even supposed to gather with one another. When I let you up, I want you to get in your car, and I want you to leave."

So I let him up. The whole Oklahoma delegation, including Jimmy, the kid Craig was supposedly going to kill, ran to their cars and drove off. They went to their camp, which was a few miles away at a place called Ghost Hawk Park along the Little White River.

I picked up the .38, went inside the house, and unloaded it. It had twelve dumdums in it. A dumdum is a bullet with lead that's been filed flat, and an X carved into its top. When a dumdum enters the body it explodes on impact, blows apart like a little bomb. These bullets were altered to kill. That's when I knew they had targeted me for execution—the fight between Craig Camp and Jimmy had been faked to lure me to the scene, to give them an excuse to assassinate me and others in the AIM leadership.

I said, "Oh man, Craig Camp intends to kill all of us."

Someone loaded that .38 pistol and got prepared for the Oklahoma guys to return.

I told the others. "Hey," I said, "anybody got any weapons here? You guys better prepare because they're going to come back." I just had that feeling.

But everybody, including the other AIM leaders present, was drunk and didn't take the threat seriously. They started laughing and patting me on the back, you know, like big heroes, "Ahhh, don't worry about it. Those guys are chickenshit."

I said, "Well, you better get prepared."

About a half hour went by, and it was getting to be daybreak. We heard a bunch of cars speeding into the compound, brakes squealing, doors slamming. The Oklahoma delegation had returned. Six or seven of them had rifles. They were laying over the hoods of their cars, looking through their scopes; they had them aimed at the door of the house.

Carter Camp, Craig's older brother, walked up to the door and knocked.

I answered. "What do you want?"

"I want you to come out and talk," he said. "You beat up my brother."

"I did what I had to do," I said. "He was going to shoot Jimmy."

"You're a fucking liar," Carter said. "Come on out. If you've got any guts come on out."

So I shouted to all of them, "If you want to talk to me, put your guns down."

They put their guns down alongside the cars and against a tree, and I walked out the door. I believe that had I not walked out the door, most of the people in the house would have been killed that morning. They would have opened fire on all of us.

Carter told everybody to put their guns down.

I walked out maybe forty feet in front of the house. Carter backed away, facing me. Craig Camp stood by his brother, holding a rifle by the barrel.

Carter said, "Why did you beat up my brother?"

I kind of grinned and said, "I didn't beat up your brother. He was trying to shoot Jimmy."

"You're a fucking liar," Craig said.

"Everybody here saw what you did, Craig, what you were going to do," I said. "I knocked you down and held you until you agreed to leave."

"You fucking liar," Craig said. He grabbed his rifle by the barrel and swung the butt at my head. I deflected it away, and just then I noticed Carter pulling a gun out of the back of his belt and—oh my God, he shot me, hit me just below the heart.

My head just started ringing. I knew I was a dead man. It was like somebody kicked me and knocked the wind out of me. There was a terrible burning in my chest. I bent over and started lurching toward the house.

"Now you won't have to fuck with my brother anymore," I remember Carter saying.

I later learned from several witnesses that Carter had tried several times to shoot me in the back as I stumbled away, but his gun jammed.

The Oklahoma guys jumped in their cars and sped off.

I crashed through the screen door of the house, lost my balance, and fell backward. I struggled to catch my breath, tripped right through the house and out the back door, fell to the ground, and went tumbling down the hill there. I couldn't stop my momentum. I rolled up against a tree trunk, which kept me from falling off a steep ledge into a deep ravine. That's when I lost consciousness.

The next thing I knew, everything was just total darkness, and no more pain.

When I came to, I was walking in that beautiful valley. I think about this all the time; I can see it, feel it, and smell it, even now, decades later. It was very still and quiet. Everything started coming to life. The sun was just breaking on the horizon. Bluebirds were singing, chirping. Butterflies were flying toward my face. I was walking into a little river, water up to my knees. I looked in the water and saw the fish. The fish came up and smiled at me. I reached down, cupped some water, and drank. It was so pure, so clean and refreshing. It had a sweet taste. I could see the flowers open up, and I could smell them.

And then I just felt somebody was with me. I looked to the left, and there was a little fawn standing in the water. I reached over and fed him. He wasn't scared of me, didn't run off—drank water right out of my hand.

I looked in the distance across the river and saw all these Indian people walking toward me from the west. In that crowd I saw my father, that giant of a man.

I was so happy to see my father. When we were little boys, we used to call my dad Pa, and my mother Ma. I hollered, "Pa," just as loud as I could. He didn't hear me. So I hollered louder, "Pa!" I could see him straining to hear. Pretty soon they all turned and walked away. I could see their heads going down over the horizon.

On the way from Rosebud to the Winner hospital that morning, Crow Dog and his girl started arguing in the back of the ambulance. Next thing I knew, they were hitting one another, wrestling around. They tipped over that blood that the Rosebud doctor had sent along. The damn container tipped over and came down and broke against my face. There was blood all over me.

One of the drivers jumped in back and broke them up and said, "What the hell is wrong with you guys? You're going to kill him. You know he needs the blood."

So they settled down. We got about twenty miles from Winner, and the goddamn ambulance ran out of gas. It was a nightmare. Finally, a highway patrolman showed up and called another ambulance.

A while later I could hear the siren of another ambulance coming in the distance. They loaded me in there, and we continued toward Winner, a town of about thirty-five hundred residents on the eastern border of the Rosebud Reservation. They finally got me to the hospital and into an operating room.

They said I was out for two and a half hours. They cut me from my chest all the way down to my crotch. Blood gushed out onto the operating table. The surgeon later said, "There's no possible way you should be alive right now."

She said when she opened me up, pints of blood poured out. It took them two hours to find the bullet. It went right through my pancreas and lodged a quarter of an inch from my spine. My spine would have been shattered by that dumdum bullet, but it had miraculously remained intact. If it had worked as intended, the bullet would have fragmented as it moved through my body.

When I came to after the operation, I could hear the medical team washing their hands. One doctor said, "We did the best we could do. It's a fifty-fifty deal now; it's up to him if he wants to live."

Another doctor said, "If he makes it, he won't have no taste for a while. Because that bullet went through his pancreas."

I was thinking, *What a hell of a way to live; you know, can't taste nothing.*

My friend Ed Bearheart later told me that at the precise time that I was shot that morning, I showed up in his bedroom five hundred miles away. He was living in the Round Lake community on the St. Croix Reservation in Wisconsin. He told me he opened his eyes and sat up, lit his kerosene lamp, and saw me standing in his bedroom.

"What's wrong, Clyde?" he asked.

He said I shrugged my shoulders, turned around, and walked right out through the wall. His daughter Beverly was laying on the couch in the living room.

She called out, "Dad! Who are you talking to?"

He said, "Clyde is here, and something's wrong with him."

Just then she saw me walk through the living room and out the door. They ran out after me, but I was gone. They hollered for me. Ed knew something was terribly wrong.

Back inside, Ed's wife turned the TV on in the living room. They heard her inside the house crying and hollering. "That was Clyde. Clyde's spirit was here," she said. "He got shot and killed this morning on the Rosebud."

They all ran to watch the TV. Just then the phone rang; it was my wife, Peggy, and she was crying. My wife had woken up in our apartment at Little Earth housing in south Minneapolis. She turned on the television. My picture was all over it with news that I was dead.

First thing Peggy did was call up Ed Bearheart, our conduit to Jack Miskwaudeis, one of the oldest medicine men around. Ed told her to get a driver and come over right away. So Peggy, who doesn't drive, found someone to take her, and they started up to the St. Croix Reservation, a ninety-minute drive from Minneapolis.

Ed Bearheart really respected the American Indian Movement. A couple years earlier his kids were facing racism in the public school system in the Cumberland, Wisconsin, area. It got so bad that they forced the Indian kids to ride in the back of the bus like it was the Deep South. One day, his daughter was taken down on the bus, and those white kids cut her hair off. The American Indian Movement went in there, and we got the Indian people to boycott that whole school system, which would have caused them to lose over a million dollars in Indian education money. Of course, they came to the table quickly. They put Indian people on the board. They hired Indian bus drivers. They started Indian studies classes. So Ed really had a lot of respect for the Movement; he was like family to me.

Ed sent his son to Spooner, Wisconsin, to find Jack Miskwaudeis. Jack had forewarned me at a ceremony about a month and a half before this that an FBI infiltrator was watching me. "Pull your curtains down," he said. "Watch what you say on the phone. Somebody in the family is watching you."

I stopped him: "What do you mean 'somebody in the family'?"

"Somebody in the AIM family is going to try to take your life."

Peggy and the old medicine man arrived at Ed's place around the same time. Ed told the old man that he and his daughter saw me walking around their house.

Jack asked, "How was he dressed?"

"He had Levi's on," Ed said, "a red ribbon shirt, hair braided."

Hearing this made the old man smile and laugh. Peggy was crying and everyone was upset. Ed was real confused—why is the old medicine man smiling? When Ed finished telling what he saw, the old man said, "You better get some venison and wild rice, make some soup."

Ed asked, "Why?"

He said, "Clyde is alive. We must have a ceremony. He needs our prayers. If he was dead, he wouldn't be dressed like that anymore."

So they started making some soup and preparing for a ceremony and a feast.

Sure enough, they looked at the TV, and it was reported that I had actually survived the shooting and that they had captured the gunman, Carter Camp.

They stayed up all night preparing for the ceremony. As the sun came up, Ed later told me, he went outside for a breath of fresh air. Ed saw this big shadow on the ground outside by the house. He looked up and here was this big eagle, about two stories tall, sitting on his garage, flapping its wings and making a *whomp whomp* like the sound of a helicopter. The sight of the gigantic eagle frightened him. Ed ran into the house and yelled, "Come on! Come out here. I've got to show you something."

Everybody ran outside and witnessed this amazing eagle as it took off and flew away.

All of a sudden, they saw something shining like a mirror on the ground beneath where the eagle had sat. Ed walked over and picked it up. It was a silver dollar, and the eagle side of the silver dollar was faceup and shining.

Meanwhile, I was in and out of consciousness at the Winner hospital as they took me down to intensive care on the first floor.

There was a big rodeo going on in Winner, which was (and still is today) known to Indian people as the most racist town in South Dakota. Cowboys were all over the place, as were armed AIM Indians there to protect me. Soon after arriving in my room, I was rolled back out. When I come to again, they were running my bed down the hallway, putting me in an elevator, and taking me upstairs. *Shit, I'm dying again*, I thought. The hospital staff had scared off somebody who had come and broken the window to my ground-floor room and was aiming to shoot me.

After that, our AIM Patrol surrounded the hospital and kept a secure perimeter.

I didn't know this until a couple days later, but Anita Wennsmen, who is a nurse in Minneapolis—an Indian woman who I consider my sister—she heard what happened to me, so she and her husband, Al, drove five hundred miles out to Winner. They stayed by my bedside for all three days I was there.

One night a nurse came in, and she was going to give me a shot.

Anita insisted on checking the prescription before she would allow the nurse to administer it. Anita said the shot that they were going to give me would have put me to sleep—forever.

She argued with that nurse. She said, "No. There's a mistake here. You're not going to put that in his body. It will kill him."

They got in a big fight about it, the nurse telling Anita she wasn't from there and had no business telling her what to do. Anita insisted she call the surgeon at home and find out if that's really what he wanted me to have. She called him, and he stopped her from killing me. It *was* the wrong medicine.

I came to the next morning, and my wife was there with Anita and Al. They were trying to figure out how to get me out of Winner alive. Man, I desperately had to find a way out of South Dakota.

I said, "Get me a phone."

I asked them to dial my dear friend the Reverend Dr. Paul Boe, head of the American Lutheran Church's Division of Social Services in Minneapolis. He had shown his values when he came to Wounded Knee, at my request, and then organized clergy all over America to come stand watch at Wounded Knee, to provide witness. Later the church turned around and punished him for his actions at Wounded Knee. I told him, you not only walk in Christ's footsteps but also in Chief Big Foot's footsteps.

Dr. Boe would know how to get me home. Dr. Boe answered the phone; he was very happy to hear from me, because it was still being reported that I was shot and killed. I started telling him what happened.

"Paul," I said, "I'm in the hospital. They tried to kill me, they tried to give me the wrong medicine. I got to get out of here before they succeed."

He said, "I heard you were dead, I can't believe I'm talking to you. Don't worry. I'm going to make arrangements."

Dr. Boe went down and talked to Hennepin County officials back home in Minneapolis. He learned of a fund that could be used to fly in people with medical emergencies. He arranged for an air ambulance out of the University of Minnesota Hospital to come to Winner. They picked me up in a Learjet and flew me home to Minneapolis, where I remained in the hospital for about ten more days. What a relief it was to have escaped racist South Dakota.

Back home I saw how big the news had become. They were talking about me on every channel; I was national news. You know: "American Indian Movement leader shot and nearly killed on the Rosebud Reservation."

Soon they reported that they had found the shooter. Apparently, Carter Camp approached a farmer in Nebraska and asked him to call a lawyer—Mark Lane. I later heard from Lane that he went out in the cornfield, and Carter Camp was laying in the fetal position, hiding and scared, because AIM was after him.

The lawyer told him, "You don't have to be worried anymore."

Carter asked, "Why?"

"Because Clyde's alive."

"That motherfucker!" Carter is reported to have said. "He's supposed to be dead."

My brother Floyd Red Crow Westerman came and saw me one night while I was recovering at the University of Minnesota Hospital. He said, "You know there's a big powwow going on in St. Paul."

I said, "Yes. Man, I wish I could go to that." I said, "Damn it, I'm going to go to that."

So I called the nurses and asked them if I could go. They said, "No, you'll have to obtain permission from the doctor when he comes to work tomorrow."

So I waited around until about six o'clock, after the hospital's dinner service. Floyd dug my jeans out of the closet. I got dressed, and we peeked down the hallway, and when the coast was clear snuck out of there, got in the car, and I went to the powwow about five miles away in St. Paul. They weren't too happy with me at the hospital, but there was nothing they could do.

The powwow was full of people wishing me well and giving me so much love. I was just so happy to be alive.

Almost as soon as I got released from the hospital, Peggy started bugging me. "You got to go to St. Croix," she said. "You got to go over to Wisconsin; they're bringing out a big drum to honor you."

Peggy kept insisting, "You got to go to St. Croix."

"Why?" I said. "The doctors told me I've got to stay right here."

"They're having a ceremony. They're bringing out one of the big drums, and they want you there."

Peggy wouldn't let it go, so I finally agreed to get in the car and go with her to Wisconsin. It was a beautiful Saturday morning when Peggy and I drove across the St. Croix River into Wisconsin.

When we arrived at Round Lake, I said, "Holy Christ, I've never seen so many people in my life." There were cars lining the roads and parked between trees in the woods.

Ed Bearheart and my old friend and mentor Eddie Benton-Banai greeted me and said, "You got to go into the sweat lodge right away."

I said, "I'm not supposed to get overheated. The doctors told me so."

"No," they insisted, "you got to go to the sweat lodge."

So they put me into the sweat lodge, and Eddie Benton-Banai was there. He started the ceremony by saying we would purify ourselves before what was to be a "making-of-a-chief ceremony." This was probably the first such ceremony among the Ojibwe people in more than a hundred years.

I asked, "Why me? What have I done to deserve all of this?"

I was told I was being honored because I fought to protect women and children, and because I had been willing to give my life for them.

They were going to make me a leader in the traditional way. But in order to become a chief, and receive my eagle feather, I first needed an Indian name. I never had one before.

I didn't know this at the time, but Eddie Benton-Banai—the man who rescued me from the hole at Stillwater State Prison in 1964—had been given tobacco by my wife and asked to pray for my name. I could not become a chief without first having an Indian name.

When I arrived for the ceremony, Eddie had already fulfilled that request. He had walked into the woods and built a little lean-to and stayed there, fasting. For the first two days he did not receive a message. On the third night he prayed real hard. He went to bed, he said, about two o'clock in the morning. In his dream he could see sheets of lightning to the west. He could see lightning through the trees and hear its distant rumble. All of a sudden that storm got close to him and a bolt struck nearby. The crack of that lightning in his dream startled him, and when he awoke the trees were blowing back and forth and it started to rain. Our true spirit names, our Indian names, are given to us in visions. This is as it has always been.

Eddie packed up his gear, returned to Round Lake, and took me into the sweat lodge the next day. In the darkness of the lodge Eddie said they were going to bring out the big drum. They were going to bring the war bustle, and I was going to dance with that war bustle. They were going to present me with an eagle feather and make me a chief.

Eddie told me the story of his nights in the forest seeking my name. He said, "From this day on your name will be Neegawnwaywidung."

I asked, "Well, what does that mean?"

He said, "The Thunder Before the Storm."

So I got out of the sweat, cleaned up, and went into the big community hall there. It was packed with people from all over.

They put that bustle on me, and as a group of singers played that big Dakota drum, they had me dance. Then they had Bill Means join me because he was a veteran of Vietnam and Wounded Knee. And they had the old medicine man dance with us. They had a big giveaway and a big feast—all kinds of wild rice and venison. It was a real celebration, a very happy time.

That night Ed came up to me and placed something in my hand. It was a silver dollar. He told me the story of the giant eagle. Ed had taken the silver dollar and drilled a little hole in it, and put it on a string. He said that for the rest of my life this silver dollar would protect me and take care of me. And it has.

At the end of the ceremony, they brought out that eagle feather, and we prayed with it. They tied the eagle feather in my hair and told me from that day on, my name would be Neegawnwaywidung, The Thunder Before the Storm, and like many of my ancestors before me, I would, for the rest of my life, be known as a chief among my people.

Peggy and me in a photo taken in New York City right after I got my name—and the eagle feather.
Chris Spotted Eagle photo

15. AIM FOR SOVEREIGNTY

LONG BEFORE HE SHOT ME, my relationship with Carter Camp was not good. We'd crossed paths several times. Carter and his brothers were involved in the Trail of Broken Treaties and BIA takeover.

During the BIA takeover, Carter approached an AIM warrior that I still know very well today. He's from the Santee Reservation in Nebraska. His name is Melvin Lee Houston; he's renowned within the American Indian Movement for his lifelong commitment. Carter approached Melvin, who at the time was a young man. He tried to get him to assassinate me. At the time Melvin didn't know what it was all about; he figured Carter was angry at me over some petty conflict and was just blowing off steam. Only after Carter shot me did Melvin reconsider the seriousness and nature of Carter's request at the BIA, and reveal to me what had happened.

There were several different factions within AIM at the time, and not everyone could move freely among all the groups. Melvin got along with everyone. He was Vernon's best friend, and Carter knew Melvin could get close to me. Also, Melvin was one of only a few AIM warriors within the BIA who had a gun. We relied on the pipe to defend us, and everybody on the inside and outside knew that. If the government knew some of us were armed, they would have had a reason to come in and wipe us out.

My suspicions of Carter grew at Wounded Knee, during that period when Russell and Dennis had left camp and went to Crow Dog's Paradise. Carter and his friends wanted to attack the feds, a disastrous plan of action, especially considering the presence of women and children in our camp.

So there is thought among some in the Movement that Carter was working for the FBI from the start of his involvement, and planted within the Movement for the sole purpose of killing me. The FBI infiltrated to disrupt, but if that failed, they were prepared to neutralize the leadership.

When they found Carter hiding in the cornfield, he got real pissed off that I wasn't dead. He was arrested and locked up in Sioux Falls, South Dakota, a city two hundred miles east of Rosebud.

A grand jury was impaneled there about six weeks later. The gunshot wound had healed enough that I could travel by then, so my attorney Ken Tilsen flew me down to Sioux Falls in a private plane.

I was the first witness. I refused, first of all, to be sworn in. I told them that the Bible doesn't mean anything to us, that the white man has used the Bible against Indian people for five hundred years. I told them, "The Bible and Jesus and the devil all came over on the same boat, and look what they have done to us. If I'm going to talk before this grand jury, then I will swear on the Sacred Pipe."

I also refused to testify, because I knew what they were trying to do—divide the Movement, turn everybody against one another. I actually faced fourteen months in prison for contempt of court—and I was the one who was shot.

Every time they asked me a question, I would ask them to repeat it. I'd ask them what it meant if I answered it yes or no. They said, "Well, information will be used for an indictment, to indict the person that we allege shot you."

I'd say, "Write down that question for me, please."

They'd write down the question, and I'd say, "Give me a few minutes, please, to talk to my attorney."

This process took about four hours, during which they asked me about twelve questions. They won't allow attorneys into the grand jury room, but you can go outside and confer with your attorney.

I'd come back in from chatting with Ken Tilsen, and I would say, "Will you repeat the question again?"

They'd repeat it again, and I'd say, "I refuse to answer the question on the grounds that it might incriminate me."

The way I thought about it was that if one of us goes down, all of us go down. We were all facing charges. We were all sunk if we started testifying against one another. I also thought that what happened within the Movement was none of their business. If we truly believed in Indian sovereignty—self-determination, self-government—then how could we ask the white man to judge things for us? That's the position I took. That is why I refused to cooperate in the prosecution of the man who tried to murder me.

Finally, they completed the questions. The prosecutor went before the judge and notified him that I had refused to cooperate.

The court thought they would try to offer me some incentive to testify against Carter. They phoned the Justice Department and requested immunity from prosecution for me. The Justice Department refused. That indicated they didn't give a shit what happened to Clyde Bellecourt *or* Carter Camp, might as well have been dead for all they cared. He was just another Indian being used by the white man. What they really wanted was to find out who all was in that camp the night I was shot, and figure how they could jail everybody present, particularly the AIM leadership, for violating the provisions of their bonds.

They had to call a halt to the grand jury. The judge got really angry and banged his gavel. He said, "I don't know what this world is coming to. I don't know what is wrong with you, Mr. Bellecourt. You're a leader of your people. You come to the state of South Dakota. You accuse the state of South Dakota of being one of the most racist states in the union. You condemn the federal government forces and the church for what they've done. A man shoots you in cold blood, and I hear you were even dead at one time. We have him in jail just a few blocks away and you refuse to testify. What is this world coming to?"

I said, "Your Honor, excuse me. Your Honor, this is none of your business. This is Indian business. We'll take over our own affairs from here."

He got so mad. He threatened me with contempt of court if I continued to refuse to answer questions. Finally, he'd had enough. He banged his gavel, ordered me to "get the hell out of this courtroom," and locked me up for contempt.

I went through the whole grand jury process twice, refusing to answer their questions. Finally, they had no choice but to release me.

Before leaving the courthouse I obtained permission to see Carter Camp. He had developed a bleeding ulcer in jail and was having a hard time with his health. I heard he'd lost several pints of blood. I went to the jail with my attorney and stood outside Carter's cell.

I said, "Why did you shoot me?"

He hung his head and refused to answer.

"Why did you shoot me? Who's really behind this? Who asked you to do it?"

He kept his head down, wouldn't look at me. Just stared at the floor.

I said, "The American Indian Movement wants to see you up in St. Paul as soon as they let you out." St. Paul was where our Wounded Knee Legal Defense/Offense Committee was headquartered. Carter told me he would be there, and we left.

People sometimes ask me about Carter and his position in the leadership at the time. There were a lot of different AIM groups operating semiautonomously around the country by 1974, and some groups considered Carter to be AIM chairman at the time he shot me.

Carter kept his word. He came to St. Paul a few days after his release from jail and stood before the American Indian Movement's grand jury. This was right in the middle of the Wounded Knee trials taking place at the federal courthouse in St. Paul. Dennis Banks and Russell Means were the first two they had on trial there. Again, Carter wouldn't tell us who ordered my murder.

Following the brief proceedings, the AIM leadership agreed on a punishment and read him his sentence: "It is the position of the American Indian Movement that you be ostracized from the Movement for life. Never again will you ever be able to carry the AIM name, have any involvement in AIM activities, or walk among those in the Movement."

We carried out justice in a traditional way. Carter was banished.

I took a lot of heat over my refusal to testify. My whole family, my wife, and my brother Vernon were very upset. But I did what I had to do. I still believe I did the right thing for the Movement and for Indian sovereignty. In fact, I had never seen Vernon so angry in his life. "What the fuck is wrong with you?" he asked. "The guy shoots you point-blank, and you turn around and let him go."

I said, "I believe in the Movement. If we really believe in Indian self-determination, how the hell can we let an all-white jury make decisions for us?"

I was later told in a ceremony that my refusal to testify against Carter was a turning point in the history of the Movement. Many of our elders and traditional people saw what I did and said, "These guys don't play around, they mean business; they really take care of their own."

Around the time we took over the Bureau of Indian Affairs, we had distributed a bumper sticker that read, "AIM for Sovereignty," the one those sellout tribal chairmen tore up. After my refusal to testify against Carter, Indian people everywhere began to understand what sovereignty means. Today, whether they ever supported the Movement or not, tribal chairs and the people they represent are using the word "sovereignty" to define who they are as independent nations and as people who demand freedom and self-determination.

I saw Carter the next year, during the Wounded Knee trials. Crow Dog brought him to the AIM National Powwow we held on the river flats at Bdote, the sacred confluence of the Mississippi and Minnesota Rivers. Several AIM members shared with me information that there was a plot to murder Carter. One of them, an old lady, came up to me and showed me that she was hiding a big butcher knife in her bag. She told me she was going to kill him.

I said, "Why are you telling me that? You've just included me in your conspiracy. If you're going to do something, that's up to you. But I'm not going to give you permission."

Another guy came up to me a few minutes later and showed me his handgun. He said if Carter wasn't gone by sundown he was a dead man. I scolded them all: "If you're going to do something like that, you should never tell me."

I went over to Carter, standing by his pickup. I said, "You're going to have to leave."

He asked, "Why?"

I said, "Because you're not going to leave here alive if you don't."

He and Crow Dog got in that truck and took off.

I no longer shy away from talking about Carter's role in my shooting. We had an opportunity to make peace with one another.

Several years after the shooting, I was at Crow Dog's Paradise for the Sun Dance. Carter Camp and his brother Greg and a lot of the people that were there when he shot me were present. I was approached by a heavyset woman who appeared to be in very bad health. The old lady gave me some tobacco, and she said, "I want to ask your forgiveness."

I asked, "Who are you?"

"I'm Mrs. Camp, Carter's mother."

I said, "What can I do for you?"

"I just want your forgiveness."

I took the tobacco, got up and gave her a hug and kiss, and said, "You're forgiven. It had nothing to do with you."

"I would like to ask you for one thing," she said.

"What do you want me to do?"

"Will you pierce my son?"

He had requested that I pierce him. I looked around, and everybody was looking at me. What was I going to say? I hugged her again and I said, "I'll do that."

So they arranged it, and word spread across the reservation that I was going to pierce the man who shot me. Hundreds of people came to the arbor to support us.

Crow Dog took me out to the tree where Carter awaited. They laid him facedown on a buffalo hide. He wanted to be pierced in the back and tied to a horse. They gave me a scalpel. I got down on one knee and cleaned my hands. Those helping me squeezed his skin together, and I put that scalpel in deep—he had these two branches as big as my thumb he wanted to be pierced with. I tied him, and stood him up. I shook his hand and embraced him. I told him I was forgiving him because I'm a Sun Dancer and we can't hold bad feelings inside us, we can't hold grudges.

There were two guys holding his arms. Someone gave the horse a pat on his behind, and when that horse took off, they couldn't hold Carter. The horse ran out of the arbor and pulled Carter along with him. The guy was somersaulting all over the village. About twenty people chased them, trying to corner the horse, but he kept running, pulling Carter by the skin of his back.

That horse returned to the arbor and stood there like he knew what he was doing all along. Carter was all beat up, caked with mud and dirt.

They set him back on his feet, and this time had five guys holding his arms and legs. They hit that horse and he pulled those pegs through Carter's skin, and that was it.

I've never had anything to do with him after that Sun Dance. I forgave him, but I could never trust someone like that. He ended up being a big drunk. I used to get reports all the time from people in Oklahoma wanting me to do something about him. There was nothing I could do. I had washed my hands of him.

Carter passed away in 2013 after a long battle with cancer. The *New York Times*, the Sioux Falls paper, and all kinds of media started calling. I said the same thing to all of them: I have no comment. I said the guy tried to kill me, now he's gone, just let it go. I said, "I feel relieved that I don't have to worry every time he's around that he might shoot me again."

But other people still carry a deep animosity toward Carter, even now, long after he's gone. My wife and my brother never forgave me for letting him off the hook. I still hear today from people in the community who come up to me expressing their regret that they never killed him. "That motherfucker," they say.

16. AMERICA ON TRIAL

THAT WEEKEND AT THE AIM POWWOW gave all of us a chance to blow off some steam. Luckily for Carter, he got out of town before that steam blew up on him. AIM had been on trial for months, and we all relished the opportunity to be together with our families, and our people, at that beautiful powwow between the two rivers.

For my activities at Wounded Knee I faced more than 350 years in prison, plus two life sentences. My case, however, never even made it to court. They chose to try Russell Means and Dennis Banks first. If they got convictions against them, of course, federal prosecutors would have the precedent to convict us all. The government thought they had us where they wanted us, and they were salivating over the notion of sending us to prison and throwing away the key.

As if it were my life on the line, I sat through the entire proceeding at the federal courthouse in St. Paul, all eight and a half months of it. *United States v. Banks and Means*, which began in January of 1974, proved one thing: that the government was desperate, and it was willing to do anything to gain convictions against the Wounded Knee defendants.

Like me, Russell and Dennis were charged with just about every crime known to jurisprudence, a whole laundry list of crimes. By the time this sham trial went to the jury, the government's case was so discredited that most of the charges had already been dismissed by US judge Fred Nichol. That doesn't mean the judge was sympathetic to our side. It took him months to finally realize that AIM and the traditional Oglala Lakota people were acting in self-defense.

We argued, every chance we got, that the United States had no authority within the Great Sioux Reservation, and thus no standing to bring these charges. Wounded Knee, our lawyers and witnesses informed Judge Nichol, is within the boundaries of sovereign Lakota lands as defined by the Treaty of 1868.

We argued this not only in Nichol's courtroom, but everywhere Wounded Knee defendants were on trial. In 1974 we had five hundred AIM people facing charges in courthouses across the region. Trials were conducted simultaneously in Rapid City, Sioux Falls, Lincoln, Minneapolis/St. Paul, and Deadwood.

For the first seven months of the Banks-Means trial the judge refused to allow the 1868 treaty into the proceedings. The document, known also as the Fort Laramie Treaty, ended Red Cloud's War and guaranteed that Lakota people had "absolute and undisturbed use of the Great Sioux Reservation." "No persons," it says, "shall ever be permitted to pass over, settle upon, or reside in territory described in this article, or without consent of the Indians."

In the long term, Judge Nichol's refusal to allow the defense to present arguments based on the treaty led to some very positive changes. As a direct result of the Banks-Means trial, the American Indian Movement would later that year form the International Indian Treaty Council. We were tired of seeing our nation-to-nation agreements ignored. Our ancestors had fought and died for what remained of Indian sovereignty, and we were no longer going to allow the United States to dishonor them.

We met for the first time in 1974 on the Standing Rock Reservation, in Fort Yates, North Dakota. Ninety-seven different Indian nations from throughout the Western Hemisphere, represented exclusively by traditional elders, showed up for the gathering. The nearly three thousand delegates in attendance made this the largest Indian treaty conference of the twentieth century. We had delegates from as far away as Chile, Argentina, and Alaska.

There was fantastic representation by traditional Lakotas, descendants of the signers of the 1868 and other important treaties that established the nation-to-nation relationship between their people and the United States. One thing that was stressed was how quickly everything was taken away from us. In the case of the Lakota, they went from nation status to reservation status in the blink of an eye. In 1868, they established the Great Sioux Nation. By 1889, the United States had carved that land mass into reservations on which the Lakota people were essentially prisoners of war, subject to the whims of the US government. The old people who spoke at the conference still believed in self-determination, in nationhood. Their words energized the Movement, and we moved forward more determined than ever to restore our treaty rights, and the sovereignty of our nations.

When the IITC was recognized by the United Nations in 1976, we became the first organization in the history of the American Indian to be a part of a worldwide governing body. Just eight years after the 1968 formation of the American Indian Movement, we had an international voice. A lot of hard work by a lot of people went into making that happen. After devoting most of his adult life to the formation and ongoing work of the IITC at the United Nations and around the world, Bill Means, an Oglala Lakota AIM leader, deserves special recognition. When it was confirmed that Indigenous people had achieved NGO status at the UN, I was blown away by how quickly things can change when a dedicated group of people comes together with a common goal.

Since 1977, the International Indian Treaty Council has been recognized as a category II nongovernmental organization, the first Indigenous NGO to gain such status. This was accomplished by the American Indian Movement, not one of the Indian organizations that carried the government's stamp of approval, like the National Congress of American Indians, or the National Tribal Chairmen's Association. In a few short years we went from being branded a militant group to having a seat on the world stage.

In 1977, before the United Nations in Geneva, Switzerland, we presented information on human rights and Indian treaty rights violations against Indian people, and we testified before several conferences within the United Nations about the continued genocidal practices against Indian people. I spent a month in Europe following the first International Indian Treaty Council meetings in Geneva, traveling around all those countries with delegations from Canada and Central and South America. We made many public appearances at colleges and universities, where we educated about Indian people and our struggle for survival in America. Because of the ongoing work of the IITC, the plight of Indigenous peoples the world over is being discussed at the United Nations and codified into international law.

I'm getting way ahead of myself, but before moving on I want to mention the IITC's crowning achievement (to date). Thirty years after the IITC gained NGO status, the world body, on September 13, 2007, adopted the United Nations Declaration on the Rights of Indigenous Peoples. The declaration asserts the rights of Indigenous peoples, fundamentally, to exist. I have included the first seven articles (out of forty-six) of the declaration below, so you can get a sense of what was accomplished when the vast majority of UN member states ratified this historic agreement.

Article 1

Indigenous peoples have the right to the full enjoyment, as a collective or as individuals, of all human rights and fundamental freedoms as recognized in the Charter of the United Nations, the Universal Declaration of Human Rights and international human rights law.

Article 2

Indigenous peoples and individuals are free and equal to all other peoples and individuals and have the right to be free from any kind of discrimination, in the exercise of their rights, in particular that based on their indigenous origin or identity.

Article 3

Indigenous peoples have the right to self-determination. By virtue of that right they freely determine their political status and freely pursue their economic, social, and cultural development.

Article 4

Indigenous peoples, in exercising their right to self-determination, have the right to autonomy or self-government in matters relating to their internal and local affairs, as well as ways and means for financing their autonomous functions.

Article 5

Indigenous peoples have the right to maintain and strengthen their distinct political, legal, economic, social and cultural institutions, while retaining their right to participate fully, if they so choose, in the political, economic, social and cultural life of the State.

Article 6

Every indigenous individual has the right to a nationality.

Article 7

1. Indigenous individuals have the rights to life, physical and mental integrity, liberty and security of person.
2. Indigenous peoples have the collective right to live in freedom, peace and security as distinct peoples and shall not be subjected to any act of genocide or any other act of violence, including forcibly removing children of the group to another group.

In September 1977, at the end of the United Nations International NGO Conference on Discrimination Against Indigenous Populations in the Americas, delegates from Indigenous communities all over the world assembled for a portrait. *Dick Bancroft photo*

The establishment of the IITC and the adoption of the Declaration on the Rights of Indigenous Peoples only happened, I believe, because of the refusal of the traditional Oglala Lakota people, and the American Indian Movement, to allow the 1868 treaty to go ignored during the Wounded Knee trials.

Many of the traditional people for whom this treaty is viewed as both spiritually and legally binding came to Minnesota from Pine Ridge for the trial. They sat in the courtroom wearing full regalia, reminding Judge Nichol by their very presence that Indian people still hold true to their history and culture. Frank Fools Crow, Floyd Red Crow Westerman, Nellie Red Owl, and Gladys Bissonette were in court almost every day. Political activists from all over the country also came to court to show their support—Dick Gregory, Marlon Brando, Angela Davis, Kwame Ture (aka Stokely Carmichael).

Every night after the hearings, we'd have a big community meeting where all the information on the proceedings was communicated to the people. We felt so confident about winning the case that these gatherings were like victory celebrations.

The government's presentation was so ridiculous and far-fetched that there were times I couldn't keep quiet. It was hard for me to control myself when lie after lie kept pouring out of the mouths of the prosecution's witnesses. I was warned several times by the judge to keep my mouth shut.

During the trial it was exposed that the government had planted a man inside AIM who had managed to gain access to the highest levels of our organization. His name was Douglas Durham, a guy who told everyone he was "one-quarter Chippewa," and yet dyed his hair black in order to fit in with the Indians. Durham had been taken into the Movement by Dennis Banks. We became aware of him after he arrived at Wounded Knee claiming to be a reporter from a left-wing newspaper. For whatever reason, Dennis really trusted him and never questioned how this guy, who looked like a career soldier, had become so skilled in just about every area where we needed expertise.

Durham was an airplane pilot, so he was able to ferry AIM people like Dennis Banks and Leonard Peltier into and out of Canada when they were laying low. He claimed to be self-trained in clandestine operations and tactical psychology. He knew how to organize people and run large, complex organizations. He became Dennis's right-hand man, despite the fact that I, and many others within the Movement, never trusted him. It got to the point where you couldn't get Dennis alone; you had to go through Durham in order to speak with him.

After Wounded Knee, Dennis and Durham opened an AIM office in St. Paul where Durham was handed the title "AIM's director of security." This gave him access to everything we were doing. It came out during the trial that Durham was a paid federal informant who was feeding the prosecution confidential information about our defense strategy.

Everybody really took a hard look at Dennis Banks after that. I've thought about it a lot through the years. There are those who have pointed fingers at Dennis, accusing him of cooperating with the government. I think Dennis was guilty of only one thing in regards to Durham: terrible judgment. To this day, whenever I see Dennis I tease him about Douglas Durham. He doesn't really respond. I'm sure it still stings to be reminded of how he let Durham into our inner circle.

Several months into the trial, the prosecution produced a twenty-two-year-old Oglala Lakota informant named Louis Moves Camp as the final government witness. This is where, after months of government lies and misconduct, their case finally unraveled. Unfortunately for the government's case, our lawyers established that Moves Camp was in California during the time he claimed to have witnessed crimes taking place at Wounded Knee.

Larry Leventhal, a member of our defense team, wrote in a scathing post-trial summation that went into detail regarding the testimony of the government's witnesses: "During the months of the government's direct case there was a scarcity of evidence linking the defendants to crimes alleged against them. When such evidence was offered, on direct examination usually the witness presenting the testimony admitted or displayed error, confusion, or reliance on what had been told by another. . . . Louis Moves Camp was unique among the witnesses offered by the government because he purported to have seen virtually every alleged incident of wrongful conduct by the defendants set forth in their indictment and the government's subsequent bill of particulars."

Our attorneys found a way to discredit Moves Camp. The prosecution had spent days coaching his testimony as they moved him around the region, supposedly to protect him from AIM. One night, while the two agents accompanying Moves Camp had him holed up in a guest ranch near River Falls, Wisconsin, the three men went out drinking.

The agents drank to excess, which they admitted in court, and left Moves Camp in the company of a young lady. He brought her back to

his room and, when he was too drunk to perform, allegedly raped her with a beer bottle. This we know because our lawyer Ken Tilsen went to River Falls and interviewed the girl and her mother in the hospital where she was recovering from the assault. We believed the FBI succeeded in convincing law enforcement officials in River Falls to drop rape and sodomy charges against Moves Camp, arguing that he was too important to the government's case in the Banks-Means trial.

These facts were brought to light by our attorneys during Louis's testimony. When that was exposed, I broke out laughing. The judge had already warned me, of course, that he would not tolerate outbursts of any kind, so he called the marshals in to clear out the row we were sitting in—the AIM row. When we refused to leave, one marshal sprayed us with Mace. When our attorneys protested, he had Bill Kunstler and Mark Lane arrested and jailed overnight for contempt.

That really pissed me off, boy. Up until then Judge Nichol tried to act as if he was at least sympathetic to the historic plight of Native people. Now he was siccing his dogs on us. I couldn't let it slide. The next week, when court reconvened, I arrived at the courthouse early in the morning and blocked the door to the building. I wouldn't let Judge Nichol through the glass doors. I looked him in the eye and called him a racist. I knew he hated that because he had presided over earlier hearings when the government had tried to shut down Heart of the Earth Survival School. He ruled in our favor, and our school remained open.

But I was so upset by the way he was handling *this* case. I told him he was no different than Joseph Bottum, one of the most racist judges in South Dakota. Judge Nichol thought of himself as a fair-minded person, and I could see his exasperation; he hated being compared to Judge Bottum, who Nichol knew well from his days as an assistant United States attorney in the District of South Dakota.

Longtime AIM attorney and treaty rights expert Larry Leventhal speaking before the J. Edgar Hoover FBI Building in Washington, DC, at the conclusion of the Longest Walk, 1978. *Dick Bancroft photo*

Judge Nichol got so angry, he walked right into that glass door and hurt his nose. He called the marshals and had me dragged away from the courthouse.

About an hour later, however, Nichol sent word to my lawyer to return me to the courtroom. From that point I knew the judge was starting to look at the case differently. I knew we were going to win.

Bill Kunstler questioned Moves Camp, presenting questions addressing the rape allegation. Moves Camp hesitated to respond to each question. He looked very uncomfortable, like a contestant on a quiz show struggling for the right answer. Mr. Kunstler got Moves Camp to admit to raping that girl with a bottle. Moves Camp later claimed he cooperated with the government because they had threatened his life.

We found out through later discovery that Moves Camp had been fed information about Wounded Knee by the Justice Department's Community Relations Division, a group that came into Wounded Knee many times to aid in communications between the government and the Indians. They were supposed to be neutral. A guy named John Terrones, he was the head of that group. Turns out they were providing information to Moves Camp on details he missed while in California. For example, Moves Camp was able to point out on a chart the location of each of our bunkers and who was responsible for them. He knew which one was manned by the South Dakota group, which by the Minnesota group, which by the Oklahoma group, and who was in charge of each group.

On August 30, 1974, Kunstler was questioning FBI agent Ronald A. Williams, one of the agents who had been with Moves Camp in Wisconsin, and he noticed the door behind the judge's bench. It was slightly cracked, which it should not have been, because behind it was the sequester room, where upcoming witnesses sit so that they cannot hear the testimony being presented. This ensures some fairness by discouraging corroboration, and influence of testimony. Set to testify next were Dennis O'Callaghan and Patrick Flynn on the same matter Agent Williams was being questioned about. Mr. Kunstler suddenly grabbed hold and yanked the door open, and those two agents came spilling into the courtroom. They looked stunned.

Everyone started laughing. Fools Crow and the other traditional people who were there from South Dakota, dressed in their war regalia, they were cracking up. The judge didn't know what was happening, banging his gavel and shouting, "Order in the court!"

It was chaos, like some slapstick comedy.

Then someone shouted, "Let's get 'em!" Those two agents knew they weren't supposed to be listening. They ran out of the courtroom, and I started chasing them with a bunch of other people. We had a strategy to make citizen's arrests on anyone who we witnessed breaking the law during the trial. Those agents managed to get away, but their conduct would not go unnoticed by the judge.

The trial lasted nearly nine months, and then finally went to the jury. During deliberations, after the jury had already voted unanimously to acquit both Banks and Means of the conspiracy charge, one juror, a young woman, suffered a heart attack and was sent to the hospital. The judge called all of the attorneys and the defendants together in his chambers to discuss how to proceed. Our side was willing to accept an eleven-juror verdict, because we knew we were going to win. We had been told during a ceremony that we would win, that Russell and Dennis would be set free. We were entirely confident. The government prosecutors demanded the judge call a mistrial, and that the case be retried. They had already spent $5 million prosecuting the case and were intent on getting something for their money.

Judge Nichol responded to their demands with exasperation. He suddenly lost his temper with the government's attorneys. He banged his gavel on the desk and said he refused to let the trial continue. He declared that he was throwing out all of the charges against Russell Means and Dennis Banks due to government misconduct.

The long list of major and repeated incidents of government misconduct relating to the prosecution of Dennis Banks and Russell Means was compiled by our attorney Larry Leventhal following the trial. Among the twenty-nine different types of violations Larry compiled, he found: the government had paid Louis Moves Camp more than $2,000 for his testimony (normal witness payments were $36 per day) and coached him to lie; the government covered up the rape allegation against Moves Camp; the government conducted illegal military activity at Wounded Knee and then covered it up; the government violated a court order by failing to produce the Nixon Wounded Knee tapes; the FBI produced erroneous witness interview accounts; the FBI interfered with media coverage; the FBI illegally wiretapped the Wounded Knee trading post; the government had covered up evidence of illegal wiretap operations . . . and on it goes.

In his September 16, 1974, decision, Judge Nichol thoroughly scolded the government from the bench. Forty-two years after he uttered these words, it still thrills me to recall them: "It's hard for me to believe that the FBI, which I have revered for so long, would stoop so low," he said. "I am forced to conclude that the prosecution acted in bad faith at various times throughout the course of the trial and was seeking convictions at the expense of justice. . . . The waters of justice have been polluted, and dismissal, I believe, is the appropriate cure for the pollution in this case."

The government appealed Nichol's decision, but the US Court of Appeals for the Eighth Circuit affirmed the dismissal of charges. AIM had set out to use Wounded Knee as an opportunity to put the United States government on trial. We succeeded in doing just that. We had won, and we were elated. The American Indian Movement was not guilty. The government was guilty—of governmental misconduct, illegal use of military forces, and illegal search and seizure.

Judge Nichol eventually threw out all the Wounded Knee cases under his jurisdiction, including mine. It was a tremendous victory for AIM. Not only were we successful in having the charges thrown out, but we had succeeded in getting at least one judge, and one federal jury in America, to take a close look at what the government was really about when it came to its dirty dealings with Indian people.

17. THE DAMN HARD WORK II

THE MOST SUCCESSFUL PROGRAMS ever developed for Indian people have been developed and run by members of the American Indian Movement. The American Indian Movement affects all Indian lives, whether they like it or not, and whether they know it or not. Nowhere is this so true as in Minneapolis and among the residents of Little Earth of United Tribes housing.

By 1975, three years after it opened its doors, 45 percent of the units at Little Earth were considered beyond repair and on the verge of fore-closure. Most of the residents had been withholding rent for months. AIM came in and did an assessment and found out there were many reasons why people were refusing to pay. For example, the builder never connected the overflow on the bathtubs. So when a kid got in and filled the bathtub, it would get up to the overflow and the water would come out in the living room. The homes also had faulty wiring, which caused several fires in the complex. Many of the units had not been insulated, and they were freezing in the winter. The residents were just being ripped off, and once they realized no one was going to help them, they stopped paying. That was not long after Wounded Knee, so AIM was seen by the government and a percentage of the public as criminals; some even considered us terrorists.

The Indian community here got together and asked Dennis Banks, who happened to be traveling through town at the time, to lead a big hearing where the residents could register their complaints. I was in Boston, Massachusetts, doing some speaking. They held the meeting at a place called Holy Rosary Church, very near Little Earth.

It seemed like everybody was after the property—major corpo-rations wanted to build expensive housing and retail complexes on the site. It was becoming a very valuable piece of land. All of these moneyed interests didn't want poor people living there anymore. The banks were considering foreclosure, and the city was considering con-demnation.

The city told the residents they had one more chance to make the Little Earth complex work, but they would have to select a new

At a protest against efforts to move Little Earth in 1975. I'm at the mic at left. My message that day: "Relocation stops right here!" *Courtesy AIM Interpretive Center*

organization to oversee and run the place. The board of directors was given a choice between the Catholic archdiocese, the Minnesota Council of Churches, and the American Indian Movement.

They selected the American Indian Movement. These guys are the ones that advocated for this Indian preference housing, they said, let them figure out a way to make it work.

I got a call in Boston from Dennis Banks and was told I had become the landlord of a 212-unit housing complex where 45 percent of the units were beyond repair, and nobody was paying rent.

Dennis said, "You always say in your speeches that 'Indians are the landlords of this continent. It's the end of the month, and the rent is due.' Now you really are a landlord."

I returned to Minneapolis and rolled up my sleeves. My first task was to find a new board of directors. I selected some of the top leadership in town. I asked Judge Miles Lord, but he couldn't serve because he was still on the federal bench. So his daughter, Priscilla Lord Faris, came on the board. I got former Minnesota governor Wendell Anderson to join. I got some of the major corporations here in town to volunteer representatives to serve on the board. I got some of the most accomplished auditors and accountants to come on board and donate their services. I had never wanted to be a landlord, but now that I was one, I intended to do right by our residents.

I did a walkthrough of the complex with the Housing and Urban Development people. They estimated it would cost a little over $2 million to do a workout agreement to get these units back up to par.

I went to a Little Earth community meeting and told people, "Some of you haven't paid rent for eight or nine months. If you intend to keep your home, you must pay next month's rent and start paying back payments on what you owe. If you don't do that, you're going to have to move, because we've got over three hundred families on the waiting list."

I had to make some hard decisions. I had to evict Indian people, Black people, and other poor people who would not, or could not, follow through on their obligations.

I also had to take care of the social crisis that had overtaken Little Earth. I had to deal with the alcoholism and the fighting and the drug dealing that was rampant in the project. So I brought in the AIM Patrol to clean up the common areas and keep the peace. AIM took complete control of Little Earth housing.

The second week after AIM took over, the Black and Native workers who managed and maintained the property went on strike. They told me they wanted comp time. They wanted back pay. They wanted an insurance plan.

I didn't have money to do that.

I said, "Look, I'm paying you what I can. That's all I can do. We're thousands of dollars in arrears here. If you don't show up on Monday morning, I'm going to have to get another crew."

They didn't believe me. They went on strike. Nobody showed up to work Monday morning. I put out a national call to all AIM chapters and brought in people from all over the country to run the management, maintenance, and security. Those people that went on strike are still on strike today. I had to let them all go.

Within eight months, things had turned around. Little Earth benefited from a very high rate of rent collection. I had convinced the people they had to make their payments regardless of the condition of their units. I gave my word that I was going to fix the entire property.

I submitted my budgets to Housing and Urban Development. They had promised to help, but when the time came they never gave me a penny. They never fulfilled their commitment. They didn't do a damn thing. They wanted me to fail. They wanted the American Indian Movement to fail. I never sent another mortgage payment in to HUD. I took every single penny that was collected and I started pouring it back into the project.

Every unit was hooked into the same little six-inch drainage pipe. I suppose the contractor who built the plumbing system must have had some leftover pipe he wanted to use rather than spend money on the proper materials. So if several units flushed their toilet at once, we had floods in all the basements. I started hiring people to correct things, putting in new pipe, putting in insulation, doing cosmetic work, putting in lawns and sod and trees and cedar bushes. Our staff started beautifying the place.

I started organizing marches downtown. I built a banner that read, "Relocation Stops Right Here." We carried it downtown. The grand-mas and grandpas and children who lived at Little Earth, and hun-dreds of other people—non-Indian people—came from all over town. We carried that banner down to HUD about once a week. Soon we had the mayor, city council, and even the local HUD office trying to help us keep Little Earth alive. The local HUD gave us advice and moral support, but what we needed most, of course, was money.

At the federal level HUD refused to help us because they believed Little Earth's tenant selection process violated federal fair housing laws. We were told by HUD officials that once Indian people left the reservation and moved into urban communities they were no longer entitled to receive the benefits—such as Indian preference housing—that were promised in the treaties. Little Earth had a tenant selection process in place that favored Indians; 90 percent of our tenants were Natives.

Jack Kemp was President George H. W. Bush's secretary of Hous-ing and Urban Development, and he came to town to do a big speech for the Metropolitan Council. The Up and Out of Poverty Now! coali-tion and some of the non-Indian groups were planning to have a big demonstration against homelessness. They called us and asked us if we would join their protest at the Hyatt Regency downtown. I agreed to speak to the protesters.

"Yes, we'll join you," I said. "We'll be there with our drum."

Kemp heard about that. He called our attorney and said, "Hey, man, I've been demonstrated against by everybody. The last thing I want in the world is to have Indian people demonstrating against me. What do I have to do?"

He said, "Mr. Bellecourt wants to meet with you. He wants you to come to Little Earth housing to meet with him and see the property."

About four o'clock that afternoon, Kemp called and said he would come over. But he would have only about fifteen or twenty minutes to spend at Little Earth.

We had just about the whole Indian community, the city council, the mayor, the local congressional delegation, priests and nuns, and all the big activists waiting when Jack Kemp pulled up in his limousine. When he got out he was shaking like a leaf. From all he'd heard about AIM, he had this impression that he needed to be scared of us. He came into the community center there. What did he find? A big friendly banner that said, "Welcome, Jack Kemp," with a cloverleaf sign all painted green in honor of his Irish heritage. We put a star blanket around his shoulders and sang an honor song for him. We had a feast all prepared for him. We had a community celebration prepared, and it kind of took him by surprise. He was really moved. He started crying, the tears rolling down his cheeks. He hugged me and said he had never been treated so well by anyone anywhere in America.

He said, "What do you want from me?"

I said, "I want to meet with you."

We went across the street into the old Indian Health Board offices. The legislative delegation, mayor, former governor, and half the gathering followed. I laid out the whole story of all the promises and commitments that were made to us by HUD that were never fulfilled.

I looked the secretary in the eyes and said, "Little Earth is not going anywhere, Mr. Kemp. I'm sorry. We're not leaving here. If we have to build a razor wire fence around here in order to defend our homes, we will. We're not going nowhere."

"What do you want?" he kept asking.

I said, "I want you to freeze this whole effort to foreclose us. I want you to put it on ice. Give us time. We'll get the money somewhere. We'll find somebody that will sponsor us. I give you my word. I'll see to it personally."

He verbally agreed we could do some type of workout agreement. After he left town, however, he never really did anything. He said that if he turned this urban housing project over to the Indian people, he'd be violating fair housing laws. He was scared of the NAACP and all these groups, like the Nation of Islam, who he believed would be coming after HUD to build homes for their communities.

So we tried to put things together without HUD. I immediately contacted the Mdewakanton Dakota community out here in Shakopee who had just launched a very successful gaming operation. I was very close friends with the Mdewakanton president, Leonard Prescott. After hearing our story, he decided he'd put Little Earth of United Tribes under the Dakota Housing Authority, which would actually give us reservation status, a federal trust status.

This shook up the whole City of Minneapolis, all of the Housing and Urban Development officials, and it caused ripples all the way to Washington, DC, because they thought if the Dakota Housing Authority puts us under their wing, we might open up some type of gaming operation in the heart of Minneapolis.

Even Martin Sabo, the longtime Minnesota congressman, who was actually a supporter of ours at the time, got so shook up about it that he put a rider on an Interior Department appropriations bill, which put a moratorium on the transfer of any off-reservation lands to reservation trust status. I think he was afraid that Indian people would buy back the entire state of Minnesota and return it to Indian Country.

Of course, Jack Kemp left office when Bill Clinton became president in 1993, and a guy by the name of Henry Cisneros came in to run HUD. Cisneros was a very good friend of ours. I met him years earlier when he was mayor of San Antonio, Texas. I attended the large luncheon meeting in Washington, DC, of the Opportunities Industrialization Centers of America, where I ran into Henry again. Now he was in a position to help us.

After the meeting, I talked to him. It was just after the courts had ruled against us in this ongoing, seven-year court battle as HUD tried to shut down Little Earth for having Indian preference. Mr. Cisneros remembered me. He pulled me aside, and we shook hands. He asked the reporters following him around for some privacy, and we went in a quiet corner to talk.

I told him the whole story. I told him about the struggle and the

promises and commitments that were made, and how Jack Kemp
came to town, and we organized a meeting with him, but he never did
a damn thing to help us.

Henry kind of chuckled about that. He told me that the Nation of
Islam had their own housing programs in Washington, DC. Hispanic
groups operated their own housing programs in San Antonio while
he was mayor there. If anybody had a legitimate claim to federally
funded housing it was Indian people because of our trust relationship
through treaties with the federal government.

Henry asked what I wanted. I said, "I want you to turn Little Earth
of United Tribes over to the Indian community, and I want you to wipe
out the $4.5 million balance of what HUD thinks we owe."

He shook hands with me and said, "We'll take care of that."

I came back and told our people what Henry Cisneros had promised me. They were disbelieving that was going to happen, but it did. It
took a few months, but he made it happen. And when it did we closed
off Cedar Avenue and held a big powwow right in the middle of the
Little Earth complex. We planted a tree to mark a whole new beginning
for our residents and our community. We signed the documents that
the Little Earth of United Tribes' debt was erased, and the project
was turned over to the urban Indian community. Our Urban Indian
Housing Authority took over, and that's been the status of the housing
complex ever since.

Today, Little Earth of United Tribes has gone through a major re-
hab. We spent up to $35,000 on each unit. Cosmetically, the whole
grounds have been taken care of, the trees, the bushes, everything
that we wanted has been taken care of.

After Little Earth was secured, we had just about *every* kind of program you can think of, taking care of any need of our Indian people.
We had programs to deal with housing, to deal with health, to deal
with education. Survival schools had started. Alternative education
programs started, rehabilitation programs, Minnesota Indian Wom-
en's Resource Center to take care of the needs of women in domestic
abuse situations. The Minnesota Indian AIDS Task Force was being

created to take care of people that were facing AIDS. All of the issues that AIM had originally laid out as our objectives and goals had
been accomplished. But we found out that the economic conditions
of Indian people remained virtually unchanged here in the city of
Minneapolis.

It wasn't any better on Minnesota's reservations. In the summer of
1976 I would learn firsthand just how hard Minnesota's reservation Indians still had it. I had been traveling with a group of AIM warriors on
the powwow circuit, providing security and spreading the word about
the good work AIM was doing in Minneapolis. I don't remember which
powwow I was at when someone got a message to me—of course in
those days we didn't have cell phones. There was an emergency at the
Lower Sioux Reservation, on the Minnesota River in southern Minnesota. A guy named David Larsen, a Lower Sioux tribal member, was
trying to track me down. The message requested that I come to Lower
Sioux, where the local Indians were under siege by a biker gang, and
to bring with me as many AIM warriors as possible.

By the time I arrived with two carloads of men, the situation was
critical. The biker gang was camped down in the river valley, and the
Indians were dug in on top of the hill. We pulled into the Indian camp,
and I asked around looking for this David Larsen. It looked like a mini
Wounded Knee up there. They had dug foxholes and armed themselves with Molotov cocktails and guns.

I found David manning a defensive post. He said, "I've never been
so happy to see anyone in my life. Thank God you're here. I fought in
Vietnam, and I've never been so scared."

David brought me up to speed. Four days earlier he had been tend-
ing bar in the little reservation town of Morton. A biker gang called
the Grim Reapers was on their way to the Sturgis Motorcycle Rally
in the Black Hills. They stopped at a campsite outside of Morton for
the night, and many of the bikers came into town to drink at the bar.
They gave David a bad feeling; he said they were filthy and looking
for trouble. The mayor and police chief were both out of town, and so
David, a bartender and college student, was, as he said, "pretty much

the ranking official in town" for the weekend. He decided to close the bar at 4:00 p.m. as the bikers became more boisterous and inebriated. This angered the bikers, who spilled out on the street and started groping some of the Indian women that happened to be there.

Just then, a young local Indian guy pulled up in his truck and thought it looked like a party. He opened his window to chat with the bikers, who tried to rip him out of his car. The guy was frightened as a group of bikers gathered in front of his truck. He gunned the engine and ran over two bikers. One man had his skull run over, but was unhurt. The other biker broke his hip.

As bikers poured into town, David ran home. Unfortunately, his home was only sixty yards from the bar. He stood in the window as the crowd outside grew. He was spotted by a biker, who shouted, "There's a fucking Indian, let's get him."

David grabbed his two small children and ran out the back, down the fire escape, and into the nearest open door. The old white man inside asked what was going on, and he provided shelter for the three of them.

David used the old man's phone to call the local cop. He had already been roughed up and run out of town. Then David called the sheriff, who claimed he had no jurisdiction on the reservation, but would have been there in an instant, of course, if there was a complaint against an Indian. David called Governor Rudy Perpich, who said he couldn't send in the National Guard until people got hurt. David called the Bureau of Indian Affairs in Washington. They placed a call to the Redwood County sheriff, who told them to leave his department out of it. David had nowhere to turn. He didn't know anyone in the Movement, but he had heard of me, and knew about Wounded Knee and many of the other actions we had undertaken to help Indian people. Through friends of friends David finally tracked me down.

First thing we did was bring out the big drum. When those bikers heard that, it scared the hell out of them. Some of them took off right away. Then I got on the megaphone, stood between the two groups, and addressed the bikers. As I spoke I was sure a bullet was going to rip through me anytime. It's a miracle someone didn't shoot me. I told them that what happened in town was an accident. No one meant anyone harm, and we didn't want no more trouble with them. And you know what, they listened. They got on their bikes and went on their way.

David and I became very good friends. He often says to me, "If it wasn't for you and AIM, I can't imagine what would have happened. People would have lost their lives."

David went on to become tribal chair. He served from 1984 to 1992. He was well known as the man who started the first Indian casino in Minnesota, only the second in the whole country. He asked me to include this in the book, and I am honored to do so. He said, "If it wasn't for you, Clyde, I never would have had the confidence to take on the State of Minnesota in our fight to legalize Indian gaming. Without Clyde, there may never have been Indian gaming in Minnesota."

Today, the people of Lower Sioux are economically self-sustaining. Their community is thriving in many ways; it has been transformed from the impoverished place I encountered when I went there in 1976 to help run the Grim Reapers out of town.

In 1978 the Indian population of Minneapolis was swelling. There were Native people coming in from all over. They heard about the Movement. They heard about the beautiful programs and the opportunities that were available to them due to our efforts. People were flooding the area. We needed to find a way to communicate directly with the local Indian community in order to help direct them to the available social and economic resources.

That year, right here in the city of Minneapolis, the American Indian Movement contributed to the founding of what was called Migizi Communications—*migizi* means "eagle" in the Ojibwe language. I arranged to provide them one of their first grants when I was on the National Indian Lutheran Board, a foundation funded by the Lutheran

Church. Syd Beane, a Dakota community organizer, and I had the authority to get together and give up to $5,000 without board approval.

We wanted to support an organization that would train Indian journalists and produce news that communicated stories that were important to Native people. Dozens of radio and television stations throughout America and Canada would soon carry the Indian news Migizi produced. One of the primary missions of Migizi was to expose those who claimed to be for Indian people, but did little or nothing for us. One of the first organizations they reported on was called the Minnesota Indian Employment Consortium, which was formed by major area foundations in 1978. It was supposed to raise the economic conditions of our people. The only problem was there were no Indian people on its board. They had people from IBM, Honeywell, Dayton-Hudson, and General Mills.

We found out that Indian people were, once again, being left out of programs like affirmative action. Indians were being left out of the America where people made enough money to feed and clothe their children, to have a car, to be able to afford rent. With the help of the Migizi media platform, our message was finally received, or so it seemed.

Big companies started holding job fairs at the Minneapolis American Indian Center. They would send their top personnel people, their human resources people, and they would encourage our people to apply to their beautiful companies.

We discovered that, over a two-year period, there were over twelve hundred applications taken from Indian job seekers in Minneapolis. But there were only ten Indian people total working at these companies, and they were sweeping floors and answering telephones.

I called a community meeting where I attacked this employment consortium. I said, "Why do they call themselves the Indian Employment Consortium? They don't have any Indian people on it. They're using us. They're using us to satisfy their multimillion-dollar federal contracts. They use these little job fairs to say, 'Oh, yes, we've got Blacks. We've got women. We've got Hispanics. We've got Southeast Asians. We've got handicapped. We've got veterans. We're doing all these efforts in the Indian community, putting these job fairs together.'"

Finally, we met with these companies at the Registry Hotel out by the airport in the early part of 1979. They voiced their reasons for hiring so few Natives, every one of them based on stereotypes: They said Indians got their checks on Thursday and didn't show up on Friday. They had alcohol problems, so they didn't come to work on Monday. If ricing season came up, they'd just leave their job and go ricing. They asked for my advice in dealing with this behavior.

I called an all-Indian caucus. I ran all these chief executive officers out of the room and I said to them, "You guys go have a cup of coffee. Let us Indian people talk about this issue. We'll come up with a solution."

They all left the room, and it got deathly quiet. I explained how and why we were being used by these corporations.

I said, "I think we ought to start our own job creation program. I think we ought to ask them right now, all eighteen of these corporations and foundations that are here with us, for $10,000 from each. We'll have $180,000 we can use for job training and placement assistance. We'll get a job pool together, and we'll start doing customized training. We'll find out what type of employees they need, and we'll train our people to do those jobs. If they need janitors, we'll train janitors. If they want to train people for higher-level positions, we'll customize the training to that."

So we called the CEOs back in there. We proposed this job training program and asked them for $10,000 payable right then and there. Of course, every one of them made excuses. They talked about their stockholders, and their boards of trustees, and this group wasn't meeting for two months, and that group wasn't meeting for six months. I expected all that. They all left to go home. They said they wanted to meet with us again.

The following day, I started calling attorneys, and I made it public that I was filing a restraining order. I was going to stop all federal funds from coming into the state of Minnesota and into the Twin

Cities area until an affirmative action program was established that would reach right down into the Indian community and start training and placing job applicants.

Amazing things happened. I was *immediately* contacted by a man named John Bolger, who ran one of the biggest printing firms in the Twin Cities. He and his wife, Genevieve, asked me to visit them in their home.

Bolger was the first white president of the Twin Cities Opportunities Industrialization Centers (TCOIC), one of the largest job training programs in the nation. It was located in the north Minneapolis Black community. He was hired to run the TCOIC because that organization was ready to go down the tubes because of general mismanagement. So they put John Bolger on as the president, and with the help of some corporations and foundations, he managed to bail them out.

He, too, recognized that Indian people weren't being served by the federally funded and state-funded affirmative action programs. He wanted to know how he could get Indian people involved.

I said, "We have to have our own job creation program. We have to see Indian faces in prominent positions. When trainees and students walk in the door, the first person they see has to be an Indian. They have to see an Indian counselor. They have to see an Indian teacher. They have to see an Indian director. They have to see successful Indian people coming in to work as mentors."

He asked, "Can you do that?"

"I can do it," I said.

"I want you to meet Reverend Leon H. Sullivan," he told me. "He's the founder of the Opportunities Industrialization Centers of America, one of the top employment training programs in the world today. He has over 170 job training programs going nationwide. He's developing and running them all over the Middle East, all over Africa. He's putting these job training agricultural programs together, growing corn and orchards out in the middle of the desert in Africa. You've got to meet him."

I didn't know who he was talking about. Turns out minister Sulli-

Reverend Leon H. Sullivan, me, Bill Lewis, Bill Means, and Mike Bonga. *Courtesy AIM Interpretive Center*

van was a major figure whose renown had escaped me. I learned he grew up the son of a small-time Baptist minister and rose to become a longtime board member of General Motors. He was not only the first Black person to break into the upper echelons of a major US corporation, he also had a hand in tearing down apartheid in South Africa.

He later wrote the *Sullivan Principles** on South Africa, where he got all of these major corporations to start divestment from South Africa. He was very powerful—one of Martin Luther King's right-hand men.

Two days later Bolger flew me to Philadelphia. Opportunities Industrialization Centers (OIC) National Headquarters was located on Broad Street. I walked in, and not only was Reverend Sullivan there, but a lot of the Black leadership from throughout America was in the room. He stood up and shook my hand. He was physically imposing, as well as intellectually impressive. He weighed 270 pounds. He was six foot nine—a giant of a man.

---

*Moving Mountains: The Principles and Purposes of Leon Sullivan, 1998

I recognized something when I walked into that room that day. I recognized that Reverend Sullivan was an Indian. I just felt it. I started telling him about the history of Black people and Indian people in America, how when they were running away from the slave owners, they went among the Cherokees, and Choctaws, and Chickasaws, and Seminoles, and Miccosukee. I told him the history of how Black people and mixed-bloods were forced into Oklahoma on the Trail of Tears. A lot of them lost their lives. When they got to Oklahoma, they were given what they called freedmen status.

I said, "The Seminole Nation right now in Oklahoma has two council seats that are held by Black people. The only freedom that Black people knew in America, they got from joining with the Indian people."

Reverend Sullivan said, "You know what? I'm half Indian." I don't know how many times I've heard that when it isn't true. But he went into his office and came back with a big photo album and showed me pictures of his grandmother and his mother. They were full-blooded Indians. He showed me pictures of his family. He was more Indian than I was. When he asked the other men in the room if they had Indian blood, most of them indicated that they, too, were part Native.

He said, "From the time I was a small child I was looked at as a Black person in America. So that's where I took my struggle."

He asked me to tell him about AIM's 1972 takeover of the Bureau of Indian Affairs and our 1973 takeover of Wounded Knee.

"The only way I could tell you about Wounded Knee is by telling you about where I was born." I told him about the White Earth Reservation. I told him how I grew up and, as a little boy, was forced into the mission school, and how my knuckles were split open. I told him about my mother, how she was taken and placed in a white-run boarding school and crippled for the rest of her life because she scrubbed floors with marbles tied to her knees, punishment for speaking Ojibwe. I told him about my father, who left Carlisle Indian Industrial School and went across the waters to fight in World War I because he believed in freedom, justice, and democracy. I told him about my own personal struggles, how I was sent to Red Wing State Training School, how I went from there to St. Cloud State Reformatory, from St. Cloud I went to Stillwater State Prison. I told him about the spiritual uplift that I got when I met Eddie Benton-Banai. I told him about my own personal family history, about my sisters and brothers that were incarcerated, that we're strong warriors, a strong family.

When I got through talking to Reverend Sullivan, this giant of a man had his head in his lap and was crying. I looked around, and all the people had tears in their eyes. He got up and embraced me, picked me right out of my chair.

He told all the other leaders in the room, "We're going to create an Indian arm of OIC of America. This young man here is going to help me make this a reality. I've been trying to do this for years," he said. "I've been to the National Congress of American Indians, and I've been to the Tribal Chairmen's Association. We weren't successful in working with these groups because we could never build that trust relationship. You know why we couldn't establish trust? Because after the Civil War the United States sent Black soldiers, the Buffalo Soldiers, to kill Indians. This drove a permanent wedge between Black and Indian people. That's why that distrust is there," he said. "We're going to work on rebuilding that trust."

I said, "Reverend Sullivan, is there some kind of document that you want me to sign as a guarantee of my good faith?"

He said, "I don't need anything signed. This handshake is good enough. I want you to come to Washington, DC, in September. We're having the OIC National Convocation. I want to introduce you to everyone. I want the government to hear the story you told here today. Will you be there?"

I said, "Yes, I'll be there."

He said, "You go back home and you tell the people there you've got my support. You don't need a letter." He said, "You're going to put together your jobs program for Indian people. I want it up and running before the first of the year." I returned home and, with the help of my new mentor John Bolger, started laying the groundwork for what would become the American Indian OIC. We started formulating a board. We picked seven people from the most powerful corporations and foundations in Minneapolis—Honeywell, IBM, 3M, Pillsbury, General Mills—and put them on my board of directors. I made sure that 75 percent of the board members were Indian. I made sure that the chairman of the board would forever be an Indian; that the executive committee would forever be majority Indian. John Bolger joined the AIOIC board and would serve for many years. Today, John's son, Charlie Bolger, has taken his place.

We started the Indian OIC program in a little cubicle, a ten-by-twelve-foot office in Heart of the Earth Survival School, in 1979. We incorporated later that year and quickly spread out into two buildings. We had a day-care program so people could train and have their kids nearby in a safe place. We ran out of space, so we spread out into churches. Soon we had an effective program. We were training people. They were going to work. They were staying in their jobs. They were getting their lives together.

We called for a capital campaign so we could build a campus for American Indian OIC. We raised over $3.9 million in eight months. Astounding. Unbelievable. We took an old building along Franklin Avenue that was being used as a telephone directory recycling warehouse, gutted it, and rebuilt it for OIC training programs.

Before his death in 2001, Leon Sullivan referred to American Indian OIC as one of the top job training programs in America, and perhaps the world. Today we have one of the highest retention rates. We've trained thousands of Indian people, most of them women, heads of households, people who had been on welfare all their life—second-, third-, fourth-generation welfare recipients.

AIM's accomplishments, like American Indian OIC, Heart of the Earth Survival School, and Little Earth of United Tribes, the Legal Rights Center, and Indian Health Board, are rarely mentioned by those who have written about the history of the Movement. They haven't taken the time to come here and find out the *depth* of the American Indian Movement, what has been accomplished here, before and after Wounded Knee.

18. ALMOST RUINED ME

DRUGS AND ALCOHOL ALMOST RUINED ME. They almost ruined the Movement. I was near death on three occasions; each time the Creator gave me another opportunity at life.

It's been a tremendous personal struggle. I know that all the time I spent in adult prison was directly related to drugs and alcohol.

As a young man I started going to Alcoholics Anonymous, drug counseling—everything failed. In the mid-1970s, I finally decided to beg for the Creator's help at the Sun Dance. Maybe that way, I thought, I would sober up.

And I did. Kind of.

Following the first year at Crow Dog's Sun Dance, I remained sober for six months. The second year, I stayed sober for nine months. The third Sun Dance I continued to struggle with sobriety, but again only for part of the year.

The fourth year I danced at Green Grass, on the Cheyenne River Reservation. I had left Crow Dog's Sun Dance because it had become a public spectacle. Reporters were allowed to come take photographs of the dancers. *National Geographic* did a big spread on it.

I drank right up to the edge of that ceremony. I hadn't had a drink for the first eleven of the previous twelve months, but I drank the whole month prior to the Sun Dance.

During those times when I was drinking and running around, my wife didn't want to have anything to do with me. She didn't want me around my kids. I was smoking marijuana. I was doing acid and other psychedelics.

I went to the Sun Dance that fourth year even though I knew I shouldn't. When I got to the community of Green Grass, maybe a mile from the Sun Dance grounds, I went up in the woods, dug a hole by a tree, and buried the alcohol and marijuana I had with me. Those things are still there today.

I arrived at Green Grass real late the night before the Sun Dance— maybe three or four in the morning. I slept in a tipi and woke up at sunrise just wringing wet. My whole body was sweating. I was sick.

I was the kind of guy that never got hangovers. I'd just be my own self the morning after a bender. I never even got a headache. But I woke up and had a terrible headache. I got the dry heaves. I had the runs. I came back from the outhouse and crawled into the tipi. I was miserable. I thought I was going to die.

Two Sun Dancers—Ted Means and Lorelei Decorah Means—came in and said, "You better get ready. We're going over to pray with the sacred White Buffalo Calf Pipe."

The Keeper of the Sacred Pipe holds a big ceremony every year—the original White Buffalo Calf Pipe is taken out for the people to behold. They go into the sweat lodge, and they bring in that pipe, pray with it, and have a feast afterward. That officially starts the Green Grass Sun Dance.

I said to Bill and Lorelei, "No way. I'm done. I can't. I've been drunk, and separated from my family, and sick; I'm carrying all these negative spirits with me."

They laughed at me. They said, "That's the reason you're here."

I said, "You guys go ahead."

A few minutes later I left the tipi to use the toilet again. Frank Fools Crow and this other medicine man, Martin High Bear, were standing by their pickup visiting. They saw me from a distance and hollered, "Nephew, come over here."

I went over and they said, "How come you're not going over to the Sun Dance? We'll go over with you. Come on."

I put my head down. I was ashamed. I told them I couldn't go; I'd been drinking and running around. I told them I was separated from my family, doing dope, and that I'd brought a lot of bad spirits. I was just going to leave.

"We'll support you," they said.

I was in need of some real strong spiritual guidance, but they both just laughed at me. They said something to one another in the Lakota language, and they both laughed. Then Martin addressed me. He said, "I'm going to tell you something, Nephew. I've been around the world. I've helped a lot of people. Not a day goes by where I'm not called to help somebody that's sick and in need of a ceremony. Just because I help spiritually everybody thinks I'm some kind of holy man. I'm not any different than you. I have the same problems you have. We gather at the Sun Dance because we're sick. We come here to heal. We come here to receive guidance. Now go get your towel. You're coming to the sweat lodge with us."

We went up to the Sun Dance grounds. The dancers, including Russell Means, were already inside the lodge. When I crawled in, they were all happy to see me. They shook my hand and encouraged me not to give up.

There were some old-timers in the lodge, and some little boys, six or seven years old. I was seated way in the back, the hottest part of the lodge. They started bringing in the rocks, more and more steaming rocks. Finally, they closed the door flap and started pouring ladles of water on the glowing pile. It got so hot in there.

Leonard Crow Dog always drilled it in our head that as AIM leaders it was our obligation to set an example. If the people had to suffer, we would have to suffer more. I could never say "Mitakuye Oyasin"— which means "All My Relations," the phrase used in the sweat lodge if you need to go out. It was searing hot, and I wanted to holler "Mitakuye Oyasin," but was embarrassed because the old people were watching, and the little boys.

The next thing I knew I started falling forward into that red-hot pit. I was so dizzy and so scared I was going to fall against the rocks. I gave myself a push and fell over sideways. There was a big guy sitting next to me, this old man. I kind of slid down his body and passed out.

It was then, at my lowest point, passed out in a sweat lodge, when the Creator came to me and gave me a vision.

I was in the Sun Dance grounds, and the four-day ceremony had just concluded. The dancers were leaving the arbor; I was the last in line. It is believed that Sun Dancers, at the conclusion of the ceremony, have the power to heal. So people bring their little children who need help. People come in wheelchairs and on crutches. Because I am known as the head Sun Dancer, I always leave the grounds after all of the other dancers.

As I left the arbor all of these people were waiting to greet us. I started shaking hands with them. At the front of the line were all people I knew that had died: Pedro Bissonette, the Oglala civil rights leader who was slain on Pine Ridge; Buddy Lamont and Frank Clearwater, who were killed at Wounded Knee. My father was there with tears in his eyes; he was so happy. My mom had died, but she was there hugging me—she was so happy about what I had done to help myself at the Sun Dance. Then I saw all the kids who had attended the Heart of the Earth Survival School over the years. And finally there were hundreds of people lined up who were old and sick and ready to die.

I was tired and weak and walking unsteadily. There was dried blood all the way down my body, down my legs. Blood on my feet.

There was a line of people queued up as far as my eyes could see. It would take hours to get through it. I wanted to get to the end of the line so I could collapse, so I could rest. All these people were hugging me, and all the little kids were just so happy. They were calling me "Uncle."

My eight sisters, some who I hadn't seen in a long time, were hugging and kissing me, telling me, "Brother, we support you 100 percent. We'll do anything to help you stay healthy." I finally got all the way down to the end of the line. I reached out to shake hands with the last individual, and it was me.

I stood there looking at myself. I had on western boots, Levi's, and a nice ribbon shirt. My hair was all neatly tied. I had earrings on, and I was really looking good. I reached out, and when I shook hands I turned into him. I looked back at the incarnation of myself that had just left the Sun Dance. I saw all the blisters on my forehead and shoulders, and blood running out of the blisters, my body completely burned. As I shook hands with myself, I looked into the eyes of the Sun Dancer and realized he was stinking drunk.

I later told Martin High Bear about my vision.

He said, "You know, Nephew, all those people that came to see you—those that are dead, they died believing in what you're doing. They believed in the cause of our people so strongly that they gave their lives. And those little children that came up to hug you—you started schools for them. You got them out of foster care. You're like a father to them. Everybody that came to see you depended on you. What they didn't know about you, however, was that between the tremendous works you're doing, you drink and run around."

He said, "Nephew, what the Creator showed you today was you're trying to ride in two canoes at the same time. It's impossible. You will never drink again. As long as you live, you'll never drink again. If you ever drink again, this vision that you saw here, this pain, this suffering that you went through, all of that will come back. The Creator wanted you to see what you're doing to those who rely on you to continue fighting."

As the dancers rested under the shade of the arbor following the first day of dancing, some women came and brought us the traditional foods, dried buffalo, ground chokecherries, and a special tea. As I rested

Dennis Banks, Eddie Benton-Banai, and me at the American Indian Center's first New Year's sober powwow, 1988. *Dick Bancroft photo*

and replenished myself, I thought, from this day forward I will never take another sip of alcohol. And I haven't.

Although I stopped drinking, I never quite gave up marijuana. I justified it, saying it was keeping me sober, it was a medicine. Phillip Deere told me around that time that marijuana was a sacred medicine. He said he used it sometimes. It helped relieve stress and could be used in a good way. He said it could also cause immense harm if abused.

I chose to continue abusing marijuana. This led me into an even deeper hole.

19. THE LONGEST WALK

THE IDEA FOR THE LONGEST WALK originated in Northern California in 1978, where Dennis Banks was operating West Coast AIM and fighting extradition to South Dakota for his role in the Custer Courthouse riot. Eleven pieces of anti-Indian legislation had been introduced in the Congress, proposing laws that would in effect terminate the tribes, stripping Native people of their treaty rights. Dennis and Lehman Brightman decided something had to be done to wake up America before it was too late. They envisioned a thirty-two-hundred-mile spiritual walk across the country to support tribal sovereignty and bring attention to the proposed legislation.

We had a lot of other business that summer as well. We had to find a way to pressure Congress and the Ford, then Carter administrations to keep the government's promises. They had agreed to conduct Senate select committee hearings on the dozens of unsolved murders that had taken place around South Dakota and across Indian Country around that time. Still today, in 2016, the FBI has yet to investigate most of these murders, even as the corpses of bludgeoned Indians continue to turn up in places like Rapid City, Seattle, and Clinton, Oklahoma.

Although Dennis had conceived the Longest Walk, he wasn't able to lead it. You see, three years before the start of the Longest Walk, in 1975, a South Dakota jury had convicted Dennis on charges of rioting and assault with a deadly weapon for his part in the 1973 Custer riot. The charges carried a maximum sentence of fifteen years in prison. Before sentencing, Dennis heard rumors about a plot to take his life in South Dakota State Penitentiary.

He fled to Northern California only to be arrested by FBI agents the following year. A massive petition movement supported by our friends Marlon Brando and Jane Fonda was circulated and submitted to Governor Jerry Brown. Governor Brown, it turns out, was friendly to our cause. He offered Dennis safe haven in California, refusing extradition requests from South Dakota. Brown informed all of the various authorities involved that he was protecting Dennis because of sworn statements that his life would be at risk in a South Dakota prison. Dennis would live in California until 1983, when the election of Republican governor George Deukmejian ended his asylum. He then sought sanctuary on the Onondaga Reservation in New York. Because reservations in the state are not under federal jurisdiction, the FBI could not arrest him there. In 1984, tired of hiding, Dennis turned himself in after nine years on the run. He was sentenced to three years in prison.

On February 11, 1978, after smoking the Sacred Pipe and praying together on Alcatraz Island, the walkers set out. As the march approached the California border, Dennis had to turn back, so he turned leadership over to a guy named Ernie Peters, the former Lakota chairman of West Coast AIM. Nobody in my circles knew much about Peters. But somewhere along the line he had apparently met with Crow Dog, who gave him the title of "Chief of All Chiefs," whatever that means, and said everybody should abide by him. And so Dennis Banks got the marchers to the California border, and watched the group march away down US Highway 40.

They started out with a very small group, about thirty or forty people. Most of those that joined the march were non-Indians—hippies, yippies, and those kind of people. US 40 is a pretty quiet road. Not many people used it anymore since they built the Interstate Highway System. On US 40 the march wasn't likely to get much attention.

They got all the way to Kansas, almost halfway across the country, and hadn't held even one single press conference. Nobody knew who they were or what they were doing. They were not passing out any literature. They would march right through towns without talking to anyone. The original plan was to meet with churches, labor unions, colleges, universities, mayors, and congressional leaders, and start educating them. None of that happened. They weren't accomplishing anything.

Dennis called me and asked me to get involved. I didn't want to have anything to do with it. I had only heard bad things about what was going on: a bunch of non-Indians marching through the middle of nowhere, acting as if they were the American Indian Movement.

Dennis said, "Indian people will join the march if they know you're in charge. The Movement will show up if you start organizing."

I said, "I'm going to talk to the community about it."

I picked up the phone and started calling around the country to gauge people's feelings. Many AIM folks told me not to get involved in the Longest Walk. It wasn't well organized, they said, and it was making Indian people look bad.

After a few days of considering various arguments, I came to the conclusion that I had no choice but to step in. I told everyone I spoke to: "It's going to fall on AIM's shoulders one way or another. They're going to say the American Indian Movement made promises that never materialized. We'll be right back to square one."

I spoke with Eddie Benton-Banai, Porky White, and some of the other traditional people who advised the Movement. None of them wanted to get involved. Even my wife told me not to get mixed up with that one. But I had made up my mind. It had to be done. I was going to travel to Kansas and take charge.

As we prepared to depart from Minneapolis, we held a ceremony at Fort Snelling State Park, near the confluence of the Minnesota and Mississippi Rivers. We put up sweat lodges there and said our prayers. We left from there with kids from Heart of the Earth Survival School and the Red School House. We called it the Run for Survival, a 560-mile journey from Minneapolis to Lawrence, Kansas. We planned a route that would take us down through Winnebago and Omaha country in Nebraska. We sent advance people to make contact with those tribes. When we arrived in those Native communities, people put us up and put on big feasts. We would also stay in places like small-town meeting halls, and Boys Town, Nebraska, where we slept in the school's gym.

The kids ran in shifts with cars traveling alongside, going a few miles an hour.

A couple days away from joining the Longest Walk, we rolled into Lawrence, Kansas. I made a phone call to the "Chief of All Chiefs," Ernie Peters, and demanded a meeting. Ernie told me that even if Dennis had asked me to take over the walk, he wasn't going to step down from the leadership role. We arranged to meet at a big park in Lawrence.

With both groups coming together it was a sizable gathering. I looked over their crew; they were 80 percent non-Indian, people with dreadlocks down to their waists, and dirty clothing, two or three filthy skirts on and unshaven legs—just a bad representation, I thought.

I questioned Ernie: Why aren't you getting any attention, or lobbying anyone, or even walking where anyone can see you? Why aren't you doing what needs to be done?

I told them all, "The literature that was supposed to be distributed has not been passed out. I've checked with several tribes; you didn't even make contact. This way of doing business is over. Indian people are going to lead this march now."

I mocked the informants among them. "If I find out you're a government agent, you're going to go all the way to DC with us, you're going to be put to work for us, but you won't eat," I told them. "And when we get to Washington we're going to dump your bones on the steps of the J. Edgar Hoover Building." I could see the expression change on some of their faces as they went ashen and started to sweat.

The next morning, I went to the store and bought shampoo, washcloths, towels, and a big box of soap—I told those people to clean up their act if they thought they were going to continue on this walk.

A bunch of people up and left that morning, and they took with them the pipe that Crow Dog had blessed for the walk. They refused to turn it over to us.

"Keep your pipe, and continue marching down these back roads if you want to," I said. "This afternoon, we're going on the freeway and that's where we'll be all the way to DC."

"Oh you can't do that," they said. "The highway patrol will arrest you."

"We're going on the freeway," I said. "Go another way if you don't like it." The real movement people stayed with me and supported me from then on.

I reminded everyone of the sacred nature of what we were doing. I told the group, "If anybody here gets caught drinking alcohol, you're out. Anybody here gets caught with weed or anything else, I'm sorry, but you're going to have to leave. That doesn't mean you can't come back, but when you come back, you're going to have to be sober. Period."

We immediately went about building an organization, putting people in charge of all the things that needed to get done. We had people contacting the labor unions, church groups, and local governments ahead of our route. We had people setting up accommodations for us, arranging places for us to stay where we could get cleaned up and get something to eat. John Thomas, a Shawnee Indian, was in charge of our advance team. He turned out to be one of the greatest organizers I've ever known. I just loved the work he did for the walk. He was always traveling miles ahead of the main group, arranging for our needs.

Because we had wasted some time trying to get everything organized, we took that walk and turned it into a run. Somebody would commit to running a certain number of miles at a time. If they pledged five miles, we'd have a car drive up ahead and put a stake in the ground at the side of the road. Another group would take off from there, and when the runner got to that stake, they picked it up and drove to catch up. And that's how we covered sometimes one hundred or more miles a day.

We sent crews out to friendly reservations all over the country. They asked tribal councils to get involved, and we started getting support. Indian people started coming by the hundreds from all over— Oklahoma, Nebraska, Kansas, South Dakota, and North Dakota— individuals, couples, and entire families.

One of the concerns that our people wanted to bring to the forefront of the Longest Walk was the case of Leonard Peltier, a Dakota/Anishinaabe political prisoner who is now very well known internationally.

I didn't know Leonard really well when he was on the outside. My brother Vern was the one that got him involved in the struggle.

Leonard was in jail in Denver, Colorado, and my brother helped get him out, introduced him to the Movement.

We sent a group up to Marion, Illinois, where he was being held at that time, to meet with Leonard and protest his incarceration. Leonard had been framed and convicted one year earlier for the murders of two FBI agents on the Pine Ridge Reservation. The killings occurred on land owned by the Jumping Bull family, near the village of Oglala. History now refers to that day in 1975 as the "shootout at Pine Ridge."

After Wounded Knee, we had asked some AIM people to stay on the Pine Ridge Reservation to protect the elders, traditional people, and other AIM supporters. That's where Leonard Peltier came into the picture.

The Jumping Bulls were well-known AIM supporters, so Leonard and a group of others camped on their land to protect them from the terror campaign taking place on the reservation.

On June 26, 1975, two white men who were not known to the Indians sped onto the Jumping Bull property in an unmarked car. Many women and children were present.

The agents stepped out of their car with guns drawn, and a firefight started. For all the Indians knew, these white men were some of the GOONs, racist skinheads, or John Birchers running around and shooting up the reservation in those days. Turns out the intruders were FBI; they were shot and killed.

From the Indians' perspective, the agents' deaths were the direct result of the agents' own actions. During the Reign of Terror on Pine Ridge, the Indians were rightfully fearful. Their understandable sense of panic led them to kill those agents in self-defense.

Joe Stuntz, one of the AIM men present, lost his life in the firefight. He was a hero to the people on Pine Ridge, but just another dead Indian to the FBI. No investigation into Stuntz's death ever occurred.

The Indians in the camp ran away and became fugitives. Out of the forty-some Indians who participated in the firefight, three men were eventually indicted and apprehended: Dino Butler, Bob Robideau, and Leonard Peltier.

During this time, I was at home in Minneapolis with my family. I had returned to Minneapolis after Wounded Knee and stayed. I was still concerned, of course, about what was going on in Pine Ridge. But my base was Minneapolis, where my family lives and where I was up to my neck working to strengthen the Indian community.

The AIM leadership had made a commitment before we left Wounded Knee: everybody was going to go home and clean up their own backyard because the women—my wife, Peggy, and many others— were demanding to have their families back. My wife said: "You've been to the BIA, you've been to Alcatraz, you've been to Wounded Knee, you've been all over the place, and now it's time for you to come home." I agreed to do that; I honored that commitment.

Peltier, Robideau, and Butler were on the run for several months. I was in communication with them, and that's how I found out Leonard Peltier had made it safely into Canada. We had to be very careful because our phones were tapped.

Canadian law enforcement eventually caught up with Peltier. He sought asylum in Canada as the United States filed for extradition. A key so-called eyewitness to the shootings was a woman named Myrtle Poor Bear, a Lakota from Pine Ridge. On the basis of her statement, that she had seen him kill the FBI agents, Leonard Peltier was extradited from Canada. This Myrtle Poor Bear, who the government claimed was Leonard's girlfriend, later retracted her testimony. At his murder trial, the judge refused to allow Leonard's attorneys to call Myrtle Poor Bear as a defense witness. Not only was Poor Bear not Leonard's girlfriend, the two had never met. In 2000, Myrtle Poor Bear issued a public statement saying that her original testimony had been coerced, the result of months of threats and harassment from FBI agents.

Robideau and Butler were apprehended in Kansas while Leonard was still in Canada. Their trial was held in Cedar Rapids, Iowa, where a miracle of justice took place. On July 16, 1976, a jury selected from a town that was 98 percent white returned not-guilty verdicts for Robideau and Butler. Their argument, that the FBI-sponsored Reign of

Terror on the Pine Ridge Reservation had led to a situation where the Indians had no choice but to defend themselves, convinced the jury of their innocence.

Had Leonard Peltier been tried along with Butler and Robideau, he would have walked away. But his fate was sealed in the fact that the FBI now had only one person to blame for the agents' deaths, and they would go to any lengths to secure a conviction. The FBI should have been on trial for those deaths, and Joe Stuntz's, too. Instead, Leonard became their scapegoat.

Leonard's defense team was able to get his trial moved out of South Dakota. Unfortunately, it ended up in the worst possible venue: Fargo, North Dakota. I attended the trial. You could just feel the hatred there, the racism. The trial was a farce. Three teenaged Native witnesses testified against Peltier. They all later admitted that the FBI forced them to testify. Even so, not one witness identified Peltier as the shooter.

The entire proceeding hinged on evidence that was later shown to have been falsified by the government. Leonard's lawyers filed a Freedom of Information Act request shortly after the trial. An FBI ballistics expert had testified during the trial that the AR-15 allegedly used by Peltier matched the shell casing that was found in the car with the agents. Turns out just the opposite was true; one of the documents showed that casing was *different* from one that Leonard's gun would have shot. Leonard's lawyers continue to seek over one hundred thousand documents that the government has refused to release. Within these documents, we are certain, is the evidence proving that the government did not know who killed the agents.

On April 18, 1977, Leonard Peltier was sentenced to two consecutive life terms on two charges of murder in the first degree. Before sentencing, Peltier gave Judge Paul Benson a piece of his mind for the way the judge had favored the FBI throughout the trial. He said, "Neither my people nor myself know why you would be so concerned about an organization that has brought so much shame to the American people. But you are! Your conduct during this trial leaves no doubt that you will do the bidding of the FBI without any hesitation!

"You are about to perform an act which will close one more chapter in the history of the failure of the United States courts and the failure of the people of the United States to do justice in the case of a Native American. After centuries of murder . . . could I have been wise in thinking that you would not break that tradition and commit an act of justice?"

As I speak, this innocent man has been locked away for thirty-nine years. I don't know who shot those agents, and it would be irresponsible to speculate. But the government doesn't know either, and they've admitted as much.

In 1985, when the Eighth Circuit Court held oral arguments on a motion filed by Peltier for a new trial, assistant US attorney Lynn Crooks, the government's lead prosecutor, admitted, "We can't prove who shot those agents."

This admission has not changed the fact that they framed Leonard Peltier and have done nothing to help set the record straight and set him free. You see, Leonard Peltier is a symbol for all Indian people in America who dared stand up for themselves. I'm sure the government feels that the entire American Indian Movement is guilty because we dared to stand up to them. As long as Leonard is in prison, Indian people will get the message that they'd better keep their heads down and their mouths shut, or risk being sent to prison for life.

Many of this country's top civil rights lawyers have had some kind of contact with the Peltier case—including former attorney general Ramsey Clark—but none of them were able to get the guy a new trial. That's all we've been asking. Based on the evidence that we found, we just asked for a new trial, because we knew he would be found innocent. We've done everything you can possibly think of to set him free.

Even Judge Gerald Heaney, who considered and denied Peltier's original request for a new trial, later voiced his strong support for Leonard's release, stating that the FBI had used improper tactics to convict him, the FBI was equally responsible for the shootout, and that Leonard's release would promote healing with Native Americans.

I've talked to Leonard several times on the phone since his incarceration began. I told him to stay strong, and that everything was being done to secure him a new trial. But I have never believed they would release him or give him amnesty.

Every president since 1977 has had an opportunity to pardon Peltier: Jimmy Carter, Ronald Reagan, George H. W. Bush, Bill Clinton, George W. Bush, and Barack Obama. Not one has dared risk offending the FBI.

More so than with any of the other presidents, there was a great deal of hope that Bill Clinton would free Peltier. With two months left in Clinton's second term, I saw an opportunity to influence his decision on Peltier. On November 21, 2000, South Africa's president Nelson Mandela came to Minneapolis on the final stop of a North American speaking tour. I knew he was scheduled to meet with President Clinton before returning to South Africa. A lot of people concerned about Peltier called me and asked me to try and get an audience with Mandela.

I put on a nice ribbon shirt and a vest embroidered with Ojibwe floral patterns, braided my hair, and went downtown to the Marriott where he was scheduled to speak. The ballroom there was just jam-packed.

I saw Mandela take the stage surrounded by very tight security. There was no way you could get close to him, but I made up my mind I was going to. I squeezed my way through the crowd and got as close as I could before the president's security detail tried to stop me. I told them it was important that I talk to Mandela. They told me to write my name down, and that I should come to the press conference the following morning. They said they would arrange to have me meet with him then; but that didn't satisfy me. I tried to push my way through, and it caused a big commotion—Minneapolis police officers started running at me. Just then Mandela got up on his toes behind the podium and saw me. He took the mic and said, "Let that freedom fighter through."

The security people spread away and I walked through. He came over to me and asked my name.

I said, "My colonial name is Clyde Bellecourt, I'm a founder and national director of the American Indian Movement, but my real name is Neegawnwaywidung."

And he asked, "What does that mean?"

And I said, "The Thunder Before the Storm."

He said, "I like that name. What can I do for you?"

I said, "I know you're very busy, but if there's any way we could have a few minutes to talk, I would like to have that."

He said, "I'm really, really tired. I've been traveling all over, and I've got to get some rest. But we're having a press conference tomorrow morning at ten at the Minneapolis Club. Come down there and we'll talk." So I shook hands with him and left.

The next morning, I went to the Minneapolis Club and found the only people they were letting in were credentialed media professionals. I ran into a reporter I knew named Al McFarland who was getting ready to go in. Al had two press passes around his neck. He took one off and put it around my neck and said, "Let's go."

We went in there, and after Mandela gave a brief speech the journalists started raising their hands for questions. A reporter from Channel 5 asked, "Mr. President, what do you think of the way the Bush-Gore election was decided in Florida?"

And he said, "That's internal business. I'm not going to come here and criticize anyone. That's for you people to figure out, not me."

I raised my hand, and he spotted me and he told me to come up and his security encircled me again. They said that was the farthest I could go, but Mandela told them to stand down. He reached down and shook my hand. I said, "Mr. Mandela, as you know, human rights groups from around the world have gathered millions of signatures calling for Leonard Peltier to receive a new trial. Leonard himself doesn't want to just be let go; he wants a new trial, so he can prove to the world that he is innocent and expose the crimes of the federal government."

He said, "I know all about Leonard's case. What do you want me to do?"

I said, "When you were in prison and the people were saying *Free Mandela* they were also saying *Free Peltier*, and when they were saying

Free Peltier they were saying *Free Mandela*. Now you're free and he's still in jail. There is more work to do. Leonard's not in good health. He's probably going to die in there unless somebody does something about it. The only thing I'm asking you to do is ask President Clinton to demand a new trial. That's all."

Mandela said he was going to be meeting with Clinton in a couple days, and he would speak to him about Peltier.

Clinton, of course, did not release Peltier. He preferred to use his power to release people like Marc Rich, a businessman brought up on charges of tax evasion and making illegal deals with Iran during the hostage crisis. Rich was in Switzerland at the time of his indictment and never returned to the United States. He was pardoned by President Clinton in January of 2001, on Clinton's last day in office, while Peltier was left to rot.

Leonard Peltier has had every major human rights figure call for his release, people like Coretta Scott King, the Dalai Lama, Mother Teresa, Rigoberta Menchu, Archbishop Desmond Tutu, Angela Davis, Danny Glover, Robert Redford, Vine Deloria, Rubin "Hurricane" Carter, Reverend Jesse Jackson, Harry Belafonte, and the list goes on and on.

Amnesty International has repeatedly called on the United States to grant Leonard a new trial. The parliaments of Belgium, Italy, and the European Union have made appeals for his release. Dozens and dozens of prominent individuals and organizations around the world have demanded justice for Leonard. Nothing anyone has done has succeeded in moving the needle in Leonard's favor.

In appeal after appeal, Leonard Peltier has been denied a new trial. He is now seventy-two years old and in poor health. I hope he will be released so he can have time with his family, his people, and his homelands. But I am not optimistic.

Over the years people have confronted me, saying I haven't done enough to help gain his release. One of the problems I've encountered in working with the Leonard Peltier Defense Committee is that they've had several people involved who were FBI informants. Every two or three years it seems like somebody else is in charge. There's a lot of infighting because the FBI has done such a good job of keeping Leonard's supporters suspicious of one another.

As much as it hurts to think of Leonard locked up, I kind of pulled away from that fight. I just don't know who in his camp can be trusted anymore.

I say to those who have criticized me: "I've been doing my work here in Minneapolis. I've dealt with hunting and fishing rights. I've dealt with racism in the schools. I've developed new schools. I've helped to start the Native American Community Clinic and the Indian Health Board. I've made job training available for Native people. I've dealt with police brutality and issues of social inequality. I've forced treaty issues on the land and in the courts."

And then I ask them: "What have you done?"

The government knows if they were to release Peltier, AIM would look like a bunch of heroes. American history would have to be rewritten and replaced with truth. Along with Peltier, they would have to release all the records showing systematic governmental misconduct against Indian people and records of how they framed Leonard and threw away the key.

In 1978, during the Longest Walk, we protested Leonard Peltier's unjust incarceration.

In 2016, as I speak, Leonard's longest walk continues.

One of the first government officials I called after taking over the Longest Walk was the mayor of Wichita. I arranged to meet with him and the city council. After the success of those presentations I started calling governors and legislators. I addressed every legislature in the states we passed through.

We'd go into the halls of government with a drum and sing our ceremonial songs and the AIM national anthem. Then we'd make a presentation, stressing the importance of passing the Indian Religious Freedom Act, a bill that was moving through Congress at the time that would legalize Native American spiritual practices. We also asked for their support in killing congressional action that would abrogate our treaties.

I always demanded, "How can you call America a democracy, then turn around and do this to Indian people? This is genocide, and it must stop now."

When I would talk about how Indian people had been forced to take our ceremonies and languages underground, the lawmakers just shook their heads in disbelief. They claimed to be unaware that anything like that had happened to us, which may indeed have been true given the malpractice of the American education system.

It wasn't just the non-Indians that needed to learn. We had to educate many of our own people, too. A lot of them had been totally Christianized. Like me, most of them had been forced as children to go to church and attend church schools.

During the Longest Walk, I met people of many tribes, Indians from all across the land who told the same story. The marchers sat around fires at night sharing our stories. We found in each other the missing history of Indian people, and how we had been mistreated, divided, and conquered by the forces of genocide.

I had my own experiences with those nuns at White Earth. Those nuns lived to break our spirits; I never gave them a moment's satisfaction. But this had been the state of affairs for Indian people since we were first herded onto reservations. Indian people were totally controlled by whichever denomination lorded over their lands. Dakota people in Minnesota mostly became Episcopalians and Presbyterians. At White Earth they brought in every denomination you can think of to convert the Anishinaabe. They had Mennonites, Lutherans, Episcopalians, and Presbyterians—everybody had their shot at our souls. On White Earth the people didn't take to Christianity at first. The Catholics decided to call in the Jesuits, who acted like the law enforcement arm of the church. They imported nuns who looked like the defensive line of the Green Bay Packers. Those white women would scare the hell out of you. We were constantly punished. That's the kind of environment—one of relentless threat—in which many of the participants on the Longest Walk were raised.

We talked about this as we wound along toward DC. Now was the time, we all agreed, to take back our spiritual ways—not just AIM leadership or certain individuals—but all Native people, all across Indian Country.

It was a long trip, and slow going, but we got a huge boost of morale every time a traditional leader came and joined—men like Phillip Deere, Crow Dog, American Horse, Red Cloud, and Cherokee spiritual leader Sam Drywater.

We built sweat lodges at many stops along the way. People who had never experienced their ceremonies returned to the sweat lodge to learn about themselves. With the help of our ceremonies, we gained strength along the way. We began to see each step as a unique prayer, dedicated to restoring our people and our communities.

Back in those days, if you didn't know your Native language there was this notion that you could not pray in the Indian way. I said to those who made this argument that the Creator gave us many languages, including English, and it's all right to pray in English. Prayer comes from the heart, not from the mind, and the heart's longing can be expressed in any language.

In the sorry powwows that were held in those days you could see how far our people had fallen away from their culture. Barely any men participated; you were lucky if you'd see two male dancers. The few men that did get out there had no regalia to speak of. They maybe had medals tied around their Levi's, and wore tennis shoes rather than moccasins. Today you see dozens of male dancers; they change costumes two, three times a day that are covered in hundreds, even thousands of dollars of beadwork. The Longest Walk helped restore this culture and spirituality to the center of our people's lives.

Phillip Deere spent a lot of time working with the people on the walk, telling the old stories and helping everyone understand their roots. Phillip had been with the Movement since 1972, when the Trail of Broken Treaties passed through his Muscogee Creek community in Oklahoma. He told this story often: In 1972, Phillip's people, like Native nations throughout the continent, had given up almost all of their land, and almost all rights to hunt and fish. Everything that was good was gone, replaced by tuberculosis, smallpox, diabetes, alcoholism, boarding schools, prisons, jails, and death.

In the early nineteenth century, the United States Indian policy focused on the removal of the Muscogee and the other southeastern tribes to areas beyond the Mississippi River. In the removal treaty of 1832, Muscogee leadership was forced to trade the last of their homelands for new lands in Oklahoma, what the government called Indian Territory. Many Muscogee Creek had settled in the new homeland after the Treaty of Washington in 1827. But the majority of Muscogee people refused to leave their sacred lands. The US Army forced the removal of more than twenty thousand Muscogee Creek to Indian Territory starting in 1836.

Deere talked about how he was from one of the Muscogee Creek bands that resisted removal, and who, at bayonet point, carried their people's sacred fire some eight hundred miles, and never let that fire go out. Through blizzards, tornadoes, and rainstorms, they carried that fire and placed it at the center of their nation at their new lodge in Okemah, Oklahoma.

Deere said he was outside of his home removing rocks from his garden one morning in 1972. He heard a drum. He went and stood out on the road and looked in the direction of the sound.

"I could hear it," he would say, "and I wondered, where's that drum coming from?"

It spooked him, like he was hearing things.

When he heard the drum again, he started thinking about a Muscogee Creek prophecy: everything would be taken from the people, and when all hope was almost lost, a new people would come forward. They would be the fifth generation following the Trail of Tears. This was the time they said a new people would restore hope to our Native nations. This was 125 years after the prophecy was given to the Muscogee Creek.

Deere said he squinted up the road, into the sun. Red dust flew into the sky and came closer and closer. From that dust finally emerged shimmering human forms—it was the American Indian Movement on the Trail of Broken Treaties.

Deere threw his wheelbarrow into a ditch that day and joined the Movement because, he said, he knew it was time to come out of hiding. At that time he had his sweat lodge underground, literally. He grew a garden over it. He wanted to have the right to be an Indigenous person, a spiritual person, to step out of the shadows, and so he left home and walked with AIM.

Due in part to the work Phillip Deere did to raise our awareness, water issues became one of AIM's priorities. He talked a lot about the coming scarcity of fresh water, and how so much of the water resources left in America are on Indian land. Phillip told us about a dream he'd had that showed him water being even more scarce than oil. He told us that in the future a pint of water would be worth more than a gallon of gasoline.

Celebrities started joining the Longest Walk to help raise the profile of our efforts. We received visits from Marlon Brando, Harry Belafonte, Senator Ted Kennedy, and Muhammad Ali. The Southern Christian Leadership started coming. The Six Nations Confederacy got involved and came in to our camps to give big talks. They discussed the reawakening of Indian pride that had been prophesied among their people.

Members of the Church of Jesus Christ of Latter-day Saints came and took care of us at several stops along the way. We learned to see them in a whole new way. We were used to thinking of the Mormons as kidnappers. They fostered many of the children that had been taken from Indian homes. By the 1970s, something like five thousand Indian children were living in Mormon homes. These AIM supporters were not *those* Mormons. These people seemed genuinely interested in helping, and in learning more about us. We talked with them about the Indian Child Welfare Act, another bill being considered by Congress at the time. ICWA, as the act is now known, would change the laws so that when Indian children were removed from their homes due to abuse or neglect, they would not be shipped off to other communities. They would stay with their relatives within their own Native communities. This kind of protection for our children was long overdue. Before enactment, as many as 25 to 35 percent of Indian children in some states were removed from their homes and placed in non-Indian homes. We used the Longest Walk to enhance people's awareness of this crisis and to gather momentum for this new law.

We were met with such enthusiasm for the changes we were after. It seemed like the time was just right for better things. Even the Mormons said they would support AIM's position on the Indian Child Welfare Act.

The Mormons asked a lot of questions. One of the things I was asked a lot was, "What is your people's religion?"

I said, "We don't have a religion. To us religion means getting hit with rulers, and standing in the corner all day with a dunce hat on while nuns shame you in front of other students. Native nations have their own spiritual ways, but most share in this simple ceremony: every day we put out tobacco for the spirits, purify our minds and bodies with sage, and pray."

When we were two hundred miles out of DC, we sent an advance team to meet with South Dakota Democratic senator James Abourezk and ask for help accommodating our group. Abourezk was the chairman of the Senate Select Committee on Indian Affairs. He was of Lebanese and Greek Orthodox descent. He was one of the first Arabs in Congress and had a lot of sympathy for the Palestinian cause. He was also very friendly to Indians. Perhaps in the plight of the Palestinians, he saw something that reminded him of our experience. He contacted the National Guard and arranged for them to take care of our needs.

By the time we got to Greenbelt Park on the outskirts of Washington, DC, we were so well organized, and so strong, we felt like we could accomplish anything.

The National Guard put up a mess tent and did all the cooking for us. They put in portable showers and toilets for us. They erected all these big army tents for us to sleep in. They put up a clinic to take care of people that were sick and injured.

On July 15, 1978, the Longest Walk entered Washington, DC, with several thousand Indians and dozens of non-Indian supporters. An estimated thirty thousand people were involved in the march into DC. We had a line of marchers that seemed to stretch for miles. Our people were very well disciplined. I had prepared them for what they were likely to face as we entered DC. I told them, "The police are going to harass you; people on the streets are going to call you all sorts of bad names; they're going to do everything they can to incite you. I don't want you to even look at them. Don't even pay attention. Instead, pray for them."

Our people were so spiritually dialed in that they didn't react in the slightest to the hundreds of policemen who lined the route. Looking at photographs today, you will not find one person in that massive procession so much as glancing at a policeman.

The government must have recalled how we took over the BIA building last time AIM was in town. They had something like eighteen different law enforcement agencies canvassing us as we marched—cops on horses, helicopters, motorcycles, and in squad cars. There was no need for all of this. We were on a spiritual mission. We were entirely peaceful. The traditional elders led us to the Washington Monument, where the pipe was smoked.

Over the following week, we held rallies and marches at various sites, such as Malcolm X Park in the heart of the Black community, to address pressing issues: the eleven pieces of legislation that would have taken our treaty rights, the Indian Child Welfare Act, Leonard Peltier and American Indian political prisoners, forced relocation at Big Mountain on the Navajo Nation, and the Native American Religious Freedom Act.

The week after we arrived, Congress passed the American Indian Religious Freedom Act. We were overjoyed to finally have these

I took a part of the advance team and, late at night, erected the Heart of the Earth Survival School's tipi on the Capitol Mall. *Dick Bancroft photo*

Muhammad Ali invited me to bring some of the children from the Longest Walk to New York City, where he had us picked up in a big limousine and took us to the foot of the Statue of Liberty for a press conference on July 18, 1978. Ali said, "I'm no longer Number One. The American Indian Movement is Number One and I am here to support them." *Courtesy AIM Interpretive Center*

important rights restored; we in the Movement felt especially proud of the work we did to bring awareness to the hundreds of years of repression of our spiritual ways. Every word of the act was paid for in the blood, sweat, and tears of Indian people.

On August 11, 1978, President Jimmy Carter signed these words into law:

> Resolved by the Senate and the House of Representatives of the United States of America in Congress Assembled, That henceforth it shall be the policy of the United States to protect and preserve for American Indians their inherent right of freedom to believe, express and exercise the traditional religions of the American Indian, Eskimo, Aleut, and Native Hawaiians, including but not limited to access to sites, use and possession of sacred objects, and the freedom to worship through ceremonials and traditional rites.

That same week the US Congress voted against the bills that would have abrogated our treaties. And just a few months later, on November 8, 1978, the federal government passed the Indian Child Welfare Act, which outlawed the genocidal practices that had stolen so many Indian children from their families and communities.

It was the Longest Walk that brought awareness to all of America regarding these issues. Not just to non-Indian people, which was important, because they're the ones that make the laws—but we brought awareness to Native people as well. There was no other time in history that that many tribal leaders ever got involved with anything in America. Never. And that unity, that focus, that spiritual campaign brought about great and lasting changes for Indigenous people.

20. HARDEST THING I EVER HAD TO DO

IN 1985, I STARTED USING COCAINE. I didn't have to buy it—a guy was giving it to me and to other people around me. Like most people who try cocaine, I found it very pleasurable, and I did not consider the severe consequences of using this drug.

I never shot it up. I snorted it, which I believed, somehow, would not be harmful. But in short order I started experiencing cocaine addiction. I got to the point where I couldn't do anything without it. I couldn't conduct a speech. I couldn't even go to a meeting.

One day around this time, while I was deeply involved in cocaine, I was living at Little Earth housing, and a young white couple approached me outside my home. They wanted to know where they could get some narcotics. They wanted to buy acid. I was running around with a crowd that was selling LSD, and so I helped them. I was not in my right mind at that particular time in my life. I was more often under the influence than not. I referred this young couple to a friend of mine who I knew was holding.

They went to that person and bought acid. Two or three times thereafter they returned for more. Turns out this was a setup; they were federal agents.

I should never have gotten involved in drug dealing, but I did. I've made mistakes in my life, and this was one of the worst; I have had to make peace with it.

Later that winter I was driving down the streets of Minneapolis and saw squad cars coming. They pulled me over and ordered me to throw my keys out the window and put my hands where they could see them. They kept me there for an hour kneeling in the snow. They searched my car and my body and didn't find anything. But they already had all the evidence they wanted. They had been tapping my phone for years and knew all of my business. They took me downtown and charged me with one count of conspiracy to distribute LSD; five counts of distribution of LSD; and three counts of use of a communications facility to distribute LSD.

I made my initial court appearance on Christmas Eve, 1985.

The story hit the newspapers nationwide the next day. I was so embarrassed. I was directly responsible for the development of almost every Indian program in Minneapolis, and I took a lot of pride in being a community leader, in taking care of business. I believe that if I'd had access to a gun, I would have put myself away.

I pleaded guilty to the conspiracy charge in exchange for a reduced sentence. The judge sentenced me to five years, of which he suspended three.

I asked the judge if I could go out of state and attend a Sun Dance, dancing for my final year at Big Mountain, before my incarceration would start. The government fought that with every motion they could conceive, but in the end, the judge allowed me to go to Big Mountain, and I danced.

When I got home, they ordered me to report to Springfield Federal Correctional Institution in Missouri. Everybody else that was busted in the case, and there were several of us, went to the federal prison camp at Duluth, Minnesota. But they sent me down to Springfield, Missouri, one of the most hard-core federal prisons in the United States—a place where they send Mafia hit men, the Aryan Brotherhood, and big gang leaders from across the country.

Turning myself in was one of the hardest things I ever had to do. My family accompanied me. We journeyed south to Springfield, about eight hours' drive from Minneapolis. Standing at the gates of the prison, my baby son wouldn't let me go. He started crying and screaming and grabbing onto me.

Law enforcement officials, of course, knew I was doing cocaine— after all, their agent had been supplying me. But they offered me no medical care during the period when they knew I would be very ill from withdrawal. At an orientation session I started feeling the pain.

I woke up that night screaming and hollering. Indian inmates held me down in my bed. This went on for a few nights. In the mornings I would go out and walk the yard, and I would put tobacco ties, little bundles of cloth containing tobacco and prayers, up in the trees, and I'd pray. I'd try to get myself tired so I could sleep. I dreamed

I was being hung, or forced into the electric chair. I needed spiritual help.

I started *demanding* that we have sweat lodges. They previously had a sweat lodge at Springfield, but the administration had shut it down—Crow Dog had been incarcerated in that institution at one time. I filed a grievance with the Federal Bureau of Prisons in DC, and soon they allowed the Indian inmates to build a sweat lodge. I had medicine men and spiritual leaders coming in from all over the country, running the sweat lodge and other ceremonies. I began to heal.

When you're in the federal system and you start causing problems, they inevitably transfer you. Pretty soon they sent me to Chillicothe, Missouri. Again I filed lawsuits demanding the institution give us the same privileges they gave Catholics, Lutherans, and Muslims—access to ceremonies, spiritual leaders, and traditional foods and medicines.

The US prison system has thousands of detainees in transit every day. They might keep you in an institution a few days or a few weeks before shipping you off again. This practice is very disconcerting for inmates' families, who are often kept in the dark as to the whereabouts of their father, brother, or husband.

Every new facility they locked me in, I would end up meeting with all the Indian inmates, and we would demand that we be given the resources to create an Indian studies program, and develop a sweat lodge and other ceremonies. Everywhere I went I left sweat lodges operating for the Native prisoners.

I did twenty-two months altogether—eleven months in Springfield, then to Chillicothe, then to Leavenworth in Kansas, back to Missouri to El Reno Federal Correctional Institution, and again to Chillicothe. I was finally put into the Rochester Federal Medical Center, about ninety miles south of Minneapolis, close enough for family to visit.

In prison I got rid of the drugs altogether. It felt good. I was working out every day. I regained my strength. I swore that if I was ever to walk the streets again, I would never allow anything to come between me and my family. My wife came back to me, started visiting me in Rochester. I was dead set on getting out, and getting on with my life.

One night I was laying in my bunk when all of a sudden I felt terrible pains in my chest. A nurse came from the hospital and examined me. I could hardly breathe.

She said, "Oh, you've just got gastritis. Nothing to worry about." She gave me some medicine to help with stomach pain.

I knew she was wrong. I was too scared to go to sleep. I stayed in a dormitory with three other Indian guys, and they all gave me their pillows so I could sit up. The pain faded some when I sat up. Finally, the guard came around and I told him I was having a heart attack. He let a nurse come from the hospital again. She examined me and said, "Wait until morning, and then go to the hospital."

I started raising all kinds of hell. I said, "If this is a heart attack, I need help now."

The guard said, "I'll tell you what. You keep your mouth shut. If you keep talking, you'll never get out of this room." So I just shut up. After a while I passed out in a puddle of sweat.

At about six o'clock in the morning I came to, and I still had terrible pain. I needed some water. I crawled out to the hallway and used the wall to guide me down the corridor. I got to the water fountain and drank and drank. I splashed water all over my face and soaked my head. I went back and sat on my bunk again.

At about seven o'clock the guards changed shifts. This young guard came in and said, "I hear you've been having some problems. How do you feel?"

I said, "I'm having a heart attack right now."

Instead of calling for the ambulance, he gave me a pass to go to the infirmary.

I started walking across the lawn in the middle of the institution and got very exhausted. I only walked maybe a block or so before I couldn't go any further. I sat down on a park bench and passed out.

I came to sometime later. A bunch of guards stood around me, asking what the hell I was doing. Instead of assisting me they said, "You better get your ass over to the infirmary." They threatened to put me in solitary confinement if I didn't move. I willed myself to make it across the compound.

There was a big line at the infirmary. I was sitting in the hallway waiting for the doctor when I heard my name called on the intercom: "Clyde Bellecourt, report to the dental office."

I had a previously scheduled dental appointment I had forgotten all about. So I went into the dental office, thinking at least a physician of some sort would look at me. I got in the chair and the guy said, "You don't look right; you don't look well." He took my temperature, and it was real high. He gave me a glass of water, picked up the phone, and called an ambulance.

About five minutes later I heard sirens coming from downtown Rochester. They wheeled me outside and took me to St. Mary's Hospital, where Mayo Clinic doctors practice.

By the time I arrived at the hospital, the heart attack was over. The doctor said I had a blocked artery. He put me in bed and let me rest for five days but would not make further treatments available. I probably could have benefited from a bypass, but I'm convinced the government preferred to see me die. Once again I disappointed.

The second day Peggy came, and she brought with her Doug Hall, one of our lawyers. Doug took a statement from me before they returned me to prison.

We filed a suit because I was afraid, after the way I'd been treated, that the feds were still out to kill me. The Department of Corrections claimed that they'd done everything they could for me. They even claimed to have driven me to the hospital and denied threatening solitary confinement. The lawsuit never really went anywhere; it's not easy for an inmate to sue the feds, even one they're trying to kill. I remained on high alert until they finally released me several months later.

21. SPLINTERED ARROW

IT STILL HURTS ME to have lost Russell Means away from the Movement, and from my life. He passed away on October 22, 2012, after suffering from esophageal cancer. He was seventy-two years old.

In 1973, after my mother passed away, I was adopted into the Means family. I was very close with Russell and his mother, Theodora Louise Feather, who loved me as her own son. At a Sun Dance at Green Grass on the Cheyenne River Reservation, with Fools Crow conducting the making-a-relative ceremony, she adopted me into her family. She didn't want me to be an orphan. So I became her son and Russell's older brother. In the Lakota way, when you are adopted, you not only become a relative to that family, you become a member of the nation.

Vernon said it was fine if I wanted to be Russell's brother, but that he would never be brothers with Russell Means. I'm pretty sure Russell felt the same way about Vernon. Our relationships got complicated, and my brother and I, and others within the Movement, came to see Russell in a negative light.

Throughout the history of the Movement there have been people on the inside suspected of being FBI agents and federal informants. A good deal of this was paranoia, induced by FBI tactics. Some of it was warranted, as we *were* infiltrated by the feds.

Perhaps the most troubling outcome of all the suspicions was the tragic murder of Anna Mae Aquash. On February 24, 1976, Anna Mae, a Mi'kmaq Indian from Nova Scotia and a dedicated AIM member, was found dead along the side of a remote road on the Pine Ridge Reservation. She had been executed by gunshot. She was thirty years old at the time of her death. In the many years following her murder there were many rumors swirling around, fingers pointing as to who may have killed her. Some of those fingers, although completely without cause, were pointed at me and my brother Vernon. Others were pointed at various AIM people. Many fingers were pointed at the FBI.

The first autopsy failed to notice the gunshot wound in her head. They said she died of exposure. The FBI claimed they couldn't identify her. They desecrated her body, cutting off her hands and sending them to an FBI lab in Washington, DC, supposedly to examine the finger-prints. This was pure terrorism. This was how they treated Indian victims. Of course, the way they mistreated her body was shocking to us and put fear into the hearts of many AIM people, the majority of whom were women.

Only after the family demanded its own autopsy was her grave exhumed and the obvious wound in her head discovered.

Some thirty years following Anna Mae's murder, two former AIM supporters, Arlo Looking Cloud and John Graham, were convicted and sentenced to serve life sentences. I don't know if the government was right to convict these two. I do know my brother and I had nothing to do with it.

Only one person ever approached me to express concerns about Anna Mae Aquash; someone told me they believed this young woman—twenty-eight years old when she arrived at Wounded Knee—was a snitch. I knew her well from when I was close to Dennis Banks, and I thought she was a fine young lady, certainly a strong supporter of the traditional people and AIM.

Anna Mae was a hard worker. She went in and out of Wounded Knee. She brought weapons. She traveled all the way across this country with weapons, ammunition, and medical supplies. I never once ever felt that she was in any way an agent.

One of the aspects of Anna Mae that was brought to my attention was that she seemed to know all of the people within Wounded Knee that weren't known to the core AIM membership or traditional Oglala people.

Another reason this individual who came to me with concerns was suspicious of Anna Mae and others, such as Carter Camp, Doug Durham (who later admitted to being a federal informant), David Hill, and numerous others, is because they were arrested and released on several occasions. This person pointed out to me that Anna Mae was from Canada. She wasn't an American citizen. If she was arrested on charges of running guns from Canada, as were the accusations at one point, she would have been deported or imprisoned immediately. Anybody from a foreign country involved with the Movement in any way would not be set free in the United States after arrest.

Law enforcement's treatment of Anna Mae did not necessarily indicate that she was giving them information. One of the ways the police and feds try to destabilize social justice movements is to make people within those movements distrustful of one another. This is called "bad-jacketing." They also do this to people inside prison.

Over the years I've grown tired of hearing this rumor and that rumor about Vernon and me having "given the order" to kill this young woman. I felt a sense of vindication when the *New York Times* published an article by Eric Konigsberg on April 25, 2014, titled "Who Killed Anna Mae?" The writer did extensive research into the case. Not only were Vernon and I not accused, our names didn't even appear in the piece.

The only people I ever suspected of being involved with the FBI at that time were Carter Camp and David Hill, who came into the Movement and caused a lot of disruption. Hill, too, had been arrested but never jailed. According to documents released long after the fact, the feds believed Hill was the guy that bombed Mount Rushmore and was involved in other bombings. Then they turned around and released him "in the best interests of justice." Whose interest? Not the interest of the American Indian Movement—we never advocated bombing anything—but the interest of the Justice Department, who didn't want their illegal tactics, their abuse of human rights and treaty rights, put on trial.

There is another person I think is a federal provocateur who infiltrated the Movement prior to Wounded Knee and is still trying to claim some authority within the Movement today. I have read that he credits his entry into the Movement to me. He claims to have first met me when I was speaking in a little place called Champaign-Urbana, Illinois—the University of Illinois—to young students. He claims he was a student at the time and was excited about the things I was saying; he came up and introduced himself as Ward Churchill.

I supposedly gave him my business card and invited him to get involved in the Movement. That's what he has claimed—and it could be true, although I don't remember meeting him. I've met thousands of people over the years.

Ward Churchill is not an Indian, although he claims to be. He has claimed membership now in several different tribal nations. He used his claim to Indian heritage to earn a six-figure salary from the University of Colorado's ethnic studies department, where he worked from 1990 to 2007, as a professor and department head.

I remember meeting him in 1973. After working for *Soldier of Fortune* magazine in Boulder, Colorado, Churchill came into Wounded Knee and hooked up with Russell Means, David Hill, Bob Robideau—these last two were part of the same group that was with Carter Camp.

As the Movement evolved in the early 1970s, I was viewed as one of the big three leaders, along with Russell Means and Dennis Banks. Because they looked the part, with their long dark braids and traditional jewelry, those guys received a lot of the attention from the press, who called them "the most famous Indians since Sitting Bull and Crazy Horse wiped out Custer." I don't know about all that. I do know that as a result of their high profile they were usually the first to be arrested.

As I think back on it now, there was a period of time when I trusted Russell, but that didn't last too long. I think I began to really question what Russell was up to after I refused to testify against Carter Camp. At that time, naturally, there were a lot of people angry at Carter, and there were a lot of people out gunning for him. I would hear reports of this person or that person running into Carter at some bar and getting into it with him. One night, I was told, Russell caught up to him and kicked his ass. Carter was drinking in Rosebud and driving around town there. Russell stopped him, crawled through the window of Carter's car, it was said, and slapped the hell out of him.

This was followed by one of the strangest and most confusing scenes I witnessed during those times. A short while after this alleged ass kicking, I was at the Rosebud Fair, and I met this little boy who was disabled. His name was Rocky. I bought him a Coke, and we went and sat in the bleachers at the powwow grounds to watch the dancers.

Just then I saw Carter Camp walking around the dance circle from one direction. Then I saw Russell coming around the circle from the other direction. They didn't know I was there. They met over on the far side from where Rocky and I sat. They were like long-lost friends, shaking hands with one another and hugging.

I thought, what the fuck? Just three weeks after Russell had supposedly slapped him up, and now they're hugging one another and shaking hands. Since that moment I always wondered how Russell and Carter were connected.

I'm going to say a few things about Russell Means in this chapter that he might have recounted differently. But this is my story, and he told his. I encourage everyone to read Russell's autobiography, *Where White Men Fear to Tread*.

It wasn't too long after I was shot that Russell pulled away from AIM and, along with Ward Churchill, who I am convinced is a CIA agent, formed what they called the *AIM* International Confederation of *Autonomous* Chapters, or "Autonomous AIM."

Russell turned against us in the Movement. He used his celebrity status to spread rumors that Vernon and I were involved in the death of Anna Mae Aquash. When in reality, I believe, he really should have been looking a little closer to home if he wanted someone to blame.

Ward Churchill used to say that I was a Stalinist because I was always singling out people, like him, that were disruptive within the Movement. Churchill was the one, along with Russell Means, who called for indictments against me and my brother, and Russell's own brother Bill, and Herb Powless, and several other respected members of the American Indian Movement, for our supposed involvement in Anna Mae's murder. This was just another FBI attempt to divide and discredit the leadership of the Movement.

In the early 1970s, we started hearing rumors that Ward Churchill had actually trained—and he later admitted this in his book—some of the police forces in South Dakota and helped them develop a profile of the American Indian Movement. Churchill claims this was cultural sensitivity training, but I have my doubts. One of the men he trained was later named head of the Rapid City Police Department's intelligence unit.

He was also suspected by people in the Indian community of being present during the infamous Incident at Oglala in 1975 (the deadly shootout between the FBI and AIM, for which Leonard Peltier took the rap). Some photographs surfaced showing Churchill getting out of an FBI helicopter, dressed in combat fatigues, at the Pine Ridge airport prior to the firefight that took the lives of two FBI agents on June 26, 1975.

Russell had resigned from the American Indian Movement on several occasions before he spilt from the Movement and formed Autonomous AIM with Ward Churchill in Colorado in 1994. First, he resigned from AIM during the Wounded Knee trials to run for president of the Oglala Sioux Tribe. There are people today who say that had he not done that, had he not publicly resigned from the American Indian Movement, he would have won that election. During the Wounded Knee trials Russell came to St. Paul, where Crow Dog admonished him in front of everybody. He told him that no one in the American Indian Movement could ever resign again. Thousands had sacrificed for the Movement. Crow Dog talked about Buddy Lamont and Frank Clearwater, the hundreds of people that went to jail, people that died, had been shot, assassinated, in cities and on reservations across the continent. Crow Dog demanded to know from Russell, "How can you resign?"

Russell promised he would never do that again.

A couple of years later, he had a very successful operation going on in the Black Hills, in a place called Yellow Thunder Camp. Russell led an effort to reclaim the Black Hills, which are sacred to many tribes and belong to the Lakota people under the terms of the 1868 Fort Laramie Treaty. Reports reached us in Minneapolis that he had told the young people at the camp that he was tired, that he was moving on to bigger things—that he left with all the money that had been donated to run the camp.

A month or two later, we found out that he was running for vice president of the United States in 1984 on a ticket with Larry Flynt, the pornographic king, the founder of *Hustler* magazine. Of course, we had to condemn him again. Women's organizations all over the United States, all over the world, started calling us, asking how we could ever allow something like that to happen. We demanded his resignation. After he lost that election he returned to AIM. Then there was the question of the Sandinistas. During Wounded Knee we received telegrams and phone calls from leaders of the Sandinista revolution, saying they were with us in the struggle. The Sandinistas let us know they cared about us, were thinking about us, and that meant so much. We certainly understood and supported their struggle. Everyone at Wounded Knee was excited to hear from the Ortega brothers, even Russell Means. I remember when that first telegram arrived. Russell was so excited. He announced to everyone, "We've got the Sandinistas!" He did nothing but praise the Sandinistas. He reminded us all the time that we had to be like the Sandinistas and never give up. He just admired them. He could not give a speech without mentioning the Sandinistas.

In 1985, after the Sandinistas won the war and sent the Somozas packing from Managua in 1979, the Ortega brothers called an international conference to draw their supporters together to help piece the country back together. The buildings and structures were bombed out and their boats were sunk, and they had only $5 million in the bank to run the country. They were having a real struggle there. One of the questions confronting the socialist government was how to deal with the land that had been liberated from the Somozas, land which now belonged to the people of Nicaragua. The Sandinistas invited leaders of the American Indian Movement, including Russell, to Nicaragua. The Ortega brothers were interested in receiving AIM's input on the best way to incorporate Nicaragua's Indigenous people into the new order. So we expected when Russell was invited to go down there and show his solidarity that he naturally would. But for some reason that I couldn't fathom at the time, he refused to go with us. The Movement put together a tremendous delegation—about twenty of us traveled down there together.

Among the delegation was Dick Bancroft, one of the many non-Indians who ended up being very important to the success of the Movement. Dick has been our photographer from almost day one. The brave, vivid imagery he has produced over these many years has given the world a window into the AIM struggle.

When he first came into the Movement, Peggy was convinced Dick was a fed. They soon became very close friends, but she still teases him about it.

I also like to clown around with Dick; I always refer to him as a reformed missionary because before we met he was living in Kenya working for the Presbyterian Church. He talks about how, as a young man, he wanted to be a Freedom Rider in the South, but he had young kids and couldn't get away. He was from a well-to-do neighborhood in St. Paul where people were set in their conservative ways. But it was the sixties, and he was hungry to learn more about social justice, to contribute to the struggle.

In 1967, when the opportunity came for him to work in Kenya, he packed up his family, his wife and four children, and moved to Africa. In Kenya, he learned what American imperialism looks like from an African perspective. I think he got a new understanding of himself as a white American and wanted to contribute to social justice in the United States more than ever.

After a few years Dick and his family returned to the United States, where he went to work for the United Way in St. Paul. At the time the organization was considering funding for our Red School House, the Indian survival school in St. Paul. He was the person they sent to go and check on the Red School House to decide whether to provide funding. That's where he first came into contact with the American Indian Movement.

Pat Bellanger and the folks there treated him really well and showed him all the good work they were doing to keep Indigenous ways alive through culturally focused education. Before he left, he told them how much he cared about what they were doing. He promised to support them and to work with the United Way to provide them some money. He wanted to know how he could become a regular contributor to the Movement.

He asked the right person. Pat Bellanger, who was at the school that day, passed away recently at the age of seventy-two. She did so much for the Movement over her lifetime that she earned the nickname "Grandmother AIM." She was instrumental in the development of the Red School House, Women of All Red Nations, the International Indian Treaty Council, and other AIM-affiliated organizations. She tended to work quietly, behind the scenes. Pat, like other prominent

Dick Bancroft shakes my hand, 1982. *Randy Croce photo*

women within the Movement, never got the recognition that some of the male leaders received. But what these women have done, and are doing, is no less important.

Pat Bellanger asked Dick Bancroft, "Well, what do you do?"

He said, "I'm an amateur photographer."

She kind of chuckled and said, "That's what we need. We need somebody to photograph all of the things we're planning to do. We'd love to have it all recorded."

So Dick Bancroft agreed to photograph our whole struggle. This was 1972. He has been with us ever since.

Dick traveled with us to Nicaragua. He photographed everything— got all kinds of pictures of Managua's bombed-out infrastructure, and the Sandinista leadership. He was on the boat with me and Vernon when we went to visit the Native people up the Rio Coco to the north of the country.

I called him about two days before we were scheduled to fly to Managua.

"Why do you always call me so late?" he complained. "Why can't you give me a week?"

I said, "Well, it just came up; we were just invited down there."

And he said, "Okay, I'll go with you."

That has always been Dick's response, whether we were visiting the IRA in Ireland or speeding off to an emergency meeting in Pine Ridge. I have heard, "Okay, I'll go with you" out of his mouth a thousand times.

Dick always teases me when remembering the Nicaragua trip. Because Vernon was along and he always braided my hair in the mornings, Dick says that I was the only member of the delegation that traveled with my hairdresser.

There were three nations of Native people who lived along the Rio Coco in the northern part of the country, along the Atlantic Coast: the Rama, the Suma, and the Miskito. The Indians were never involved in the revolution—it all took place in the cities, in the south of the country.

The Sandinistas said they wanted us to help establish policies that

Dick Bancroft took this photo of me and a child on an earlier trip to Nicaragua, in 1981.
Dick Bancroft photo

would apply to their Indigenous peoples. They were thinking about developing some institution just to deal with "the Indian situation." We told the Sandinistas that regardless of whether the Indigenous people had contributed to the revolution, they should be able to maintain their culture, and they should have schools and health programs available to them just like anyone else in the country. We made a very strong point that they must not establish another institution like the Bureau of Indian Affairs.

The Sandinistas started a counter-antirevolutionary program. They started with the Miskito, Rama, and Suma. They didn't give them a seat at the table on the land reform commissions that would decide how the country's newly freed lands would be used and distributed. That's why our AIM delegation went down there, to make sure the Sandinistas treated the Native people of Nicaragua fairly. We demanded to visit with the Rama, Suma, and Miskito people. The Sandinistas agreed to accommodate our request and arranged travel for us.

We went up the Rio Coco in big speedboats. Cruising alongside the speedboats were young people from the Sandinista army wielding AK-47s. They sent the army to protect us because the United States had an active counterrevolutionary program in the north; the Sandinistas didn't want anything to happen to us. Wherever we went, wherever we slept, the army showed up. They were just kids, some of them only fourteen or fifteen years old, their AKs nearly as big as they were. They came on motorcycles sometimes, two or three of them per bike—boys, girls. They watched over us the whole time.

We spent several nights in Indian Territory, visiting from one village to another. It was a wonderful experience. At night, in every village, the people would build big bonfires about as tall as me. Everyone from the local area would come in to hear us speak.

These were beautiful, healthy people—perfect teeth, and not a one of them wearing glasses. They told us they had a fish soup that contained medicine which kept their eyes strong. They took us out in their canoes to show us how they fish the Rio Coco in the old way, with bows and arrows. We met their traditional leaders and their spiritual leaders; we understood each other and got along well.

Although they had no electricity or roads in the region, everywhere we went there was a church. The Samosa regime had mostly left these Natives alone, but the church, acting as a pseudogovernment, moved in and took control of the area during his reign.

The Indians had been exposed to US government propaganda that had them convinced the Sandinistas were going to take their land. They were accepting shipments of arms from the United States and aligning with the US-sponsored Contras (short for *la contrarrevolución*), who sought to overthrow the socialist revolution. The Indians, although they could speak two or three languages (native, Spanish, English), were illiterate and susceptible to the CIA's false claims. That was one of the ways Somoza kept the people of Nicaragua pacified—by refusing to provide education.

When the Sandinistas came in, they received the aid of hundreds of Cuban doctors and educators. The Cubans worked with poor people on both sides of the conflict, the Sandinistas and the counterrevolutionaries. This was a fantastic contribution to the nation, improving the literacy rate dramatically.

When we returned to Managua, we told the Sandinistas that the Indian people should be provided schools and health care, like any other citizens, and they should be protected from corporations and other entities trying to exploit them, but should otherwise be left alone on their land to live as independent Indigenous peoples. They listened to us carefully and gave their word that they would follow our guidance.

We returned home and went to work, spreading word that American Indians should support the Sandinistas. They were fighting, as we had at Wounded Knee, against a covert operation of the US government.

Of course, our efforts were countered by the CIA, whose agents followed us into those Indian villages warning the people about the American Indian Movement. They told the people that we didn't represent Indian people in America; that the BIA took good care of American Indians, gave them new homes and jobs and good educations. They spread propaganda that we were a bunch of Cuba-trained communists.

A year later, Russell and Ward Churchill ran into the Native American rights activist Suzan Shown Harjo in Washington, DC. She later reported back to the AIM leadership, through Vernon, what the two men had told her. They said they had just come from a meeting at the Pentagon with Elliott Abrams—an assistant secretary of state under Ronald Reagan who was later implicated, along with Colonel Oliver North, of having carried out the Iran-Contra affair (also known as Arms for Hostages). Harjo said she was told they were trying to get logistical support from the federal government to take "AIM warriors" into Nicaragua to join the Contras—and their Indigenous allies—in the war against the Sandinistas. The US government was supplying funds and weapons to the Contras so they could get rid of the Sandinistas. When Congress outlawed the support, the Reagan administration continued it illegally, through the National Security Council and the CIA, selling arms to Iran in order to fund the Contras. With this admission, Russell and Churchill had finally come out in the open and shown everybody exactly who they were; they were directly connected with the CIA.

Once Russell and Churchill announced their plan to fight the Sandinistas, we had the Irish Republican Army and revolutionary movements around the world calling us in Minneapolis and asking what the hell we were doing.

According to national news stories, Russell told reporters in Washington, DC, before he left for Nicaragua in December of 1985, that he and one hundred "American Indian Movement members" would help the Costa Rica–based Misurasata Indian Organization and the US-backed Contra rebels battle Nicaragua's Marxist-led government.

"If it was possible for the Marxists to justly deal with the Indian people, I would very strongly champion the Sandinista government. But you can't even consider it, because the Marxists are racists," he reportedly said. I don't know who these so-called American Indian Movement members were—CIA mercenaries in headbands, I suppose.

The Sandinistas were our great allies when we were battling at Wounded Knee. Now Russell wanted to kill them for being racist. It made no sense. If he wanted to fight racism, he should have stayed in South Dakota.

As far as I know, the government never gave them the money, but the two of them went to Nicaragua anyway. The Sandinistas heard Russell and Churchill were there and in short order had them cornered in the northern jungles, and were prepared to do them in. Russell got word to his brother Bill that they needed our help. Despite everything that had happened, I always took my role as Russell's brother seriously. Bill Means and I placed a phone call to the Ortega brothers and asked them to provide safe passage for Russell and Churchill out of the country. I am convinced that had we not done that, those two would have been killed that very day.

In 1987 Russell resigned from AIM to run for president, but he lost in the Libertarian primary to Ron Paul and returned to the Movement yet again.

Russell and I were guests of a television show hosted by Jesse Jackson in Washington, DC, on September 29, 1990. It took us five hours to tape a one-hour segment because I had to stop the taping repeatedly to correct him and make him state that he was no longer a member of the American Indian Movement. I had to correct Jesse Jackson more than once for referring to Russell as the leader of the American Indian Movement.

A couple years later, in 1992, he was back again with AIM. Until, that is, we saw him running around on the big screen in a breechclout alongside Daniel Day-Lewis, acting as if he was the last of the Mohicans. After that the phone at our Minneapolis AIM office rang off the hook. We had actual, living Mohican people calling us, condemning us, condemning Russell for what he had done. We had to ask for his resignation again.

Russell continued to align with Churchill and represent himself as an AIM leader into the 1990s. Finally, in 1993, at a meeting of AIM's founding members, we took action to ban Russell Means and Ward Churchill from the American Indian Movement for life.

We spelled out the terms of their banishment in a letter we later released to the press. It read:

> At this point we do not know for sure if you are out and out agents. What we do know for sure is that your actions clearly fall within the method of operation of Operation Cointelpro of the FBI and Operation Chaos of the CIA. If you are not on the payroll of these, or other agencies, you should be—because it is clear to us you are doing their work.
>
> In conclusion, we want to make it perfectly clear, effective September 3, 1993, both of you are expelled from the American Indian Movement. Furthermore, you are prohibited from using the name of the American Indian Movement in your phony credentials, and you are never to say that you are, or were a leader, or a member of the American Indian Movement. In your public appearances and speeches, you are not to represent the American Indian Movement. Both of you are not to use these expulsions to further disrupt or divide the Indian or non-Indian community. This decision is final.

The directive was signed by the AIM leadership at the time: Vernon Bellecourt, Herb Powless, Carol Standing Elk, Sam Drywater Jr., and myself.

This directive was not the last time we would deal with Russell Means and Ward Churchill.

In 1994, we started hearing about something called Autonomous AIM of Colorado organizing throughout the Southwest. They held meetings and invited everyone to attend. They registered people from all over the country, Indian and non-Indian, as AIM leaders of various states, regions, and cities, and called this bogus network "AIM International Confederation of Autonomous Chapters." All of a sudden all of these fake AIM chapters started popping up everywhere. If anyone sent him a donation of $10, Russell would send them a membership card to Autonomous AIM. That membership card gave them access to a free barbeque and a Sun Dance in the Black Hills.

Russell had been soliciting money from non-Indians ever since Wounded Knee. He claimed the money would go to build a culturally based school on the Pine Ridge Reservation, like the ones AIM had established in Minneapolis and St. Paul. The Pine Ridge school was never built, but that's the way he made his living for many years.

In response to their banishment from the Movement, Russell and Churchill tried to discredit the legitimate leadership of the American Indian Movement. In March of 1994 they called for a tribunal to be held against me. They found an old church in Oakland, California, to hold it in. I was supposed to go there.

The Movement held a big meeting in Minneapolis to discuss this. It was led by Elaine Salinas, Laura Waterman Wittstock, and people that had worked with me and trusted me for years. Spiritual leaders, medicine people, and elders came from all over the Great Lakes area to Minneapolis. They held a big feast. They had all their drums and pipes there.

The elders instructed me not to go to that hearing in Oakland. I was not to respond, they said. They warned that I would be lowering myself into their cesspool if I responded.

At the meeting, as I recall, Elaine Salinas got so upset. She stood up and demanded, "Who are these bastards that would dare say these things about our leaders? They have never been through the battles that we have been through to develop our schools, and job training programs, and our legal services. Who are they?"

Elaine is a beautiful person, like a little sister to me, and I never imagined she was capable of standing up like that and using such powerful language. When she called Russell and them bastards, it really got my attention.

She said to me, "You don't have to go nowhere. You stay here with us. You don't have to answer to anything. They can go to hell with their fake subpoenas."

When the meeting was over we held a ceremony, and we smoked the pipe.

I thought about it all that day and the next. I thought, you know, somebody has to go down there and educate the young people about who these guys really are; how they're all about disrupting the Movement, attempting to destroy the Movement. It bothered me so much that I went and saw this old medicine man, Archie Mosay, over at the St. Croix Reservation in Wisconsin. I went and saw him late at night.

Archie knew I was coming. He knew that this issue was still on my mind. He had been at the ceremony the previous day.

I said, "I thought I'd come and talk to you once more, because I just feel that I have to go down there. I have to talk to these people, and I have to let them know the truth."

Archie said, "Clyde, I've been taking care of people for years. I'm an old man now. The same people that I've taken care of all these years are now talking about me behind my back, working with this other AIM. If you feel that you *have* to go down there and it will bother you if you don't, then I'm going to prepare a medicine bundle for you. I want you to take your pipe, and take this medicine."

Laura Waterman Wittstock and Elaine Salinas wrote a brief history of the American Indian Movement and provided me with a bunch of other documentation on Ward Churchill and Russell Means, so that I could expose them.

We left the next day. Who went with me to Oakland? Bill Means, Russell's brother, decided to accompany me, provide me with support. I'll never forget how Bill responded when I asked him about the things his brother had been doing to discredit AIM. Bill said, "Russell is AIM's Comandante Zero." He was referring to the Sandinista commander who was one of the founders of that movement. Comandante Zero, whose real name is Eden Pastora, after years of fighting for the Sandinistas, joined the Contras and fought against the Sandinistas.

We flew into San Francisco and were met by the Los Angeles AIM leaders and a delegation from the International Indian Treaty Council. The following morning, we went to the hearing in Oakland. It was really pitiful.

First of all, they had tried to pay people to come. They sent a bus to Pine Ridge and asked people to get on there by offering them a vacation in California, if they would come and testify, and condemn

Vernon, myself, and others within the Movement. I later heard this story from several of my Oglala friends. Not *one single person* in Pine Ridge, Russell's home reservation, would get on that bus. In fact, the people on Pine Ridge reminded them that when they were suffering before Wounded Knee, when they were being raped and murdered and their houses burned down, that Russell didn't stand up; none of their warriors would stand up. It was the American Indian Movement, Clyde Bellecourt and Dennis Banks, that came down here and forced the Oglala warriors to make a stand.

At that Oakland church where the meeting was held, they had real tight security, like they were scared somebody was going to get shot. They shook everyone down with metal detectors. We got in the room and everything was in a military fashion, just like a courtroom, with the judges' chairs elevated above the rest. There were mostly white people in the audience who, I suppose, were members and leaders of Russell's Autonomous AIM. There were also a bunch of children in the room.

I refused to go along with the hearing the way it was. I wanted the whole room rearranged in a circle. I told them I had brought my tobacco with me, and my pipe, and before we'd conduct any kind of a trial we were going to have a ceremony. I started taking out my pipe and they got so scared. Many people started taking off, running for the door. They were bouncing into one another, trying to get out of there before I opened my pipe and took my medicine out. Russell and Churchill and everyone on their side ran out the door and were gone for about an hour. They would not return for that ceremony, not one of them.

There was an old man named Coyote who they maintained was one of their local spiritual leaders. He stayed with us. There was another old guy named George Martin, part of that Autonomous bunch, and he stayed with us.

I said, "You know, before the American Indian Movement does anything, we always pray and extend our hand in peace and friendship." I explained to this old man why we were doing what we were doing.

While they were gone, and with the help of George Martin and this

284 THE THUNDER BEFORE THE STORM

Coyote fellow, I rearranged the whole room, put everything in a circle. We set up an altar there in the middle of the room, and we smoked the pipe.

Russell returned, looked at the configuration of the room, and just went completely berserk. He wanted to know who the hell I thought I was.

"This is my tribunal!" he shouted.

It was no longer a people's tribunal or an Autonomous AIM tribunal. It was Russell's tribunal.

"You come down here and you try to tell me how to run my courtroom," he ranted. He acted just like Judge Fred Nichol and some of these racist judges who had tried to put him away for the rest of his life. He just went completely nuts. It kind of blew everybody's mind, even his supporters. They didn't know what do. They were all looking at me like they were embarrassed. Finally, he settled down.

So we started, and Russell had the floor. He came at me with a whole litany of charges that the Movement had done wrong. He even brought up the incident where I was shot. He attacked every detail of my history, trying to prove somehow that I was dishonest. He even claimed, for some reason, that Carter Camp shot me with a rifle.

I just kind of started laughing. "Russell," I said. "Hell, no. You were laid out drunk when I was shot. Don't you remember that? You didn't even know what the hell happened. I was shot with a .38 dumdum."

"Oh, yes, yes. That's right," he stammered.

I had to correct his charges against me to make sure everything that he was saying was correct, the dates and the times and all the facts. He rambled on for about thirty minutes, then finally sat down.

I was supposed to get up and respond. So I walked up and I stood right in front of him. I told him that he was my brother, and I felt really bad, but I had to do what I had to do. I had to let these young people in the room know who he really was.

I asked him why he even wanted to call his organization "AIM International Confederation of Autonomous Chapters." If they hated the American Indian Movement so much, and they hated the Bellecourt brothers, his own brother Bill, and other people so much, then why in the hell don't they get themselves another name, get themselves another organization?

"Call yourself Larry Flint's Brigade or something, but don't associate yourselves with the American Indian Movement," I said. "An American Indian Movement warrior doesn't resign to run for tribal government. An American Indian Movement warrior doesn't resign, as you have, to run as vice president of the United States with Larry Flynt. We don't do that. The American Indian Movement never gives up on a treaty issue, as you did when you left Yellow Thunder Camp and absconded with all these young people's funds. An American Indian Movement warrior doesn't resign to join the Libertarian Party. An American Indian Movement warrior doesn't resign and threaten to take a hundred warriors and go join the Contras in Nicaragua, or meet with the CIA. We don't do that in our Movement."

I just went on and on.

I said, "The American Indian Movement is taking on this whole mascot issue. You filed a lawsuit, Russell. Remember that? Yes, you filed a lawsuit against the Cleveland Indians. Everybody is wondering whatever happened to that. We threatened to file a lawsuit here, too, a few months ago. Do you know what they told us? We couldn't do it because you settled that lawsuit. Did you ever tell the people, Russell, that they gave you $30,000 to settle and give up?

"You became the new Judas, sold out for thirty pieces. You got $15,000 and the lawyer got the other $15,000. Did you ever tell the people how you sold out? You named all these national organizations that you said you represented, and it was agreed that they could never come back with a lawsuit, because you sold out. You made that settlement, and then you resigned.

"You resigned when you went to play that Indian stereotype in your role as Old Indian in *Natural Born Killers*. Remember that disgrace?

"We don't want you. We don't want you in the Movement. We don't want you around us. I'm sorry. You're my brother, but I have to tell you that."

Then I went and stood in front of Ward Churchill. I said, "You claim to be a Native person and yet you have been rejected from all these different tribes. You worked for *Soldier of Fortune* magazine. You were seen wearing fatigues and exiting an FBI helicopter at Pine Ridge. You went to meet with Elliott Abrams at the CIA and tried to get money and weapons to fight the Sandinistas. Who are you? Who do you really represent? Do you represent Indian people, or do you represent the FBI and Central Intelligence Agency?"

"I was at a meeting the other night," I said, "and this young lady got up. Her name is Elaine Salinas. Russell, do you know Elaine Salinas? She's just a beautiful young woman, well respected, a fine young lady." I said, "Do you know what she said the other night? She wanted to know who you *bastards* think you are. She shocked the Indian community with her language. She wanted to know who the hell these *bastards* were that would dare to do this to one of their community leaders—and she started crying. She was so embarrassed that she said something like that, but she was so upset she couldn't help it. She couldn't be here, and so I bring her question to you right now. Who are you bastards?" I pointed my finger at them: "Who are you?"

By this time, they started hitting the gavel, telling me I was out of order.

"I didn't come here to answer to any charges, plead to any charges, or listen to any charges," I continued. "But I did come down here to set the record straight. I condemn you for what you have done. Someday, you're going to have to stand before the Indian people and answer to that."

I started picking up my pipe and my bundle, putting it back in order.

I said, "I came here to talk to these young people. I want these young people to respond. I want them to be warriors. I want them to be proud to be members of the American Indian Movement. There's no such thing as the AIM International Confederation of Autonomous Chapters. There's only one Movement. There will always be only one American Indian Movement."

Bill Means and I, and the rest of our delegation, walked toward the door. Everybody in our party was just jubilant. A lot of other people walked out, too.

The following year, in 1995, Russell came out in the Disney movie *Pocahontas*. He voiced Chief Powhatan in a Hollywood film that once again depicts Indians as racial stereotypes. That became the laughingstock of Indian country. Even some of his own family thought he'd gone completely loco and wondered if he might be back on alcohol and drugs.

Russell's gone now, yet this group that he spawned is still in operation today. One of his most unfortunate legacies is the prevalence today of these non-Indian, self-proclaimed shamans. I get calls from AIM people all over the country who want to talk about all the white people that are conducting ceremonies. These people are no more Indian than Jesus Christ, but they're claiming that they were welcomed into the Movement by Autonomous AIM, and given powers by our medicine men to conduct ceremonies. These white poseurs charge $300 or more to go into a sweat lodge. You pay money, and they'll teach you how to smoke the pipe, how to smudge.

Just recently, I was in Washington, DC, where I go every year for World Peace and Prayer Day. It's usually held in September and, boy, there's a lot of Indian people that go. I decided I needed to address this issue of non-Indians selling access to our ceremonies. I told all the non-Indian people that were there, and the Indians, that if anybody charges you more than a pinch of tobacco and some sage for a ceremony, they're a phony. The Creator, I said, doesn't charge you a penny when you ask for help. I wish my brother Russell had understood that.

22. THE COFFEE CONSPIRACY

IN 2007, I BEGAN TO REALIZE that with each breath I was beating the odds. I had reached the age of average life expectancy for a Native American male of seventy-one years. I had survived being shot at point-blank range, and a prison heart attack, and was still going strong.

Looking at life expectancy alone, you can see the hard work of the Movement. In 1968, the year the Movement began, you might recall that average life expectancy for a Native American was just forty-four years, compared with sixty-four for white Americans. By 2007—although we still lagged six years behind white Americans—we were living twenty-seven years longer than before. That's a significant improvement over a relatively short period.

Although I struggled with diabetes and the nagging effects of the bullet that tore through me in 1974, I remained energetic and deeply committed.

I was more engaged in the people's struggle than ever, working in the community and serving on many boards: American Indian OIC, Indian Health Board, American Indian Movement Grand Governing Council, Federation of Native Controlled Charter Schools, International Indian Treaty Council, Heart of the Earth School, Legal Rights Center, Migizi Communications, National Coalition against Racism in Sports and Media, Little Earth of United Tribes, and Native American Community Clinic.

If you had asked me at the time, I probably would have told you my days of being arrested and jailed were behind me. And I would have been wrong.

I was at home on the south side of Minneapolis on the morning of December 24, 2012, when I received a call from Frank Paro, who works with me in the Movement. He told me that there was an Idle No More gathering, a round dance, taking place at the IDS tower, downtown at noon. Frank asked if I'd come down and support these Native women. I said of course; those are all my nieces. Of course I support them and the mission of Idle No More, a movement that was started in Canada by First Nations women seeking to restore sovereignty to Indigenous Canadians.

When I walked into that huge skylit lobby they call the Crystal Court, at the base of Minnesota's tallest building, the event was already half over. A group of Native women were dancing in order to publicize the actions of a chief up in Canada that was fasting outside Parliament.

This chief, Theresa Spence, was from the Attawapiskat First Nation near James Bay in northern Ontario, one of the poorest tribes in Canada. She had pledged that she was going to fast until she died unless the prime minister and the provincial governor met with First Nations leaders and started recognizing the treaties they'd made with Indigenous nations. When Chief Spence started her fast, word spread across the globe almost overnight. People sprang into action, holding these Idle No More gatherings in public places like big shopping malls and border crossings.

Everybody was just happy to see me when I arrived at the IDS tower. I had recently gone through a gallbladder operation, so I had a walking stick. I was seventy-six, a real elder. It was slow getting around, but I was happy to be there to observe and show my support.

I looked over in the corner of the Crystal Court and saw all these security guards gathering. Pretty soon members of the Minneapolis Police Department arrived, and I knew right away some kind of police action was about to take place.

I later found out, after obtaining transcripts of everything that happened that day, that my presence had spooked the police. A temporary commander of the downtown precinct, a Lieutenant Christianson, was in charge that day. When he identified me, he put out a call to all of the officers in his precinct and ordered them to report to the IDS tower. He even called his off-duty officers, saying that Indian people were protesting and there were going to be major arrests. Then they called their audio and video people to document the arrests, and a booking bus to process all of us. They even called the fire department, and those guys showed up in all their riot gear, you know, gas masks and everything. After they made all those calls, I saw them converging on the gathering.

We weren't harming anyone. We weren't even blocking foot traffic in the building. These women were going to sing five or six songs and it would be over. They had about three songs yet to sing.

Lieutenant Christianson walked right up to me and he said, "You have to break this up."

I said, "Why are you asking me?"

"Because you're the big chief," he said. It kind of got me upset, you know, calling me big chief.

I said, "I'm not colonized, so I don't do your work for you; you're going to have to do that yourself."

He tried to go over and speak to the dancers, but the drum was so loud nobody could hear him.

I went over and told Christianson, "Listen, just let it go. You're trying to get a confrontation going here. There's not going to be a confrontation here today because these people know what they're doing; they know they can't block entrances and all that." I said, "If there were a bunch of people caroling down here for Christmas Eve, I don't think you'd bother them."

He kind of backed up and took an aggressive posture, and I thought I better get out of there. The police were trying to get a confrontation going with me because they knew the people would back me, and it would be on.

I looked up to the second floor of the atrium and saw there was a coffee shop. I went up to Starbucks and ordered coffee. The people at the shop asked me what was going on. I told them what was happening, and everybody clapped in support. And they said, "It's good, what you're doing."

I stood on the balcony overlooking the courtyard, and pretty soon I noticed the dancers were disbursing. I took my coffee, went down the escalator, and sat on a bench in the middle of the Crystal Court. I started drinking my coffee and here they come again: it's Christianson, and he has IDS tower security guards with him.

"I thought I told you to leave," Christianson said.

"Well, you know what?" I said, "When I've finished my coffee, I'm out of here. I don't hang around the IDS tower. I haven't been in this damn building for five or six years. I'm going to go home, it's Christmas Eve."

"You're not going home," he said. "You're going downtown."

I started chuckling. I got up and walked toward the exit, and he grabbed me and repeated, "You're not going home; you're going downtown."

"What did I do?"

"You're trespassing."

"Trespassing?" I said, "There's hundreds of people here. Why me?"

Some of the dancers saw what was happening and started to gather. I told them to get out of there, go home before the police start making more trouble.

When the cops put their hands on me, I went limp, down on the floor.

They told me to roll over because they wanted to put handcuffs on me. I told them I couldn't. I just had a hip replacement, and had my gallbladder taken out. So they put the handcuffs on, and then they attached another set to them to haul me up by. They started pulling me up, and the cuff caught on my wrist, and it really hurt.

I let them know how bad it hurt, and they dropped me on the floor. They shouted at me, "Are you going to get up?"

"No," I said, "I'm not getting up. I didn't do anything."

Ten minutes later an ambulance crew arrived with a stretcher. They pushed me onto my side, put the thing under me, rolled me onto the stretcher, and cranked it up. The police asked me again if I was going to walk out, or if they had to take me in an ambulance.

I said, "If you're going to take me in an ambulance, take me to the hospital." I told them I'm diabetic.

They assigned a cop to ride inside the ambulance with me. They put an IV in my arm, and they took me downtown to the jail.

When we arrived, the cop said, "Well, you made your point; are you going to walk in or do we have to carry you?"

I said, "I'll walk in." I've been arrested enough times to know that once they get you inside the jail, and they decide you're not cooperating, they will beat the living hell out of you.

I made it inside with the help of my cane. There were about six or seven deputies there, four of them women. The head guy told me to get up against the wall; he went through my hair and pockets. He started patting me down, you know, so he could make sure I didn't have any weapons.

As he worked his way to my crotch, the cops were all joking with me, trying to get me mad.

"How come you always end up down here at Christmastime?" they asked.

I said, "I had no intentions of getting arrested. I went down to support these ladies. I didn't cause no disturbance. I didn't assault nobody. I didn't do anything. I don't know why I'm here."

I said, "I guess sometimes you got to go back to where you came from to find out where you're going."

By this time the guy got up to my crotch, and they were all laughing at my humor, and about the whole situation.

As he was feeling my crotch, I said, "You know what, deputy?"

"What?" he said gruffly.

"You should have been a Catholic priest instead of a sheriff." Oh shit, that comment cost me about six hours in a cell.

Larry Leventhal, my attorney since the Wounded Knee days, arrived. It was getting late in the afternoon, and a lot of judges were leaving for the holiday. Larry said, "I'm going to run upstairs before all the judges go and get them to release you."

So he took off and found a judge just closing up. He was the last judge remaining in the building. Larry said, "Your Honor, a very dear friend of mine just got arrested and I don't want him sitting in here over Christmas. He should be home with his family."

The judge asked, "Well, who is it?"

He said, "Clyde Bellecourt."

The judge, who knew me quite well, called his court back into session, sent his bailiff to get the city attorney, and told the city attorney he wanted me out of there immediately.

When Larry came back up they started booking me—fingerprints, pictures. They wouldn't release me until that process was over. But they stretched it out. All these new detainees were coming in, and they took them ahead of me. It was after midnight before I was finally released.

Soon thereafter we went to court, and they offered to drop the charge from a misdemeanor to a petty misdemeanor and just forget about it—no time, no fine, nothing.

I said, "Your Honor, I'm sorry, I can't do that. I didn't do anything wrong; the police are the ones that did something wrong here. I want to go to trial."

He asked me if I wanted a trial by judge or jury. I said I want a jury trial, which ended up being very expensive for the City of Minneapolis.

Even though the city attorney resisted, because she said it was too costly and time-consuming, the judge granted our request for a complete transcript of the record of everything that happened that day. In addition, the city ended up with an $800 tab for the ambulance, the cost of a jury trial, and what must have amounted to thousands of dollars in overtime and equipment costs for the massive law enforcement response to the Crystal Court.

Had they just allowed these women to carry on peacefully, there would have been no cost at all—not to mention that all the cops they had lining the Crystal Court should have been working the streets. There's all kinds of serious crime going on in the city of Minneapolis. In 2012, there were thirty-nine murders in the city; that's ten murders for every one hundred thousand residents. And these guys wasted precious manpower oppressing dancing Indian women and an elderly man with a walking cane. Honestly, the fact that the police recognized me as a resistance figure, and singled me out for prosecution, is quite a compliment, an honor.

Of course today, through the social media, photographs of me being handcuffed and arrested went all over the world. About three days after the incident my son called me, "Dad! Dad! Come over."

He showed me on his computer that down in Chiapas, Mexico, the Zapatistas—the Indigenous revolutionaries—had a big demonstration. They were in some big mall, over seven hundred of them, all dressed in black with white serapes and face masks. And they were carrying signs of me being arrested in Minneapolis.

Another week went by and I got word of another demonstration, this time from Barcelona, Spain. Four thousand people showed up at a bullfighting arena in support of the American Indian Movement and the Idle No More women. All over Indian America, from Tulsa to Michigan, South Dakota, North Dakota, these demonstrations sprung up that week after I was arrested. It really made me feel good because I was reminded how much people all over the world have been inspired by the American Indian Movement.

This was not the first time an overreaction by the Minneapolis Police Department has proven them to be among the greatest organizing tools of the American Indian Movement. We don't have to organize that much, you know, the Minneapolis police have been doing it for us for decades.

My case finally went to trial, and after hearing all the witnesses, it should have been a slam dunk in my favor. It was a six-man, six-woman jury. There was a woman on the jury from India who grew up under British colonial rule. She had very strict ideas about private property and the definition of trespassing. She was the one juror who found me guilty. And even though the court gave her all the transcripts, all the video, and all the audio, she could not be shaken from her belief that I was guilty.

Finally, the judge called a mistrial and sent it back to the city attorney's office. About ten days later a city attorney decided not to retry the whole mess.

23. NO HONOR IN RACISM

PEOPLE ASK ME ALL THE TIME why we picked Washington's National Football League team to take down first—when I say *we*, I mean the National Coalition against Racism in Sports and Media—an AIM-offshoot organization that my brother Vernon formed back in 1991, and whose work I, and many others, carry on today.

I have a very easy answer to that question: Redskins is the most horrific name in sports history. We believe that the term was used to refer to the bloody scalps taken by bounty hunters from the Indians they killed, starting in the 1500s and continuing through the 1800s. The English and Dutch found it more convenient to pay bounties on scalps, rather than the entire heads of the Pequot and Raritan people they wanted eliminated. Minnesota paid bounties on scalps after the US–Dakota War of 1862. Colonizers have consistently used "redskin" to denigrate and dehumanize the original inhabitants of this continent, so they could justify killing us off.

For centuries, we've been portrayed in books and movies as the enemy—people that had to be done away with. So maybe it's not surprising to see that kind of frontier mentality still existing in America today, where it's perfectly acceptable to mock Indigenous cultures, and particularly in professional sports, where fans come to the games wearing Mohawk haircuts, chicken feathers in their hair, and caricature images like Chief Wahoo, mascot of the Cleveland Indians baseball team. Fans are coming to games with their tomahawks, and performing mass rituals like the "tomahawk chop," where they look like Nazis saluting the Führer. We Indians know tomahawks as the weapon whites utilized to scalp our innocent people.

The history books used in Minnesota and across the United States do not tell the true story of this land. The books still push our story aside, hide it so the white children don't have to feel bad, but what about the Indian kids? In the 1960s, when AIM was starting, textbooks portrayed Indians as subhuman. There used to be a history text widely used here called *Minnesota: Star of the North*, by Antoinette Elizabeth Ford and Neoma Johnson, published in 1961. In their chapter on the US–Dakota War, they called the Indian people "savage," "lazy," "thieving," and "heathen." There was another book I was assigned in school which showed an Indian man holding a white woman by the throat, and a little girl was holding her leg and crying, and a farmer laying in a field with arrows in his back, and a barn burning in the background.

If the history books told it right, they would show that the real savages were the European settlers, the over two hundred thousand white squatters that moved onto Little Crow's land after the Dakota were forced to sign the treaties of 1851 and 1858. They came in and started to push the Dakota people around, taking even the tiny bit of land that was supposed to be their reservation and failing to deliver treaty payments, so that Dakota people were starving. In 1862 the young warriors, in an act of desperation, rose up against the white settlers to try and force them off the land. Some six hundred settlers and soldiers were killed. The number of Dakota casualties remains unknown. After the three-week conflict ended with the defeat of the Dakota, the United States took revenge on the entire Dakota nation. Minnesota governor Alexander Ramsey told the legislature, "The Sioux Indians of Minnesota must be exterminated or driven forever beyond the borders of the state." And then the soldiers tried to make that happen.

Many of the Dakota who had been fighting fled west and to Canada. Those who stayed and surrendered at Camp Release suffered terribly. The men were tricked into giving up their weapons, then taken off to prison camps at Mankato and Davenport, Iowa, and given hasty trials. Three hundred eight were condemned to death. Abraham Lincoln approved the hanging of thirty-eight Dakota men on December 26, 1862. Lincoln signed their death warrants even though he knew they hadn't been given fair trials.

And what happened to the women, children, and elders? In November, they were marched through all these little white, Christian, German towns, and settlers came out in droves to express their hatred for the Dakota. Some stood on rooftops and poured hot water on them as they marched past. Others stoned them. In Henderson a white woman came out of the crowd, grabbed a little baby right out of an Indian woman's arms, and smashed its head against a wall, murdering that baby. They held these poor people in a concentration camp on the swampy Mississippi River bottoms beneath Fort Snelling. Close to three hundred people, most of them children, died of diseases that winter.

The next summer, a settler and his son shot at two Dakota men who were picking berries and killed one of them. It was legal—encouraged—within the state of Minnesota to kill Dakota people in those days. They didn't even know it was Little Crow, but still, they desecrated his body. They scalped him, then put him on display down in Hutchinson. People came and spat on him, clubbed him, put firecrackers in his nose and blew his nose off. After authorities discovered that the murdered Indian was Little Crow, the desecration continued. The sheriff who had his scalp turned it in for a $25 bounty, and the men who shot him later got $500. Two different doctors took possession of his skull and the bones of one arm, and they held on to them as trophies. Later on, the doctors turned them over to the State of Minnesota, which put the remains on display in the state capitol in St. Paul until 1915.

When the American Indian Movement formed in July 1968, Little Crow's remains were still locked in the collections of the Minnesota Historical Society. David Beaulieu, a young man from my reservation, was working there in 1969–70 while he was going to college. He says the staff there didn't think he was an Indian because of his light complexion. One day they told him to bring a box that had been nailed shut out of the storage area to the photography area. They had him open it, and he was shocked at what he saw. Little Crow's grandson had been asking to have his grandfather's remains returned to the family since 1962, and now he wanted proof that they were still there. A man from Flandreau had come to take photos. David got really upset when he saw what was in that box, and he started doing research on the whole story. He made copies of everything he found, and he gave us copies, so we were learning this history and making members of our community aware of it at the same time. One of AIM's goals was to force the return of our prayer bundles, human remains, and drums that had been confiscated in earlier days and were held in museums.

David was talking about these remains, asking questions about them in his history class, and the people at the historical society didn't like it. A reporter from one of the TV stations got interested in the story. David finally went into the office of the historical society's director and told him he should stop dragging his feet. "WCCO is interested in doing a story, and I don't think you want AIM demonstrating on the capitol mall." Right after that, they found a way to return Little Crow's remains to his grandson.

Dennis and I pored through the materials David gave us, piecing together for ourselves a timeline and a narrative of the genocide upon which Minnesota was founded. It was a new and different story. We wanted this story told right, finally. We wanted *Minnesota: Star of the North* taken out of the curriculum. We went to the state education department and demanded they remove this racist book. We did not receive a warm reception. They said that each school district would make its own decision on the book. Minneapolis schools had dropped it in 1968, but other schools didn't. So we took our fight into the public sphere, taking advantage of every opportunity to talk about the book and the resulting miseducation of our children.

On college campuses across the United States we talked about how this book, and others like it, treated us. That's why we were targeted for so much hatred, and why there was so much ignorance about Indian people. They had this George Armstrong Custer mentality that the only good Indian is a dead Indian. And stories like this, taught all over the country to the people who are now the ones in power, are why we still have all the racism in sports and in the media—because great numbers of people still don't know the truth.

It turns out we didn't need to win that fight to get rid of the book, because the students did it for themselves. In the Robbinsdale school district, on the north side of Minneapolis, some students had heard of our campaign against *Minnesota: Star of the North*. These white students called on every student who had a copy to show up after school for a book burning. Their dramatic action caused tension statewide. Everybody heard about it and started debating it.

Finally, Robbinsdale quit using it, and the other school districts in Minnesota followed. We in the Movement were so pleased by the proactive stance taken by these students to get rid of that awful textbook. The only problem is, too many schools just stopped teaching Indian history. So instead of having students engage in a perverted discussion, there was no discussion at all.

I can still feel the pain of being an Indian child in a Eurocentric classroom. I felt very bad, and I rejected education. I remember the first day I went to school. I was six years old, in the first grade. I walked in and there was a picture of a white guy on the wall. By white I mean totally white, ghostly white: white hair, with powder on his face and rouge on his checks. He had on a little ruffled shirt, black knickers to his knees, white silk stockings like panty hose, and high-heeled shoes with shiny buckles on them.

The teacher said, "This is George Washington. He's the father of our country."

The classroom also had an American flag hanging on the wall. Every morning we'd put our hands on our hearts, as instructed, and pledge allegiance to the United States of America. That's the way we Indian kids were educated. I wondered why my grandfather, one of the principal chiefs of the White Earth Anishinaabe Nation, didn't look anything like old boy George. Instead of education providing clarity, it caused confusion.

As the grades came and went, the confusion about world history just compounded. They taught us, a classroom full of Native children, about Christopher Columbus and Ponce de León and all those explorers that came here and, we were told, "discovered" America. I always wondered how they could discover America when we were here all along. From a very early age I wondered why they didn't teach us anything about us.

One day I finally mustered the courage to ask my teacher: "What about Indians? Why don't we learn about our people?"

"Oh, forget about that. That's in the past," I was scolded. Since those days I've heard the same misguided sentiments thousands of times.

When the American Indian Movement formed, I started telling people that we had to go back to our past, and that if we ever forget about our past, we will never have a future. I still say that today because we still get that question: people wonder how come Native people don't become more involved with the American democratic system. I respond to that question with one of my own: What has American democracy done for us? It has never benefited us.

We have to start teaching our young Native people that we're a strong civilization that practiced our own form of democracy. When our young people show up in the classroom, we've got to help them understand where they come from and make them feel good about themselves.

As I'm sitting here talking to you, there's a major archaeological dig going on in Teotihuacán, Mexico. They've found a city down there where upwards of one hundred thousand people lived in modern metropolises, where the residents had running water. They found a pyramid down there built at the time of the Roman Empire that's three times larger than the pyramids along the Nile River. European Americans talk about us as uncivilized people. But they stole everything we had, and because of their guilty feelings, they depict us as subhuman savages.

I didn't start learning this history until I was in Stillwater State Prison. I was in my late twenties before I started learning the truth. They always say in America that the truth will set you free. But I guess they don't want Indian people to be free yet, because they're still hiding the truth. That's where many of our children are today, still lost.

The very fact that we have months set aside for different ethnic groups is an indictment against the whole educational system. They set aside one month to study Indian people, one month to study Blacks, and one month to study Hispanics. They minimize everyone's contributions and cultures. They have them bring out their ethnic foods, and their arts and crafts, and put pictures up of Emiliano Zapata or Martin Luther King or Chief Joseph. Soon they'll have to make a month for the Hmong community, then another for the Somalis, because they've become very numerous in Minnesota.

Why the hell don't they just throw all that junk out the door and start celebrating Indian culture year around, Black culture year around, Hispanic culture year around? If we did that, young people would start feeling good about who they are.

In our Indian schools today we're teaching kids that they're going to be Indian for the rest of their lives. No matter what kind of education they have, when they get up in the morning, jump out of bed, and look in the mirror, they're still going to be Indian. They had better feel good about it. We tell them, "We love you, and want you to stay in school." We hope they will love themselves and their heritage for the rest of their lives.

I remember being a little boy: When people played cowboys and Indians, nobody wanted to be an Indian. Cowboys were glorified, even in our own communities. Indian kids grow up seeing their cultures disrespected in sports and media, and this contributes to low self-esteem and psychological problems and subjects them to bullying in school—non-Indian children take these societal messages and turn them into violence.

The Black community has been successful in removing derogatory images from teams and media across America. You know, Little Black Sambo, and the use of blackface. The same way with the Hispanic community. They went after racial stereotypes in media, where they were always shown as lazy, laying under some cactus with a sombrero over their face. But somehow it is still acceptable, in 2016, to portray Native people as stereotypes. We knew when we started this campaign that the problem went much deeper than just getting rid of mascots; we'd have to go after the curricula, as well, and force the schools to portray Native people as human beings.

We figured if we could get the well-known teams to change their racist names and mascots, that would push communities across America to take on this issue. Using this strategy, we have had a great deal of success changing team names in collegiate and high school sports.

In 2012, the University of North Dakota dropped the use of "Fighting Sioux" and its Indianhead logo. That major victory came on the heels of a National Collegiate Athletic Association decision to ban racist mascots. There have been over two thousand racist team names in high schools, colleges, and universities that have been changed since we began our fight over forty years ago to transform the perception of Native people in America. We haven't been able to crack the professional teams yet, but I think we're on our way.

We've seen lots of people come to our aid after their awareness was raised by our efforts. That was well demonstrated in Minneapolis on November 23, 2014, when the Washington football team came to town to play the Minnesota Vikings. Thousands of concerned community members from every walk of life showed up—senators, congressional leaders, and celebrities joined with college students, high school groups, and concerned men, women, and children of every race, economic status, and religion. They came out in force against the use of the R-word by the NFL.

When we saw the success of what we were able to do here the last time the Washington football team played in Minneapolis, we decided we had to help other cities whose professional teams play under racist names. We are helping local communities take down the Kansas City Chiefs, Atlanta Braves, and Cleveland Indians.

We know that we've been successful because the Washington team's owner, Dan Snyder, has been organizing busloads of tribal members to attend his games, taking care of all expenses, getting them choice seats, and trying to get them to speak out against their own people. At the same time we have resolutions from those tribes that he's calling in for support; they have taken up positions against the Washington team as well. For instance, the Standing Rock Sioux Tribe in North and South Dakota—Snyder brought two busloads of tribal members to Minneapolis when his team played the Vikings.

We were very concerned about that, because if it hadn't been for Standing Rock taking a strong position against the Fighting Sioux, that name would have continued. The NCAA said that if the two Sioux tribes in North Dakota supported the use of the Fighting Sioux, UND would be able to continue using the name—but Standing Rock stood firm.

Snyder brought the tribal chair and vice-chair of the Navajo nation, the largest tribe in America, to Phoenix for the 2014 game his team played against the Cardinals. Still, we have a resolution from the Great Navajo Nation, whose council voted 9 to 2 to support changing the mascot. This shows just how desperate Snyder is.

We've done our historical background checks on the roots of this racist organization. George Preston Marshall, an earlier owner of the Washington franchise, was deeply connected to right-wing forces in America. His team was the last in the NFL to hire nonwhite players. The American Nazi Party marched in support of Marshall outside RFK Stadium in 1961 when the federal government attempted to force the team to hire Black players, which they finally did later that year. The Department of the Interior, you see, owned the land under the team's new stadium. The federal government threatened to rescind the lease if the team didn't desegregate. Finally, Marshall gave in—the team selected their first African American player, running back Ernie Davis, in the 1961 draft—but he never changed his racist views.

On his deathbed, Marshall rewrote his will so that not a penny of his money would go to anyone that supported integration. That's the legacy Dan Snyder and his family are extending today. It's confounding to me that a member of an ethnic group that lost six million innocent people to the Nazis would not sympathize with the genocide of Native American people.

Our campaign got some help from the US Patent and Trademark Office in the summer of 2014. That agency revoked the team's trademark and confirmed that the five American Indians who brought the suit proved "the term 'Redskins' was disparaging of Native Americans, when used in relation to professional football services. . . . Federal trademark law does not permit registration of trademarks that 'may disparage' individuals or groups or 'bring them into contempt or disrepute.'"

So momentum has been building; we know we're hurting Snyder in the pocketbook. The NFL is a business, and when we impact their bottom line, they start to pay attention. Over the past few years sales of Washington team gear has shrunk almost 50 percent. That represents millions of dollars lost.

And now we're hitting him from another angle: the National Indian Gaming Association, which represents over five hundred tribal casinos, has proposed a ban on the sale of all NFL-related products within its members' retail outlets. So there's a lot of pressure being exerted.

Another amazing thing that's happening is many major sports announcers, people like Tony Dungy, Keith Olbermann, and Phil Simms, are now speaking out against Snyder's team and refusing to use the team's name during broadcasts. Newspapers across America are refusing to use the Washington team's name or show their logo.

The beautiful thing I see coming from all of this is that we're rewriting history. Millions of people are starting to find out the truth. I was recently interviewed on local television with Joey Browner—a former Vikings safety who is now part of the Movement. Mike Morris, the host (who used to be the long snapper for the Vikings), asked me where the Washington team got its name. I gave him a fifteen-minute response; he was so captivated he couldn't even blink. He was totally stunned. He said this was the first time he'd heard the story. The interview was picked up by ESPN, and about five days later just about every sportswriter in America was talking about the name change. So that's strong evidence our efforts are working.

Our determination has encouraged some prominent former professional athletes to speak out against racism in sports and media. Joey Browner was a six-time Pro Bowl safety for the Minnesota Vikings—one of the most dominant players ever to man the position.

He was a hero to me when he played (1983–91). I didn't know he had Indian blood until after I met him several years ago at a Midewiwin ceremony up in northern Wisconsin. I got a chance to shake his hand and tell him how much I admire him. I was surprised to learn that he is an Indigenous person—he refuses to use the word "Indian" to describe himself. He says, "I'm indigenous to the Western Hemisphere." When he was playing football, fans and media assumed he was black. He knew how much harder it would be for him to succeed in the NFL if he were to challenge that assumption and assert his actual Native heritage—Polynesian and Cherokee on his mother's side, and Seminole and Blackfeet on his father's side.

Joey has become a tremendous spokesman. He plays a very prominent role, traveling across the country with me, speaking to crowds with great eloquence and intellect. He is always coming up with angles and ideas I had never considered.

Everywhere we go, people know who Joey Browner is. On a recent trip to Washington, DC, this young police officer approached him. He knew about Joey's whole career and told him how much respect he has for him. The officer asked to take a picture with him. When the young officer told his chief who Joey was, the chief asked for pictures, too. This happens everywhere we go, from tiny tribal communities to major metropolitan areas.

We have another former athlete working with the National Coalition against Racism in Sports and Media. He is one of the greatest players in the history of hockey, and he is Anishinaabe, from Warroad, Minnesota—a small town on the Canadian border. I'm talking about Henry Boucha, an Olympian and silver medalist in the 1972 Sapporo games. He also played in the National Hockey League from 1971 to 1977.

Henry lost one of his eyes in a hockey game against the Boston Bruins in 1975 when an opposing player jabbed him in the face with his stick. This was at a time when most NHL players didn't wear helmets. Henry played with nothing on his head but a headband. Henry continued to play after that horrible injury and was able to return to the NHL, but never really returned to top form.

We're really lucky to have athletes like Joey Browner and Henry Boucha on our team. Professional athletes often find it impossible to speak out. They're getting paid millions of dollars, but in so doing give up a lot of their rights. As much as they'd love to speak up, they have to honor their contracts. Once they're retired, like Joey and Henry, we see them coming out to support us.

It takes a lot of education to get people to take a stand. We're not against football, basketball, or baseball. Being called warriors and braves, that's actually a nice thing. It's the behavior you see in the stands that's generated from those kinds of team names that's the real problem. You see fans of these teams, when they get a little behind in a game, they'll start hollering, "Scalp those f-ing Vikings."

I was walking at the head of the 2014 march opposing the Washington team's visit to Minneapolis. I went alongside a young man named Jerry McAfee; he's a Black minister here in Minneapolis, a longtime civil rights activist, and the pastor at New Salem Missionary Baptist Church on the north side. He just kept grabbing my arm and squeezing it, saying, "Man, this is unbelievable." We were up front looking back at all the people behind us. He said, "I've never seen anything like this in my life."

I was just thinking, "Man, we finally did it; we finally did it."

I had predicted we would get five thousand people to come out and march with us. And we topped that. Some estimates from newsmen and an assistant police chief said we had as many as seven thousand protesters out there.

As important as the powerful showing of grassroots support was that they represented a wider spectrum of support from both Indians and non-Indians than we had ever seen before. There were human rights organizations from across the continent: the National Congress of American Indians, National Indian Gaming Association, NAACP,

Protesting the Washington football team, 2014. *Jose Lopez,* The Corsair *(Santa Monica)*

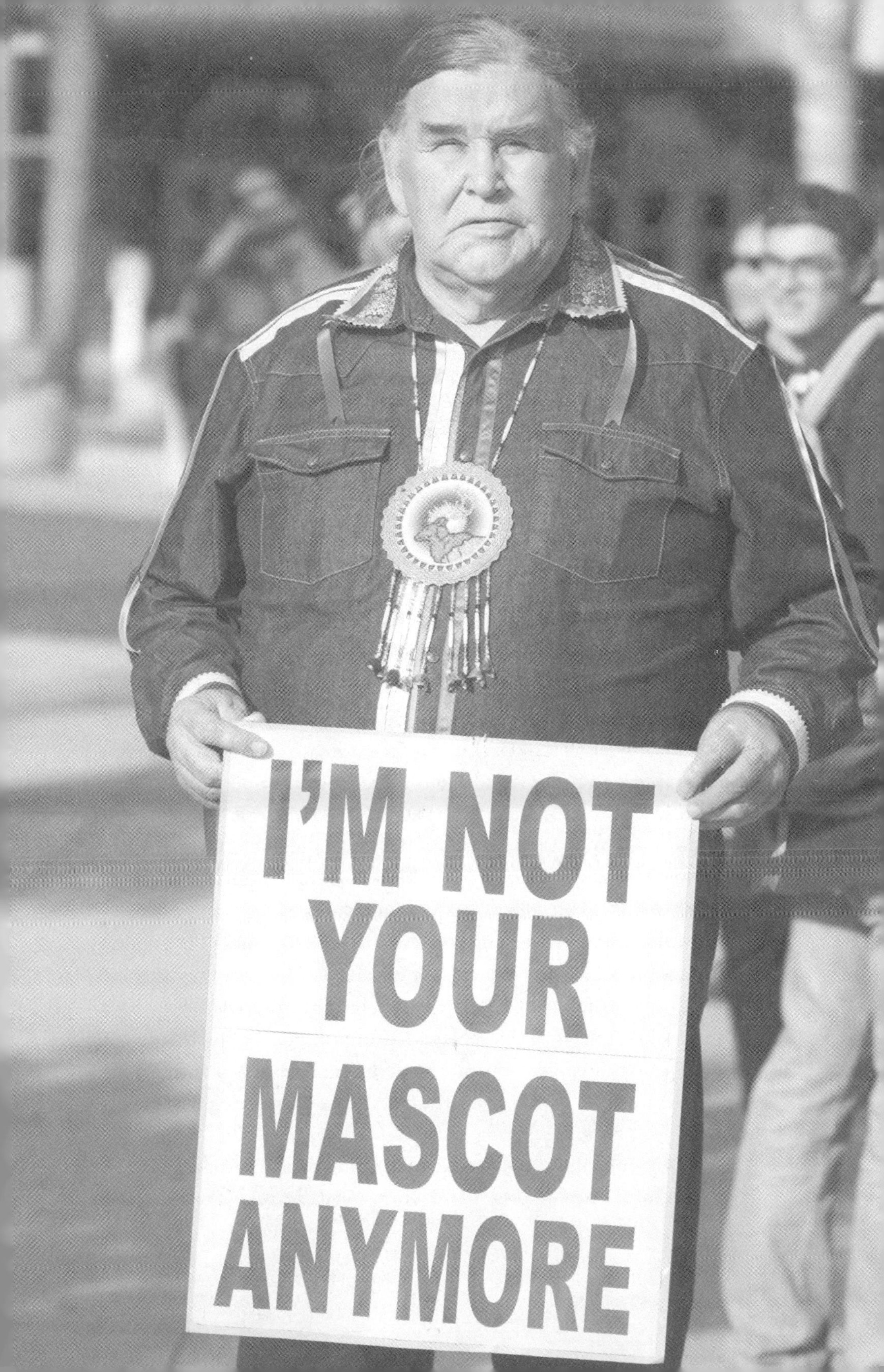
I'M NOT
YOUR
MASCOT
ANYMORE

Idle No More, Honor the Earth, Not Your Mascot, International Indian Treaty Council, and dozens more. Innumerable churches, temples, synagogues, and mosques participated.

I got up to the stage and looked out at that massive crowd. I took the microphone and, as I always have, spoke from the heart. I said, "There's no other place in the world I'd rather be but right here with you."

The feeling was unbelievable. I saw people with smiles on their faces, waving and hollering. I saw grandmas bringing their new grandsons, granddaughters, still in diapers. Some families brought little kids who were just learning how to do the hoop dance; they wanted to perform to show people they were there supporting the cause. I felt so good I didn't know what to say. I kind of locked up, so I said the only thing that came to mind, and that was to express my gratitude for what I was seeing.

I was also overjoyed with all the tribal leadership and other political figures who showed up. Jesse Ventura, the ex-governor of Minnesota, was all smiles. He patted me on the back and hugged me. Jesse just wanted everybody to know that he was there, that he supported us. The local NAACP leadership was present, and longtime activists from the Black community, like Jerry McAfee and Spike Moss, were in the crowd. The actor and activist Dick Gregory came. Young people that I never even met before asked if they could say a few words to the crowd, and so they did. That's what this movement is all about, engaging people of all colors and from all walks of life.

I saw many people wearing homemade AIM T-shirts. They didn't have access to AIM gear where they were from, but they wanted everyone to know they felt like they were a part of the Movement.

As I looked out over that crowd I thought, you know, this is the result of a forty-five-year history of activism and organizing. I never thought this day would come, but it's here. Our people are finally together.

One morning, about two weeks before the protest, I had an unbelievable dream: I was at a big march composed entirely of women and children. We stopped in a park, and I sat down at a picnic table. All these little kids were coming up and shaking hands, taking pictures with me. Everybody was happy. It was a beautiful, sunny day. Some guy came up to me and pulled my arm. I could see right through his body to the trees and grass behind him.

He said, "Hey, there's a couple guys up there in the bleachers who want to talk to you."

I looked up in the bleachers and saw my brother Vernon sitting next to Floyd Red Crow Westerman. In life, Floyd was a very well-known singer, probably best known for his song "BIA I'm Not Your Indian Anymore." He and Vern died precisely two months apart in 2007—Vern was seventy-five, and Floyd seventy-one. They were both very prominent in forming the National Coalition against Racism in Sports and Media three decades earlier. In my dream they were both smiling and waving at me. They were standing on some bleachers, and I could see the benches right through their bodies. I was so happy to see them. I started walking up there—I heard Peggy calling out from the living room of our home, "Sundance is here! Sundance is here!" Her shouts woke me up just before I reached Vern and Floyd.

I got out of bed and greeted my son Wolf, my granddaughter Sundance, and my daughter-in-law Jennifer.

I was kind of stunned from the dream. It was so vivid and reminded me how much I miss my brother and my old friend. Peggy thought I was sick.

"You wouldn't believe what just happened to me," I said.

She said, "Please, tell me about it."

I told her all about the dream.

She said, "You know what that means?"

"No, tell me." I knew what it meant, but I wanted to hear her interpretation.

She said, "It means you're going to put the women and the children up front when Washington comes to town. Your work is not about the American Indian Movement anymore, it's about the people. It's about the women and children."

I said, "I agree. That's exactly what's going to happen. The women and children will march up front at the rally."

I commissioned this big banner for the women and children to carry at the head of the march. It said: "We honor women and children, our great leaders of tomorrow." And I announced at the beginning of the march that this is the way it's going to be; from now on, we're going to put our women and our children up front. This lesson resonates far beyond our community. In the NFL earlier that year they had Baltimore Ravens running back Ray Rice knocking his fiancée unconscious in an elevator, and Minnesota Vikings running back Adrian Peterson beating his son bloody with a switch. Both situations were handled badly by the league and cast a spotlight on the problem of domestic abuse in America.

After our successful march here, I brought that banner with me to San Francisco, where the Washington team was playing next. When the marchers saw the beautiful banner, many people started arguing about who would march with it.

I said, "I want the women and children to carry it up front."

I told them the vision Vernon and Floyd had sent. I told them that I knew my brother was very pleased and honored that we were carrying on his work.

Vernon didn't get a lot of attention for his enormous efforts. He didn't write any books or make any documentaries, but during Wounded Knee and after he traveled all over the world, attracting support for the Movement. He went to foreign countries, addressed the World Council of Churches—he didn't shy away from anything. He went down to Central America and met with the Sandinista leaders—the Ortega brothers—in Nicaragua; he met with Fidel Castro in Cuba, Muammar Gaddafi in Libya, and he went and met with Yasser Arafat in Palestine, to talk about the plight of the American Indian. He spread word all over the world about who we are and what the Movement is all about. I can't even explain how much I miss him.

I was driving down the road about two weeks after he passed, and I needed to know something right away, and so I called Vernon. It hit me very hard; he's gone. But his phone was still active. I heard his voice: "Sorry I can't be here right now but leave a message and I'll call you back as soon as possible." I pulled over on the side of the road and started crying, you know.

Vernon was so smart, like an encyclopedia. Anybody could call him, I don't care what the issue, what the question—he always had the right answer—could tell you the right course of action. If you didn't do what he suggested and something went wrong, he would always say, "I told you so."

I know Vernon is very happy today knowing how his efforts have led to so many people coming together in a spirit of cooperation. We're working very closely today with the Tribal Chairmen's Association, the National Congress of the American Indian, the national Indian education community, and the NAACP. We have every major civil and human rights organization behind us today. They want to be part of this effort to get rid of racism in sports and media.

One of the things people still don't understand is that we continue to be a very spiritual movement. Before every one of our meetings that we had leading up to this major demonstration, we started out with a prayer, and with a drum, and honor songs. We asked the Creator to sit with us, plan with us, stand with us, walk with us, and guide us in everything that we do.

Dick Gregory said it very clearly at the rally outside TCF Bank Stadium. He said, "They might have all the weapons, but they don't have one thing the Indian people have." He pointed up to the sky. He said, "They have the Creator, and the Creator is watching over us."

I think sooner than later even the corporate sponsors are going to stand with us. They're going to withdraw their money from the NFL and take a stand against racist team names. They're going to come out publicly, as they did when the Adrian Peterson child abuse case happened, and take a stand. The public is starting to realize, plain and simple, this is racism.

Fifty Democratic senators signed a letter and sent it to NFL commissioner Roger Goodell about six months before the Minneapolis demonstration. The letter said, "The N.F.L. can no longer ignore this and perpetuate the use of this name as anything but what it is: a racial slur. . . . The Washington, D.C., football team is on the wrong side of history."

The National Football League has said repeatedly, in response to this and other petitions, that the only person who can change the name of the Washington team is their owner. Dan Snyder, unfortunately, has said repeatedly that he will never do so. But we have received encouraging messages through the NFL's back channels.

Lester Bagley, the Minnesota Vikings' executive vice president who oversees the team's public relations, let us know that we are going to prevail. There's no doubt in his mind, he said, that we're going to win this thing. And it's going to be a major historic shift; it's going to affect professional and amateur teams all over America. And it's going to allow new generations of Americans to finally see Native people as who we are: human beings.

24. NEEGAWNWAYWIDUNG

I GET A CHARGE WHEN I READ BOOKS written about the Movement: *In the Spirit of Crazy Horse* by Peter Matthiessen; *Like a Hurricane: The Indian Movement from Alcatraz to Wounded Knee* by Paul Chaat Smith and Robert Allen Warrior; and *Crossbloods* by Gerald Vizenor. These writers, and many others, like to think the American Indian Movement rolled over after 1973, that Wounded Knee was our final act, after which AIM ceased to exist. I'd like to take them on a tour of Minneapolis and St. Paul some day and show them all the beautiful things we've developed here since Wounded Knee.

Most of these authors forget the real purpose AIM formed in the first place. Although we were prepared to give our lives for our people, AIM wasn't just a bunch of militants walking around with rifles. We founded AIM in order to upgrade the conditions of Indian people, their health, education, and welfare. Opening schools and clinics, for instance, were natural extensions of the American Indian Movement's core values.

I wanted to mention many more events than there is room for here. But I tried to at least highlight those actions that have been most important to the renewal of Indian life, brought about by the sacrifices of thousands of AIM supporters, most of them anonymous. It's a little embarrassing to receive the kind of attention I've gotten for AIM's achievements when so many others deserve credit as well.

People always ask me why I haven't appointed the next AIM leader to take my place when I'm gone. I have heard a lot of criticism about that. I tell people it's not up to me who steps into the leadership after I go home. I have helped to create the conditions necessary for young people to develop leadership skills. The current generation has all sorts of advantages I never had, the greatest of which is access to their culture and ceremonies. It is up to the people to decide who to follow, not up to me.

We have come a very long way, but the struggle continues.

Every day of the week AIM is participating in some way in the battle against racism. The AIM Patrol is still alive. Our job training program is the top in the nation. Our housing is secure. Economic development is taking place. We have the largest Indian Chamber of Commerce in North America, right here in Minneapolis. We have health facilities that tend to the specific needs of Native people. Over three hundred Indian businesses that never existed prior to the Movement forming in 1968 are going today. Casinos are thriving here and in many places where Native people exercise their sovereignty.

Our legacy can also be seen in the string of accomplishments on the Pine Ridge Reservation following Wounded Knee. They have the Porcupine Clinic, the brainchild of some of the women of the American Indian Movement. They did this to eliminate the fears people had of going to the Indian Health Service hospital.

KILI Radio, the voice of the Lakota Nation, was established in 1983 and is celebrating its thirty-second year. A lot of the problems that happened on Pine Ridge happened because of lack of communication.

In the schools, the Native children are now learning Lakota, and singing Lakota flag songs to start each day.

Most importantly, in the wake of Wounded Knee, there has been an explosion in the number of traditional ceremonies. On the Pine Ridge Reservation today they have dozens of different Sun Dances.

None of this would have occurred had the traditional women of Pine Ridge not taken a stand. When Gladys Bissonette, the Oglala Sioux civil rights leader, called and asked AIM to come defend the women and children on Pine Ridge, a great alliance was born that resulted in all of these positive changes. I'll never forget a statement Gladys made at Wounded Knee in 1973. "I lived here seventy-seven years," she said. "This whole reservation was in total darkness and somewhere these young men started the American Indian Movement, and they came to our reservation, and they turned that light on inside, and it's getting bigger now—now we can see things."

From day one AIM took a position that the land was sacred, and we were going to do everything in our power to protect what little we had left. We made a commitment to regain the natural resources that had been stolen from us. It was a solemn commitment where we said if it was necessary, we would lay down our lives for what we believed. *Many times* we faced guns. We faced the threat of death. But that never turned us away from our goal of total self-determination; that the Indigenous people of this continent would once again control our own destiny.

It has been a tremendous fifty-year campaign during which AIM inspired unbelievable change. One of the people that deserves the most credit is my wife, Peggy. We have one of a few marriages that survived the Movement. Most families have broken up. It's been very difficult. I've spent a lot of time away. We made tremendous sacrifices. She made tremendous sacrifices.

We just celebrated our fifty-second wedding anniversary. That's quite a milestone. I have such gratitude for Peggy. I would not have been able to maintain my sanity with all the stress we were under. I would never have recovered from the alcohol and drugs. I would not have been able to resist thoughts of suicide, had I not had such a beautiful wife standing by me. Peggy is one of the most respected Indian women in America. I'm very fortunate to have such a relationship.

I'm also very fortunate to have met a young man by the name of Eddie Benton-Banai. Without Eddie, the American Indian Movement would not have arisen from within solitary confinement at Stillwater State Prison. AIM started when this young traditionalist, young spiritual person, came to visit me and told me he believed in me. From that day forth, I've been with the Movement.

My children are very proud of me, and that makes me feel good. My grandchildren are proud. There's hardly a day goes by without a nephew or niece telling me they read my name or saw my picture somewhere. That all means a lot.

The most important work I've done has been encouraging parents to give their kids Indian names, because that goes counter to the genocidal policies of the United States government which sought to terminate us and force us to live like them.

They put our children in boarding schools and took their names away. They called them Kyle and Joseph and Mark and Luke and John, all these biblical names. They called me Clyde!

One day recently I held a meeting to get our people organized and ready to protest the Washington football team that was coming to Minneapolis. I asked the attendees to introduce themselves, and, to my complete surprise, every Indian person in the room introduced themselves by their Indian name. I couldn't believe what I was hearing; I was totally blown away.

I sat in that meeting looking into the faces of the children, and at the same time looking back through four decades, to when nobody had an Indian name. I was one of the first to be given that since the times when our people were forced to take our culture and spirituality underground. What a beautiful feeling to see Indian people coming back to themselves, and knowing I played a small part in that.

I want to thank Eddie for bestowing upon me a powerful name, a name that I've carried with me since 1973, when the medicine man Jack Miskwaudeis presented me with an eagle feather and recognized me as a war chief. He said I earned the honor because I had gone into another nation's territory, and defended their women and children against the tyranny of the United States government. All these years later I am still humbled to recall that ceremony in the woods near Round Lake, Wisconsin.

The name Eddie bestowed upon me I will carry with pride the rest of my life and into the spirit world. That name is Neegawnwaywidung. I am The Thunder Before the Storm.

Neegawnwaywidung. *Courtesy AIM Interpretive Center*

ACKNOWLEDGMENTS

Peggy Bellecourt, Susan Bellecourt, the Bellecourt family, Eddie Benton-Banai (Bawdwaywidun), Bill Means, Dick Bancroft, Diane Gorney, Norma Renville, Melvin Lee Houston, Michael Davis, David Larsen, Elaine Salinas, Joey Browner, Lydia Caros, Larry Leventhal, Ham Muus, Father Frank Kenney, Ann Regan, Jack Swanson, Eric Byrd, Shannon Pennefeather, Malcolm Lurie, Jose Perez, Sally Hunter, Keith Ellison, Frank Paro, Douglas Hall, Leonard Crow Dog, Phillip Deere, Gladys Bissonette, Lenny Foster, James Donahue, and Bill Kunstler.

INDEX

Page numbers in *italics* indicate illustrations.

ment misconduct during, 210–12; government presentation, 206–7; judge, 201, 202, 206, 209–10, 211, 212; Moves Camp discredited, 208–9, 210; number and locations of, 201–2
Federal Water Power (1924), 93
firewater, 81
"First Encounters: Spanish Exploration in the Caribbean and the United States, 1492–1570" (exhibit at Science Museum of Minnesota, St. Paul), 90
fishing, 18
Flannigan, Del, 31
Flannigan, Glen, 31
Flynn, Patrick, 210–11
Fonda, Jane, 147, 237
Fools Crow, Frank: make-a-relative ceremony, 265; and Sun Dance, 101, 232; and Wounded Knee occupation, 142–43, 146, 148–50; at Wounded Knee trials, 206, 211
Ford, Antoinette Elizabeth, 297–98, 300–301
Fort Laramie Treaty (1868), 82, 138, 201, 202, 206, 270
Fort Lawton takeover, 86, 92–93
Fortunate Eagle, Adam, 82–84
foster care in Hennepin County, MN, 105, 108
Frontline documentary, 128

Ghost Dance shirt, 161
Gildersleeve, Agnes, 143
Gildersleeve, Clive, 143–44
Goodsky, Harold, 46
GOONS (Guardians of the Oglala Nation), 127–28, 133–34, 135, 162
Gordon, NE, abduction and murder in, 129–30
Graham, John, 266
"Grandmother AIM," 273
Great Anishinaabe Migration, 37
Great Sioux Nation, 202–3
Green, Helen, 75–76
Green Grass Sun Dance: and addic-

tions, 231–32, 236; vision, 233–35; White Buffalo Calf Pipe ceremony, 232
Gregory, Dick, 147, 206, 310, 314
Grim Reapers, 221–23

Haldeman, H. R., 124–25
halfway house, 44–45
Hall, Douglas, 54, 69, 165, 168, 263
"hang around the fort Indians," 133–34
Hare, Leslie, 130
Hare, Melvin, 130
Harjo, Suzan Shown, 278
health: AIM projects, 108–10, 316; BIA expenditures, 80; life expectancy, 173–74, 289; state of Indian, 81
health, of Bellecourt, 289; attempts on life while hospitalized in South Dakota, 186; and drugs, 231, 236, 259–61; healing ceremony for, 185–86; heart attack, 262–64; shooting of, on Rosebud Reservation, 177–84
Heaney, Gerald, 245
Heart of the Earth Survival School, 106–8, 209, 239
Heidi (niece), 75–76
Hendricks (Catholic priest), 19–20
Hennepin County General Hospital, 64
High Bear, Martin, 232–33, 234–35
Hilaire, Peter (priest at St. Cloud State Reformatory), 32
Hill, David, 267
History of the Ojibway Nation (Warren), 36, 37
Holder, Stan, 151
Holmes, Peggy Sue, *191*; at Alcatraz Island takeover, 84–85; background, 61–62; and Bellecourt's addictions, 231; characteristics, 61, 65; harassment of family during Wounded Knee occupation, 162; as incentive to change in Stillwater, 38; and Longest Walk, 239; and making-of-a-chief ceremony, 188–89; marriage to Bellecourt, 45, 67;

The Thunder Before the Storm was designed and set in type by Judy Gilats in St. Paul, Minnesota. The text face is Turnip.